Ordering the City

Ordering the City

Land Use, Policing, and the Restoration of Urban America

Nicole Stelle Garnett

Yale University Press

New Haven & London

Set in Adobe Garamond by Westchester Book Group, Danbury, Connecticut.
Printed in the United States of America by Sheridan Books, Ann Arbor, Michigan.

Library of Congress Cataloging-in-Publication Data

Garnett, Nicole Stelle.
   Ordering the city : land use, policing, and the restoration of urban America /
Nicole Stelle Garnett.
      p.   cm.
   Includes bibliographical references and index.
   ISBN 978-0-300-12494-1 (pbk. : alk. paper)
  1. City planning and redevelopment law—United States.   I. Title.
   KF5729.G37 2009
   346.7304'5—dc22

                                     2009028348

A catalogue record for this book is available from the British Library.

This paper meets the requirements of ANSI/NISO Z39.48–1992 (Permanence
of Paper).

10 9 8 7 6 5 4 3 2 1

For Rick, Maggie, Thomas, and Libby

Contents

Preface

From January through June 2007, I lived in Hyde Park, a neighborhood on Chicago's South Side. While Hyde Park, the home of the University of Chicago, is both relatively affluent and stable, most other South Side neighborhoods are neither. But the South Side was changing during those months. I witnessed what appeared to be a remarkable transformation whenever I drove north toward the downtown area along Lake Shore Drive. Luxury townhouses were popping up in neighborhoods that were recently home to the densest concentration of public housing in the country. Hyde Park's traditional "safety zone" was expanding on all sides, and the high-rise condos of the wealthy Loop were moving toward the South Side as well. Still, when I left Lake Shore Drive to explore, it became clear that in some neighborhoods the transformation was proceeding in fits and starts. Beautifully renovated brownstones sat next to burned-out, abandoned ones; storefronts remained empty; back streets were strewn with litter. What, if anything, I wondered, echoing Jane Jacobs from almost fifty years before, could reverse the cycle of neglect and even despair palpably present in these struggling neighborhoods? What made them so different from the vibrant immigrant communities that I had explored a decade before as a young lawyer representing West Indian "dollar van" drivers in Brooklyn? As Jane Jacobs mused in *The Death and Life of Great American Cities*, why do "some slums stay slums and other slums regenerate themselves even against financial and official opposition"?

My book explores one possible answer to these questions. In a sense, it is my effort to explore Jacobs's answer: Namely, city officials destroy the fabric of urban neighborhoods with a misguided effort to impose order on them. My conclusions are more tentative than Jacobs's, and, I admit, than my own convictions when I began this project. As I hope the pages that follow illustrate, the intersections and conflicts between the ideas of "order" and "disorder" in urban policy are as many, varied, and complex as the cities where they are played out. A humble and honest effort to understand them, however, forms the foundation of the kinds of urban policies that I believe can transform our cities into healthy, vibrant, and orderly places to make our lives.

Many, many friends and colleagues helped shape this book. I regret that I cannot thank all of them for their insights, encouragement, and support, because I am deeply grateful to them all. I am particularly indebted to Peg Brinig, Lee Anne Fennell, Sonia Katyal, Rick Garnett, John Nagle, and Julian Velasco, who generously offered to read previous drafts of the manuscript in its entirety. I also benefited tremendously from the comments of and conversations with Judge Morris Arnold, Jane Barden, Amy Barrett, Benjamin Barros, Vicki Been, A. J. Bellia, Patricia Bellia, Philip Bess, Gerry Bradley, David Brady, Richard Briffault, William Buzbee, Peter Byrne, Alejandro Camacho, Eric Claeys, Marcus Cole, John Coughlin, O.F.M., David Dana, Nestor Davidson, Lou DelFra, C.S.C., Tex Dutile, John Echeverria, Ingrid Gould Ellen, Robert Ellickson, Sheila Foster, Richard W. Garnett III, Jacob Gerson, Clayton Gillette, Bernard Harcourt, Michael Heller, Todd Henderson, Michael Jenuwine, Bob Jones, Bill Kelley, James Krier, Saul Levmore, Michael Lykoudis, John McGreevy, Mark McKenna, Tracey Meares, Thomas Merrill, Mary Ellen O'Connell, Eduardo Peñalver, Mark Poirier, Claire Priest, Carol Rose, Peter Schuck, Christopher Serkin, Henry Smith, Stephen F. Smith, Steven D. Smith, Carter Snead, Stewart Sterk, and Lior Strahilevitz. I also received valuable input on draft chapters from faculty workshops at Emory Law School, Notre Dame Law School, and Seton Hall Law School; at the NYU School of Law Colloquium on the Law, Economics, and Politics of Urban

Affairs; and at the 2008 Property Works in Progress Conference at the University of Colorado Law School. My editor at Yale University Press, Michael O'Malley, provided invaluable guidance throughout the publication process, and Kate Davis improved the manuscript tremendously with her sharp copy-editing skills.

I could not have completed this project without the financial support of Notre Dame Law School or the research assistance of Notre Dame Research Librarians Dwight King, Patty Ogden, and Warren Rees and of a number of law students, especially Eric Babbs, James Burnham, Rob Driscoll, Jessica Laux, Derek Muller, and Jaclyn Sexton. My administrative assistant, Sharon Loftus, kept me organized and sane during the writing process. I learned about the Maricopa County Human Services Campus (discussed in chapter 5) during a conversation with my father-in-law, Richard Garnett, and about the zoning reforms in East Harlem (discussed in chapter 4) in an excellent seminar paper written by my former student Scott Bibb.

I owe a particular debt to the three people—Judge Morris S. Arnold of the U.S. Court of Appeals, David Brady of Stanford University, and Bob Ellickson of Yale Law School—who inspired me to a consider a life of teaching and scholarship. A mentor is a great gift, and I am thankful to each of them for the encouragement that led me to a vocation that has brought so much joy. Finally, my husband, Rick Garnett, is my most important colleague—my constant sounding board, editor, critic, and friend. He also made possible the happy, if chaotic, challenge of writing this book as a mother of three small children.

This book includes, in substantially revised and reordered form, portions of several articles of mine that were originally published in law reviews: "Suburbs as Exit, Suburbs as Entrance," *Michigan Law Review* 106, no. 2 (2007): 277; "The Neglected Political Economy of Eminent Domain," *Michigan Law Review* 105, no. 1 (2006): 101; "Unsubsidizing Suburbia," *Minnesota Law Review* 90, no. 2 (2005): 459; "Relocating Disorder," *Virginia Law Review* 91, no. 5 (2005): 1075; "Ordering (and Order in) the City," *Stanford Law Review* 57, no. 1 (2004): 1; "The Public-Use Question as a Takings Problem," *George Washington Law Review* 71, no. 6 (2003): 934; "Trouble Preserving Paradise," *Cornell Law Review* 87, no. 1 (2001): 158; and "On Castles and Commerce: Zoning Law and the Home-Business Dilemma," *William and Mary Law Review* 42, no. 4 (2001): 1191. All are reproduced with permission.

Introduction

[C]ivilization . . . is achieved because city dwellers . . . have smoothed the edges of private desire so as to fit, or at least work in with all the other city dwellers, without undue abrasion, without sharp edges forever nicking and wounding, each refining an individual capacity for those thousands of daily, instantaneous negotiations that keep crowded city life from being a constant brawl or ceaseless shoving match. When a city dweller has achieved that truly heightened sensitivity to others that allows for easy access, for self and others, through the clogged thoroughfares of urban existence, we call that smoothness urbane. . . . Through the several millennia of our Western culture, to be urbane has been a term of high praise precisely because cities are such difficult environments to make work.

—*A. Bartlett Giamatti*

The walls of the Palazzo Pubblico in Siena, Italy, are graced with Ambrogio Lorenzetti's striking frescoes contrasting the effects of "good government" and "bad government" on fourteenth-century city life. In the city under good government, men work to repair stately buildings, women socialize in the streets, and merchants sell their wares in a busy marketplace. In the city under bad government, the buildings are crumbling, men stand idle (save one crafting weapons), bandits terrorize the innocent, and the bodies of murder victims lie in the streets. The goals of urban policy, it appears, have not changed in more than six hundred years.

Over the past three decades, however, the ascendance of two ideas has revolutionized thinking about how to achieve these goals. The first and most influential idea is James Q. Wilson and George L. Kelling's "broken windows" hypothesis, which was articulated in a 1982 *Atlantic Monthly* essay.[1] This now-familiar theory suggests that uncorrected manifestations of disorder, even minor ones like broken windows, signal a breakdown in the social order that accelerates neighborhood decline and generates serious crime. The response to this theory, and to a growing disillusionment with modern policing practices generally, has been a proliferation of policies focusing on curbing disorder, such as former Mayor Rudolph Giuliani's "quality of life" and "no tolerance" programs, as well as ubiquitous "community policing" efforts. The second idea is Jane Jacobs's argument, popularized in recent years by the self-styled "new urbanists," that mixed-land-use urban environments might be safer and more orderly than single-use ones because a diversity of land uses helps guarantee an around-the-clock presence of people who provide "eyes upon the street" and enforce the social norms that the order-maintenance literature suggests are critical to disorder suppression. A central goal of my book is to explore how these two important ideas intersect and conflict in American land-use and policing policies. In so doing, I hope to unpack what these intersections and conflicts teach about the efficacy and wisdom of prevailing land-use and order-maintenance policies and to better understand disorder by learning about how its different manifestations affect urban life.

Broken windows policies have generated a vast academic literature, most of which focuses on police efforts to restore order by enforcing criminal laws. This scholarship falls into two broad and overlapping categories: First, "social norms" scholars argue that order-maintenance-policing strategies are needed to shore up important nonlegal social controls because disorder is a precursor to more-serious deviancy and crime. As Dan Kahan has observed, "[c]racking down on aggressive panhandling, prostitution, open gang activity and other visible signs of disorder may be justifiable on this ground, since disorderly behavior and the law's response to it are cues about the community's attitude toward more-serious forms of criminal wrongdoing."[2] Efforts to test this claim have generated a voluminous empirical literature, with scholars sharply divided over the meaning of the available data. Second, criminal-procedure scholars focus on the questions raised by the discretion afforded police officers by order-promoting criminal laws. Many worry that order-maintenance-policing techniques threaten to undermine hard-won civil-liberties victories and open the door to police abuses, especially by eroding the constitutional limits on police discretion. In response, order-maintenance proponents assert that skepticism of the police is both outdated and harms the very population it is intended to protect, that is, poor minorities living in disorder-ravaged inner-city neighborhoods.

While important, these debates about the wisdom and efficacy of order-maintenance-policing techniques tend to overlook the complex and important role of property regulation in order-maintenance efforts, as well as what might be called "land-use" benefits and costs of the order-maintenance agenda. Land-use and order-maintenance policies intersect in important ways. Many order-maintenance policies *are* land-use policies. Some property regulations, such as housing and building codes and nuisance laws, serve a *disorder-suppression* function. They target the physical (and related social) disorders that signal and contribute to urban decline. It is hardly surprising that city officials eager to curb disorder have seized upon the disorder-suppression function of property regulation (as discussed more completely in chapters 4 and 5). Social scientists have long linked property conditions with community health. Put most simply, the presence of an "eyesore" is a negative indicator of neighborhood health, as Wilson and Kelling's precursor to spiraling disorder—the broken windows—suggests. Furthermore, constitutional rules governing police discretion limit, for good or ill, a community's ability to curb disorder through flexible criminal laws, such as loitering and vagrancy prohibitions. As discussed in chapter 5, the fact that the tools of property regulation offer vast enforcement flexibility without raising the same constitutional concerns makes them all the more attractive to city officials.

American property regulations, however, do far more than suppress disorder. Indeed, our dominant form of land-use regulation—zoning—serves an "*order-construction*" function. Zoning reflects a long-standing judgment that the appropriate way to order different land uses is to separate them from one another into single-use zones. Although there is no particular reason to equate the two functions of property regulation—disorder suppression and order construction—the order-construction enterprise has from its inception been predicated on the belief that ordered land uses suppress disorder. City officials have long assumed either that economic activity *is* disorder or that it fosters disorder, and they have therefore sought to shield residences from disorder by segregating them away from "incompatible" (that is, commercial) land uses.

Untangling the order-construction/disorder-suppression equation is no small task, but this is an opportune time to tackle the challenge. Today, city officials acting as developers have begun to embrace diversity and vitality as important planning goals. Yet when acting as property regulators, these same city officials continue to cling to the century-old order-construction apparatus, viewing zoning as an important piece of the order-maintenance puzzle. The elevation of disorder suppression as a primary urban policy goal, combined with the failure to systematically consider the many and varied intersections between land-use and order-maintenance policies, may lead city officials to reject reasonable land-use reforms that might help make urban neighborhoods vibrant, more socially cohesive, and safer.

This book's exploration of these difficulties is animated by a belief that urban policies, and land-use policies in particular, succeed when they achieve three important goals. First, they make neighborhoods healthier by fostering social capital and what sociologists and social psychologists call collective efficacy, that is, residents' ability to organize and maintain private social controls. Second, they help cities compete with suburbs for both businesses and residents. And third, they improve our poorest, most struggling urban neighborhoods—and not just those ripe for gentrification.

Land-Use Policies and Social Capital

This book explores the connection between land-use policies and social capital in two contexts. First, it expands the order-maintenance discussion beyond the narrow question of whether disorder is criminogenic. Specifically, by examining how well the order-maintenance agenda fares as land-use policy, the book asks whether and when disorder-suppression efforts generate social capital and foster collective efficacy. This discussion suggests that disorder suppression is an important land-use goal. Not only does disorder weaken neighborhood social controls, but it also generates fear, which is correlated with low levels of collective efficacy. The discussion suggests, however, that policymakers need to carefully heed the nuanced distinctions between different order-maintenance policies. Land-use policies that directly suppress disorder, for example, may improve neighborhood life while bypassing some of the risks associated with the most aggressive order-maintenance-policing policies.

Similarly, order-maintenance-policing policies that promote social capital—either directly, by organizing community efforts to curb disorder and crime, or indirectly, by increasing the frequency and quality of citizen-police interactions—

also hold great promise for improving urban neighborhood life. In contrast, some policing strategies may undermine the social fabric of a community by straining the relationship between police and the urban residents that they are charged with protecting.

Second, this book also unpacks the connections between land-use patterns, disorder, and social capital. That is, the book examines whether and under what circumstances order-construction efforts serve a disorder-suppression function. The relationship between neighborhood health and land-use patterns is contested. Scholars debate, in particular, whether the traditional urban form, with its mix of commercial and residential land uses, fosters or undermines social capital. Urban policymakers have long assumed that regulations segregating land uses by function suppress disorder, in part because they view economic activity with suspicion. Jane Jacobs influentially challenged this traditional view, arguing that economic activity will increase, not undermine, neighborhood-social ties and will suppress disorder.

The record supporting Jacobs's contrarian view, however, is mixed. On the one hand, there is some empirical evidence suggesting that exclusively residential neighborhoods are safer, are less disorderly, and have higher levels of collective efficacy than mixed-use environments. On the other hand, the needs of poor communities may suggest a different recipe for land-use "success" than those of wealthier communities. For example, the same research suggesting that commercial land uses are generally detrimental (that is, generative of crime and disorder) also suggests that commercial land uses are beneficial (that is, disorder-suppressing and social-capital-building) in poor neighborhoods. Furthermore, many intentional order-construction efforts, including especially the reordering efforts that characterized development policy during the urban renewal era, backfired and destroyed the strong community ties that existed organically, even in apparently disorderly mixed-use urban environments.

Land-Use Policies and City-Suburb Competitiveness

A second assumption animating the discussion in this book is that urban policies, including land-use policies, should empower cities to compete effectively with their suburban counterparts. The discussion suggests that the same order-maintenance policies that reduce fear are also likely to improve city competitiveness: Not only is fear of crime a major factor influencing individuals' residential decisions—leading many to leave the city for the suburbs and dramatically curtailing the likelihood of in-migration to the city—but fear exerts the greatest influence on the residential decisions of the educated middle-class families with children, who may prove critical for building healthy urban neighborhoods.

The effect of order-construction efforts on city-suburb competitiveness is, again, more complicated. If, rather than generating more "eyes on the street," commercial uses *generate* disorder and crime, perhaps the traditional assumptions about order-construction regulations are correct: Cities *should* focus on building strong residential communities, not hip urban ones. On the other hand, it is precisely the mixing of land uses in traditional urban neighborhoods—and the vibrancy that the mixing fosters—that allow cities to offer a distinctive alternative to suburban life. And there is a strong case to be made that cities should capitalize on that distinctiveness precisely because they, in most cases, are probably better at being cities than at imitating suburbs. Redevelopment policies that seek to reimpose the traditional urban form in places where it was eliminated by previous generations of planners suggests that city officials now believe that mixed-use communities give them a competitive advantage, or at least represent the best available strategy for attracting and retaining residents.

Land-Use Policies and Poor Urban Neighborhoods

A third essential goal of land-use policies must be to improve poor neighborhoods and the lives of the residents who live in them. Until quite recently, this goal was widely regarded as unachievable; some urban communities were viewed as so mired in poverty, crime, and disorder as to seem unredeemable. For reasons that are not completely clear, and which may include some of the policies discussed in this book, many cities can point to one or more remarkable "success stories," even in the poorest neighborhoods. Neighborhoods that appeared to be declining, or had declined, have begun to regenerate. Some of these successes have been complete enough to generate concerns about gentrification, as poorer residents are replaced by wealthier ones. Without discounting the seriousness of these gentrification concerns, city governments do have reason to boast (or at least to breathe a sigh of relief) about their successes. Those who believed two decades ago that urban centers were socially and economically obsolete must now confront communities that have returned to life just as they appeared to be hanging on by a thread at the edge of the abyss. It remains to be seen, however, how well they will weather challenging economic times. Poorer city neighborhoods, for example, have been particularly hard hit by the foreclosure crisis attending the current recession.

Despite the signs of hope, focus on the effect of land-use policies in the *poorest*, least "gentrifiable" communities is particularly important because urban centers will always have poor communities and life in these communities will always be difficult. Urban poverty declined precipitously during the 1990s, after increasing dramatically during the 1970s and 1980s. The number of high-poverty neighborhoods (that is, neighborhoods with poverty rates of 40 percent or more) fell by more than one-fourth, and the number of people living in such neighborhoods declined by 24 percent (from 10.4 million in 1990 to 7.9 million in 2000). Importantly, the decline in concentrated poverty spanned racial and ethnic lines: The most significant decline was among African Americans; the percentage of poor African Americans living in high-poverty neighborhoods declined from 30.4 percent to 18.6 percent between 1990 and 2000. These declines are *not* attributable to the decline in the overall poverty rate: The poverty rate did decline, but only by about 1 percent. (In fact, the total number of poor people in the United States actually rose slightly.) What happened was that poverty was spatially redistributed, a trend generally regarded as positive by social scientists and poverty advocates alike.*

Not all cities, however, enjoyed the benefits of the national trend away from concentrated poverty: The number of high-poverty census tracts increased in seven cities, including Los Angeles. And even the vast majority of cities that saw a decrease in concentrated poverty hardly saw the problem of poverty disappear. All central cities continue to be home to many poor people living in very poor neighborhoods. The 2000 census found that, in the central cities anchoring the 102 largest U.S. metropolitan areas, nearly one in five individuals had incomes below the poverty level, compared to one in twelve individuals in the suburbs. Even the relationship between population change and poverty is not straightforward. During the 1990s, cities that lost population were nearly as likely to experience declining poverty as those that gained population. And although the decline of concentrated poverty among minorities is hopeful, African Americans and Native Americans continue to suffer the highest concentrated poverty rates, with African Americans disproportionately living in highly segregated urban ghettos.[3]

It is precisely because poor communities face so many problems and because efforts to improve them encounter so many obstacles that the success of

*American suburbs, interestingly, became poorer during the 1990s, a trend that might be interpreted as either a hopeful indicator that poor people are overcoming barriers to intrametropolitan mobility or a harbinger of the inner-suburban decline that concerns many scholars of local government.

city land-use policies should be measured against their effects in those communities. Not only do the detrimental effects of concentrated poverty on neighborhood life suggest that the need for success is greatest in poor neighborhoods, but, as Robert Bruegmann has argued, city life has always been easier for the rich than the poor. Since ancient times, wealthy urban residents have been able to purchase the luxury of space, leaving the poor crammed into dangerous and disease-ridden slums. Indeed, it was from these slums that the first true suburbanites fled during the late nineteenth century. And while smokestacks and overcrowding are no longer poor city dwellers' primary concerns, crime, education, and employment are. Indeed, one reason why suburban life is so attractive to those of modest means is that the suburbs offer the good schools, economic opportunities, and environmental amenities that wealthy urban dwellers can afford to purchase and poorer ones cannot. The poor residents of poor neighborhoods not only find city life most difficult, but they also face the most significant obstacles to leaving it behind. The health of these neighborhoods and the well-being of their residents must therefore always be a primary consideration of our land-use policies.

I

Order in the City

The current focus on restoring order in our cities arises against a backdrop of a century-long debate about when, how, and if local governments generally—and police officers in particular—should address the constellation of problems now known as "urban disorder." This chapter briefly outlines that debate in an effort to place contemporary disorder-suppression efforts in their legal and historical context.

The Re-Revolution in American Policing
(or There and Back Again)

Over the past century, American policing practices have woven a curious course, from a focus on proactive peacekeeping, to the "professionalization" of response-oriented police forces in the mid-twentieth century, to a renewed emphasis on preventing and curbing disorder (that is, a partial return to peacekeeping) in the past three decades. The story of this journey has been ably told elsewhere and need only be briefly recounted here. For most of American history, laws against vagrancy, public drunkenness, and related misconduct served as the primary legal check on urban "disorders." These laws empowered local officials to "keep the peace" in a number of ways, including arresting individuals who were thought to threaten it. After their establishment in the latter half of the nineteenth century, municipal police forces became the primary regulators of public order, and vagrancy-type laws became their primary *legal* enforcement mechanism. That is, from their inception until the latter half of the twentieth century, municipal police forces focused primarily on regulating and minimizing disorder in public spaces. As Debra Livingston has observed, prior to "the constitutional reforms of the 1960s and 1970s, police operated, at least as a legal matter, under a broad delegation of legal authority that licensed them to maintain order in public places largely as they deemed appropriate." In 1960, for example, more than half of all arrests in the United States were for vagrancy, public drunkenness, or disorderly conduct; even as late as 1969, one in four arrests was for public drunkenness.[1]

These statistics tell only part of the story, however. Arrests for public-order offenses were never the primary way that police officers "kept the peace." Most peacekeeping and order-maintenance efforts were undoubtedly informal. In his classic study *Varieties of Police Behavior,* James Q. Wilson wrote—a decade and a half before penning "Broken Windows"—that a patrolman "approaches incidents that threaten order *not in terms of enforcing the law but in terms of 'handling the situation.'*" The availability of legal sanctions for breaches of the public order did, however, provide an important backup to these informal order-maintenance efforts. Wilson and Kelling tellingly observed in "Broken Windows" that "[u]ntil quite recently . . . the police ma[de] arrests on such charges as 'suspicious persons' or 'vagrancy' or 'public drunkenness'—charges with scarcely any legal meaning. These charges exist not because society wants judges to punish vagrants or drunks but because it wants an officer to have the legal tools to remove undesirable persons from a neighborhood when informal efforts to preserve order in the streets have failed." Vagrancy, loitering, and public drunkenness prohibitions gave police officers vast discretion to decide when to arrest an individual for a breach of the peace. As William Stuntz has observed, "Prior to the 1960s, vagrancy and loitering laws made it possible for police to arrest pretty much anyone, or at least anyone on the street: the laws were so broad as to plausibly cover anything anyone might do in public." Since vagrancy laws rendered people deemed a threat to public order perpetually subject to arrest, the threat of a formal arrest was what most frequently motivated compliance with officers' informal order-maintenance requests.[2]

Even strong proponents of modern-day order-maintenance policing acknowledge that the order-maintenance regime was not always a just one. Egon Bittner's famous study of the police on skid row, for example, noted the "restricted relevance of culpability": Many individuals encountered by a patrol officer were apt to be technically guilty of a public-order offense; arrests occurred only when an officer decided to remove the "person whose presence is most likely to perpetuate the troublesome development"; and the poor and, especially, minorities most frequently were deemed "troublesome." Uneven and discriminatory enforcement abounded. Police officers, who were almost exclusively white, used the vast discretion afforded by vaguely worded laws criminalizing public-order offenses to target "undesirables." As Debra Livingston has observed, the old-style public-order regime "was politically acceptable for an extended period of time because the police . . . used their authority primarily against traditional subjects of heightened police surveillance who lacked effective political power to complain: undesirables of various sorts, and especially minorities, the poor, and the young."[3]

Moreover, as Caleb Foote's seminal study devastatingly illustrated, the legal system all too frequently turned a blind eye to the myriad injustices perpetrated in the name of public order. Foote observed hundreds of legal proceedings in Philadelphia misdemeanor court between 1951 and 1954, an experience that led him to condemn the order-maintenance regime as the "garbage pail of the criminal law." Foote recounted how Philadelphia police officers conducted sweeps to "clean up" neighborhoods and make them "out of bounds for undesirables." When the "bums" arrested during these sweeps appeared in court, they were rarely given an opportunity to speak; the presiding magistrate would give each defendant less than a minute's time. Foote observed, "[p]rocedural due process does not penetrate to the world inhabited by the 'bums' of Philadelphia." One judge asked, "Where are you Martin?" The man replied, "Right here." The judge announced, "Well, you aren't going to be 'right here' long. Three months in the House of Correction." Another defendant was released after producing a bus ticket out of the city. "You'd better get on that bus quick," observed the magistrate, "because if you are picked up between here and the bus station, you're a dead duck."[4]

These realities formed the backdrop of the radical deregulation of our urban public spaces. This deregulation was accelerated by the Warren Court's "criminal procedure revolution," which vastly expanded the constitutional rights of the accused. Concerns about uneven and discriminatory enforcement practices also led the Supreme Court to impose what Meir Dan-Cohen and Carol Steiker

have called "conduct rules" governing police-citizen interaction. These new restrictions directly impeded the ability of police departments to continue old-
style order-maintenance policing. In a series of Fourth Amendment cases, for
example, the Court dramatically curtailed police officers' ability to conduct discretionary searches and seizures without individualized grounds for suspicion.
And, perhaps most importantly, the Court began invalidating public-order offenses on due process grounds, reasoning that many were too "vague" to place
citizens on notice of what conduct was prohibited or to properly constrain police discretion. For example, in the well-known *Papachristou* decision, the Court
invalidated a Florida vagrancy ordinance on "vagueness" grounds, ruling that it
"fails to give a person of ordinary intelligence fair notice that his . . . conduct is
forbidden" and that it "encourages arbitrary and erratic arrests and convictions." *Papachristou* and related decisions demanded that criminal laws closely
constrain police officers' discretion to enforce the law, thus depriving them of
the single most important weapon in the traditional order-maintenance
arsenal—namely, the unfettered discretion to keep the peace. In so doing, these
cases called into question the legality of the entire order-maintenance regime.[5]

But the Warren Court was not solely, or even primarily, responsible for
shifting police priorities away from public-order efforts. On the contrary,
the Court's decisions—especially decisions demanding constraints on police
discretion—also were in keeping with contemporary policing theory. From
the early twentieth century police reformers had argued that patrol officers'
focus on minor victimless crimes served little purpose and spawned corruption, unequal enforcement, and public resentment. The very real connections
between the "beat" system and urban "machine" politics, graft, and racial discrimination certainly lent credence to these concerns. Indeed, elite thinking
about policing practices coincided neatly with Foote's conclusion that the
only possible justification for the order-maintenance system—the fact that "its
flexibility gives the police a residual discretionary power to control suspicious
persons"—was an "illusory" one that permitted the "substitution of harassment for the more difficult job of obtaining the evidence necessary to convict
criminals . . . [and] encourages superficial and inefficient police work." By the
early 1970s, the old-style public-order enforcement regime largely had been
eliminated by reforms downplaying officers' traditional peacekeeping function.

These so-called reform-era strategies emphasized crime fighting rather than
crime prevention. To prevent the corruption and abuse endemic to the old-
style order-maintenance system, the professionalization and control of officers
took paramount importance. Police departments replaced foot patrols with

"rapid responders" in patrol cars. Officers were sequestered from contact with civilians and dispatched to investigate crimes and disturbances only once they had occurred (usually after they were reported to the 911 dispatcher). Some cities even banned officers from engaging in idle conversation with citizens. Police officers became law-enforcement experts, with investigative detectives at the pinnacle of departmental structures. Foot patrols, in many departments, became a form of punishment.[6]

Frustration with this new law-enforcement model of policing began to build by the 1970s. Despite the focus on "solving" crimes, many (perhaps most) perpetrators remained undetected. Police departments became frustrated that rapid-response tactics, driven by 911 calls, tended to dictate policing priorities. These tactics almost by definition also did nothing to prevent crime: However rapidly a responder arrived at the scene of the reported crime, she inevitably arrived *after* the crime generating the report was committed. Moreover, even when official policies downplayed or prohibited peacekeeping, police officers found that circumstances on the ground dictated that they continue to play an order-maintenance role. And when departments succeeded in limiting this role, the physical and social distance imposed by reformers appeared to spawn resentment and misunderstanding between police and citizens. Indeed, in the wake of the massive race riots of the late 1960s, President Johnson's National Advisory Commission on Civil Disorders—commonly known as the Kerner Commission—laid the blame for racial tension in part on police neglect of community relations and inattention to minor crimes.[7]

Perhaps most importantly, crime rates rose dramatically during the 1960s and 1970s—just as the reform-era tactics became entrenched—and then remained at unprecedented levels despite increases in police expenditures. And as the crime rate rose, so did fear of crime, especially in urban areas. While the increasing crime rates did not necessarily result from changes in policing strategies, the police began to appear at best powerless, or, at worst, part of the problem. Most Americans began to take ever-spiraling crime rates as a given during this time. Private security forces—from paid security guards to the controversial Guardian Angels—began to patrol the streets. Along with the high crime rates, other factors—including the decriminalization of public drunkenness and vagrancy and the deinstitutionalization of the mentally ill—contributed to a crippling fear of urban disorder. By the end of the 1980s, many of those who could do so chose simply to avoid urban public spaces. The opening lines of the 1981 blockbuster film *Escape from New York* captures well the popular sentiment about our urban places:

In 1988, the Crime Rate in the United States rises four hundred percent. The once-great city of New York becomes the one maximum-security prison for the entire country. A fifty-foot containment wall is erected along the New Jersey shoreline, across the Harlem River, and down along the Brooklyn shoreline. It completely surrounds Manhattan Island. All bridges and waterways are mined. The United States Police Force, like an army, is encamped around the island. There are no guards inside the prison: only prisoners and the worlds they have made. The rules are simple. Once you go in, you don't come out.

Around this time, I remember hearing my grandmother warn my mother not to take her purse to downtown Kansas City, Missouri. She was quite certain that a thug would snatch it away immediately as soon as she stepped out of her car.[8]

By the time that Wilson and Kelling published the "Broken Windows" essay in 1982, these realities had set the stage for new experimentation with order-restoration strategies. Thus, just as one revolution in policing philosophy had ended in triumph, another "quiet revolution" began to refocus police efforts on maintaining order. The seed for the "Broken Windows" essay was planted by the Newark Foot Patrol Experiment, a mid-1970s New Jersey program that funded additional foot patrols on city streets in an effort to measure whether increased police presence reduced crime. Kelling participated as a researcher in the official evaluation of the project. The study, which was based upon controlled evidence taken primarily from Newark, found that foot patrols did not, in fact, reduce crime. This finding coincided with prevailing wisdom about police practices, which held that foot patrols were a cumbersome and inefficient means of conducting police work. Researchers also found, however, that residents of neighborhoods where foot patrol officers were deployed felt more secure, took fewer steps to protect themselves from crime, and, importantly, *believed* that crime rates had declined (even though they had not). Residents of the foot patrol areas also expressed a more favorable attitude toward the police than those living elsewhere.[9]

In "Broken Windows," which is at heart a reflection on the Newark Foot Patrol Experiment, Wilson and Kelling first articulated a version of the social-norms justification for order-maintenance policies. "Disorder and crime," they argued, "are usually inextricably linked, in a kind of developmental sequence." Wilson and Kelling reasoned that "one unrepaired broken window is a signal that no one cares, and so breaking more windows costs nothing." The logic, in other words, is that a single broken window has a multiplier effect: "If a window in a building is broken *and is left unrepaired,* all the rest of the windows will soon be broken." Similarly, according to Wilson and Kelling, "untended behavior also leads to the breakdown of community controls." Communities that fail to curb physical and social disorder (that is, "untended behavior") become vulnerable to serious crime for at least two related reasons. First, unchecked disorder frightens law-abiding citizens, causing them to avoid public places, and eventually leads those with financial means to move away from the disorderly community. The law-abiders' departure, first from parks and sidewalks and eventually from struggling communities to more stable ones, in turn further weakens social controls. (The reasons for this, which are fairly intuitive, are discussed in much greater detail in chapter 6.) Second, disorder sends signals to would-be offenders that communities plagued by disorder are "safe" places to commit crimes: The community's failure to check disorder suggests that residents cannot, or choose not to, control socially detrimental behaviors and conditions. In Wilson and Kelling's words, "If the neighborhood cannot keep a bothersome panhandler from annoying passersby, the thief may reason, it is even less likely to call the police to identify a potential mugger or to interfere if the mugging actually takes place."[10]

"Broken Windows" represented more than a rallying cry for residents of struggling neighborhoods to "take back" their communities by controlling disorder. The essay challenged nearly a century of thinking about the role of police in urban communities. Both of Wilson and Kelling's core recommendations stood reform-style tactics on their head: They asserted, first, that police should integrate themselves into the social fabric of the communities that they protect, and, second, that police should prioritize efforts to control minor crimes and disorder over the "fighting" of serious crime. According to Wilson and Kelling, in other words, the reformers had it exactly backwards— the withdrawal of the officers from the beat and prioritizing of crime fighting over peacekeeping had proven to be a death knell of urban community life. But it was not too late: Police intervention to enforce the kinds of antidisorder norms that operate naturally in healthy communities would both check the spiral of urban decay and also reduce more-serious crime. By intervening to check disorder, officers could help communities send the right signals—those proclaiming "residents here do not tolerate social deviancy." Moreover, the disorder-control efforts of the police officers, Wilson and Kelling argued, also would kick-start the informal social norms needed to check deviancy—norms that had been crippled by the disorder plaguing all too many urban neighborhoods. There was more than one irony lurking in these distinguished researchers' arguments: In his 1968 essay "The Urban Unease," James Q. Wilson argued that fear (or unease) brought about by the failure of community was the root of the so-called urban crisis. While this thesis is certainly in keeping with the broken windows hypothesis, Wilson further argued (as discussed in greater detail in chapter 6) that police can do little to help communities that lack the organic norms needed for healthy urban life. A decade later, Kelling was the principal researcher in the Kansas City Preventive Patrol Experiment, an empirical study of police practices that rejected the idea that preventative patrols will prevent crime and that embraced reform-style tactics.[11]

Irony aside, "Broken Windows" is, without question, one of the most influential magazine articles in history. While "Broken Windows" was not the only catalyst for the order-maintenance revolution, its influence can hardly be overstated. Since its publication, police departments across the nation have implemented literally tens of thousands of order-maintenance policies. Policies inspired by the broken windows hypothesis are numerous and diverse. Some, such as former New York City Mayor Rudolph Giuliani's famous "quality of life" campaign and the antigang ordinance at issue in the *City of Chicago v. Morales* decision, directly target perceived "disorders"—gang members, "squeegee men," turnstile jumpers, dope smokers, and the like. Others, such as ubiquitous "community policing" efforts (discussed in greater detail in chapters 6 and 8) build upon Wilson and Kelling's arguments about the importance of police-citizen interaction. Community policing efforts seek to build stronger relationships between police officers and the citizens whom they protect, both through policing techniques that ensure more-frequent informal interactions and by soliciting citizen input about policing priorities. While community policing practices influence all aspects of police operations, they are closely intertwined with order-maintenance efforts for at least two reasons. First, removing officers from patrol cars and replacing them with foot and bike patrols encourages police-citizen interaction, but it also maximizes officers' ability to monitor and control disorder and enables officers to intervene early and prevent serious crime before it occurs. Second, and perhaps most tellingly, when citizens are asked to help shape policing priorities, they frequently prioritize the elimination of "prevalent and low-key troubles"—loitering, vandalism, prostitution, and gangs—the very "disorders" at the heart of the order-maintenance agenda.[12]

Order-maintenance policies have found their most forceful and articulate support among social-norms scholars in the legal academy. Social-norms proponents of order-maintenance policies extrapolate the following causal chain from the commonsense observation that our behavior is shaped by, and frequently conforms to, our perceptions of others' behavior: First, it is reasonable to assume that people tend to be law-abiding when they perceive that their neighbors are obeying the law; second, relatively minor disorders like vandalism and public drunkenness signal that neighbors are *not* obeying the law; third, these signals create an environment that fosters serious crime. Disorder, according to social-norms scholars, has a negative "social-influence" effect. As Dan Kahan argues, disorder "erode[s] deterrence by emboldening law-breakers and demoralizing law-abiders." Put differently, the social-norms scholars argue that by failing to curb disorder, a community signals to wrongdoers that the informal social controls that tend to keep disorder and crime in check in healthy communities are broken. A would-be wrongdoer may therefore infer from the presence of disorder that the community plagued by it also does not, or cannot, control serious crime. If so, he is likely to perceive that the disorder-plagued community is a "safe" place to commit crime, that is, that the risks of criminal behavior are low and the rewards high. Disorderly neighborhoods are also dangerous ones, social-norms scholars argue, and the danger is a direct result of the presence of disorder.

Although it is worth noting that many residents of disorder-plagued communities are likely to view curbing disorder as good in and of itself, social-norms scholars argue that order-maintenance policies will do more than curb disorder. If the social-norms scholars have it right, and disorder is causally linked to crime, curbing disorder will make our communities *safer* as well as more orderly. Order-maintenance policies, in other words, have a positive social-influence effect—they act as circuit breakers that disrupt the causal relationship between disorder and serious crime. Moreover, social-norms scholars assert, echoing Wilson and Kelling, that order-maintenance strategies can also help reinvigorate the important informal social controls that keep disorder in check. If disorder emboldens lawbreakers, then, social-norms scholars reason, governmental (usually police) efforts to curb disorder will over time embolden law-abiders. As law-abiding citizens begin to assert control over their communities, the need for governmental intervention will wane.[13]

The Debates

The broken windows hypothesis and its order-maintenance-policy progeny have generated two heated debates: The first concerns the civil-liberties implications of the order-maintenance enterprise; the second, the efficacy of order-maintenance tactics. These debates are briefly reviewed below:

The Civil-Liberties Question

Proponents and opponents of order-maintenance policing both recognize that the old-style order-maintenance regime, described above, was plagued by corruption and characterized by widespread police abuses, especially of marginalized members of our society. And proponents and opponents both recognize the uncomfortable reality that police qua "peacekeepers" were historically armed with—and, perhaps more frequently than we want to admit, abused—sweeping discretion to enforce vague laws criminalizing breaches of the "public order," such as vagrancy, loitering, and public drunkenness. Both sides of the debate also recognize that order-maintenance policies reintroduce some of the factors that led to corruption and abuse: Especially in contrast to reform-era "law-enforcement" techniques, they tend to increase police-citizen interaction, vesting police officers with greater discretion to act upon their judgments about the "harmfulness" of individuals and activities.

It is at this point that the two camps sharply part company. Order-maintenance proponents strongly resist the suggestion that they advocate the re-enactment of Elizabethan-era vagrancy laws. But they do assert that police officers necessarily exercise discretion in the course of their peacekeeping duties and that the law generally should trust them to do so responsibly. As George Kelling and Catherine Coles have asserted, "we must recognize and accept the legitimate use of police discretion, while finding ways to shape and limit its exercise." Order-maintenance proponents argue, moreover, both that skepticism of police discretion is outdated and that it actually harms the very population it is intended to protect. With respect to the first argument—that judicial discretion of police discretion to control disorder is outdated, at least insofar as it stems from a concern about racially discriminatory enforcement practice—proponents point to changing attitudes about race, the increasing racial diversity on urban police forces, and the growing political power of minority groups. These factors, they assert, make it far less likely that police officers will abuse their discretion to control disorder. Dan Kahan and Tracey Meares also note that inner-city minority residents consistently exercise their increasing political clout to demand order-maintenance policies, signaling a desire for more police intervention in their communities. Moreover, concerns about protecting citizens from the *risk* of police abuses may expose them to the *certainty* of crime and disorder by depriving police officers of the discretion needed to address the serious problems facing our most vulnerable communities. Randall Kennedy has argued, for example, that the main problem plaguing African Americans is "a misguided antagonism toward efforts to preserve public safety." In other words, at a time when the risks of police discretion are lower than ever, the need for it has reached an all-time high in the inner-city communities most plagued by disorder and crime. In these vulnerable communities, police indifference may be a greater concern than aggressive law enforcement. "Courts," Debra Livingston has written, "cannot solve the problem of police discretion by invalidating reasonably specific public order laws . . . without seriously impairing legitimate community efforts to enhance the quality of neighborhood life."[14]*

Other legal scholars, as well as judges faced with constitutional challenges to new order-maintenance offenses, worry that the order-maintenance agenda threatens hard-earned civil liberties. These skeptics counter that new order-maintenance policies raise many of the same concerns as old ones, especially about police discretion to control disorder. Bernard Harcourt, for example, asserts that "regularity on the street depends on irregularity in police practice—mixed, of course, with some regularity in the choice of suspects. The need for regularity, in turn, triggers a demand for police discretion and expertise." Harcourt echoes Caleb Foote when he warns that "[t]he order-maintenance strategy also depends on arresting people on meaningless charges. What makes the system work is the availability of broad criminal laws that allow the police to take people off the street because they look suspicious." In response to the claim that the evolving sociopolitical reality of major cities diminishes the concern that officers cannot be trusted to exercise discretion to control disorder responsibly, critics accuse order-maintenance proponents of viewing the world through rose-colored glasses and ignoring the reality that inner-city minority residents continue to face a disproportionate risk of discriminatory enforcement and police brutality. They worry that today's order-maintenance policies will lead to the very police abuses that motivated previous generations of police reformers to curtail officers' discretion to keep the peace. As Margaret Burnham asserts, poor minorities are "twice victimized" by order-maintenance policies that vest police with unchecked discretion to control

---

*Even in the days of old-style order-maintenance policing, police sometimes exercised their discretion to protect vulnerable citizens. In his classic study of skid row, for example, Egon Bittner found that many police officers came to see themselves as "protectors" of an otherwise forgotten community. Bittner chronicled police efforts to gain detailed knowledge of the individuals living on skid row and noted that the prevailing view among the patrol officers was that they should protect vulnerable skid row inhabitants. Bittner, "The Police on Skid Row," 707–9.

disorder—first by crime and disorder, and second by police tactics that threaten civil liberties in the name of protecting them from crime and disorder. Opponents link instances of police abuse—like the notorious Amadou Diallo incident—to order-maintenance strategies. After New York City police officers shot Diallo, an unarmed African immigrant, forty-one times, popular accounts widely questioned whether Mayor Rudolph Giuliani's "zero tolerance" regime was to blame.[15]

Skeptics also worry that order-maintenance policies tend to reinforce negative stereotypes of black criminality. Robert Sampson and Stephen Raudenbush's troubling findings on perceptions of disorder lend support for this final concern. Sampson and Raudenbush compared survey evidence measuring social perceptions of disorder with systematic, recorded observations of actual disorder in urban neighborhoods. They found that race was the single biggest factor influencing perceptions of disorder. Not only did blacks perceive less disorder than whites living in the same neighborhood, but, far more disturbingly, the perception of disorder increased as the percentage of black residents increased. This held true across races: Blacks, whites, and Latinos perceived more disorder in predominantly black neighborhoods, regardless of the level of measurable disorder.[16]

While order-maintenance policing appears to be carrying the day politically, judges continue to listen to the critics, at least often enough to make judicial skepticism of the "new policing" a significant impediment to implementing the order-maintenance agenda. Perhaps most importantly, the Supreme Court has resisted invitations to soften its stance toward laws that grant the police broad discretion to define and control behaviors that may threaten the public peace. *City of Chicago v. Morales,* decided in 1999, is the most significant recent opinion reflecting continued discomfort with police discretion to maintain order. In *Morales,* the Court considered a Chicago ordinance that made it a crime to "loiter" with a "criminal street gang member." A majority of the justices found the ordinance's definition of loitering—to "remain in any one place with no apparent purpose"—too vague to adequately channel police-enforcement discretion. In response to *Morales,* the City of Chicago attempted to channel police discretion by incorporating a specific-intent element into the offense of gang loitering. To do so, the city changed the definition of loitering to "remaining in any one place under circumstances that would warrant a reasonable person to believe that the purpose or effect of that behavior is to enable a criminal street gang to establish control over identifiable areas, to intimidate others from entering these areas, or to conceal illegal activities." Thus far, this ordinance has—as Chicago hoped and Justice O'Connor's concurring opinion in *Morales* hinted—survived a subsequent challenge. This effort to use specific-intent requirements to remedy "vagueness" problems is in keeping with legislative trends, although, much to the frustration of local officials, judicial opinion about specific-intent public-order ordinances has been mixed.[17]

Morales addressed the vagueness doctrine—a *procedural* rule that limits police discretion. While concerns about the scope of police discretion follow naturally from efforts to give the police greater authority to restore order, the legal issues raised by the order-maintenance agenda are not purely procedural in nature. Cities seeking to implement the order-maintenance agenda have also faced challenges alleging that public-order policies run afoul of the *substantive* rights guaranteed by the federal and state constitutions. For example, courts have ruled that anti-panhandling laws unconstitutionally curtail free speech rights; have invalidated juvenile curfews on right-to-travel and parental-liberty grounds; have held that laws prohibiting sleeping in public spaces criminalize homelessness in contradiction of the Eighth Amendment's prohibition on "status" crimes; and have ruled that efforts to use trespass laws to exclude drug dealers from troubled neighborhoods infringe upon the freedom of association.[18]

The Efficacy Debate

The second debate sparked by the order-maintenance agenda concerns the *efficacy* of order-maintenance tactics. In "Broken Windows," Wilson and Kelling hypothesized that disorder and crime are causally linked—that unchecked disorder leads to more serious crimes and that police intervention to check disorder will reduce crime. The debate over these predictions, which form the theoretical foundation of the order-maintenance enterprise, is reflected in a sizable empirical literature. Some scholars have sought to test the broken windows hypothesis itself, that is, to measure whether any connection exists between disorder and serious crime. Others seek to measure whether order-maintenance tactics work *in a broken windows sense,* that is, whether real-world efforts to curb disorder in fact curb more real-world serious crime. Critics argue that the available data does not support a disorder-crime nexus and challenge as flawed any studies suggesting that it does. These scholars argue, therefore, that there is no reason to believe that curbing disorder will lead to the reduction in serious crime, which social-norms scholars promise.[19]

Criminologist Wesley Skogan's work provides the springboard for most empirical discussions of the broken windows hypothesis. In his influential

book *Disorder and Decline,* Skogan collected and analyzed data from forty urban neighborhoods with dramatically different crime rates. Skogan's work
sought to understand broadly the effects of disorder on urban neighborhood
life. He explored, for example, the impact of disorder on property values, residential stability, and neighborhood collective efficacy (that is, as discussed in
greater detail in chapter 6, the ability of a community to address social problems, neighborhood stability and housing markets, and the fear of crime).
Most influentially (and controversially), however, Skogan also purported to
find a strong positive correlation between disorder and robbery rates, even after controlling for race, poverty, and other demographic variables that are
commonly associated with crime. Indeed, Skogan found, after he controlled
for the effects of disorder, that these other variables did little to explain the
robbery-rate variation between neighborhoods. Skogan further found that
perceptions of crime also tracked the presence of visible disorder. Skogan's
findings have been sharply challenged, notably by Harcourt, who replicated
and found numerous flaws in Skogan's study. Harcourt faulted Skogan for ag-
gregating studies that relied upon different variables to measure disorder. He
also criticized Skogan's decision to exclude data on crimes other than robbery
(including assault, purse snatching, sexual assault, and burglary), especially
because the statistical relationship between disorder and these other crimes
vanished when neighborhood demographic factors—neighborhood poverty,
stability, and race—were held constant. In fact, Harcourt noted, the relationship between disorder and robbery would also have disappeared save for data
from five Newark neighborhoods. Harcourt concluded that "in the end, the
data do not support the broken windows hypothesis."[20]

Robert Sampson and Stephen Raudenbush's exhaustive study of the effects of disorder in Chicago tends to support Harcourt's conclusion. Rather
than relying, as had Skogan, on previous studies based primarily upon surveys designed to elicit perceptions of neighborhood disorder, Sampson and
Raudenbush undertook an intensive effort to systematically record observable
disorder. They enlisted trained observers, driving sports utility vehicles, to
videotape and catalog visible disorder along nearly twenty-five thousand blocks
in urban Chicago neighborhoods. They then compared these observations
both to official crime data and to survey responses designed to elicit information about neighborhood "collective efficacy," which they defined as the "link-
age of cohesion and mutual trust with shared expectations for intervening in
support of neighborhood social control." Sampson and Raudenbush initially
found a strong correlation between disorder and both crime and collective

efficacy, that is, more disorder correlated strongly with higher crime rates and lower levels of collective efficacy. The direct correlation between disorder and crime largely disappeared, however, when they controlled for neighborhood structural factors such as race, income, and residential stability. The direct nexus between disorder and crime held true only for robbery rates, a finding consistent with Skogan's earlier work. Sampson and Raudenbush also found, importantly, that disorder reduced collective efficacy and that weak collective efficacy is strongly predictive of higher crime rates. Thus, they concluded, even if disorder and crime are not directly causally linked, disorder may have a "cascade effect" that indirectly affects crime rates by undermining neighborhood collective efficacy.[21]

More recently, Harcourt and Jens Ludwig sought to test the broken windows hypothesis using data from the U.S. Department of Housing and Urban Development's "Moving to Opportunity Program." Since 1994, the MTO program has enabled very low-income families living in public or subsidized housing projects in five large cities (Baltimore, Boston, Chicago, Los Angeles, and New York) to move to low-poverty, low-crime communities. Each of the forty-six hundred families that applied to the program between 1994 and 1997 was assigned randomly to one of three groups: One-third were offered housing vouchers that enabled them to rent private housing in a low-poverty census tract; one-third received vouchers without any geographic limitations attached; and one-third received no vouchers. Presumably, Harcourt and Ludwig posited, if disorder generates serious crime, then individuals moving from high-disorder to low-disorder communities should commit fewer crimes than those who remain in more disorderly ones. Harcourt and Ludwig, however, found no statistically significant differences in arrest rates for MTO participants that lived in neighborhoods with dramatically different levels of physical and social disorder. They found a slight (but not statistically significant) decline in criminal activity by younger women who moved to less disorderly neighborhoods and a slight (but again not significant) increase in criminal activity among younger men in the corresponding group. Harcourt and Ludwig concluded that "[t]he findings from MTO suggest either that declines in community disorder do not translate into reductions in individual criminal behavior or that any effects . . . from less disorder are outweighed by the countervailing effects" of a reduction in relative socioeconomic status of the program participants vis-à-vis their neighbors.[22]

Each of these studies sought to test the broken windows hypothesis by measuring the extent of the connection, if any, between disorder and serious crime.

Other studies have sought to test the broken windows hypothesis by examining the effectiveness of order-maintenance policies. Presumably, if Wilson and Kelling and their social-norms allies are correct, then real-world efforts to curb disorder should reduce serious crime. New York City has served as the laboratory for many of these studies. Beginning in the early 1990s, the New York City Police Department began focusing intensively on public-order offenses, including vandalism, aggressive panhandling, public drunkenness, unlicensed vending, public urination, prostitution, and misdemeanor drug possession. Crime rates declined dramatically over the same period: Between 1990 and 1998, murder declined by more than 70 percent; robbery, by more than 60 percent; total violent offenses, by more than 50 percent; and property felonies, by more than 60 percent. Crime rates fell precipitously throughout the United States during the same period, but New York City's decline was more than twice the national average. Order-maintenance proponents quickly seized on the New York City experience, claiming that it demonstrated unequivocally that curbing disorder did in fact reduce serious crime.[23]

The empirical support for this conclusion is, not surprisingly, mixed. In a 2001 study, George Kelling and William Sousa concluded that the New York City Police Department's order-maintenance agenda, especially its aggressive misdemeanor-arrest policy, did in fact account for the significant drop in serious crime that the city experienced during the 1990s. Kelling and Sousa conducted a precinct-by-precinct analysis of the effects of order-maintenance policing on crime rates in New York City. They found that, in virtually all precincts, order-maintenance policing correlated with a decrease in violent-crime arrests. In fact, according to Kelling and Sousa, the number of precinct misdemeanor arrests was the "strongest predictor" of violent crime rates during the relevant period. They asserted that the average precinct could expect one fewer violent crime for every twenty-eight additional misdemeanor arrests. Kelling and Sousa concluded that between 1989 and 1999 aggressive misdemeanor arrests prevented over sixty thousand violent crimes. They also argued that the reorientation of policing priorities to focus on problem solving, crime prevention, and community relations—all staples of the order-maintenance agenda—also contributed to a remarkable overall reduction in crime experienced in the city during the same time period.[24]

Kelling and Sousa's findings are consistent with a more recent study by Hope Corman and Naci Mocan. Using citywide data, Corman and Mocan attempted to measure how different factors—including improving economic conditions, increasing the size of the police force, rising incarceration rates, and broken windows policing tactics—contributed to New York City's dramatic reduction in violent crime during the 1990s. Corman and Mocan found that misdemeanor arrests did have a statistically significant effect on motor vehicle theft, robbery, and grand larceny (but not on other serious crimes): "A 10 percent increase in misdemeanor arrests decreases motor vehicle thefts by 1.6 to 2.1 percent, robberies by 2.5 to 3.2 percent, and grand larcenies by .5 to .6 percent." Corman and Mocan cautioned, however, that the other factors (especially felony arrests and incarceration rates) contributed more to falling felony rates, that the reductions attributable to misdemeanor arrests were modest and limited to certain categories of crimes, and that crime rates fell significantly in other cities—including Los Angeles (50 percent), San Diego (56 percent), and San Francisco (41 percent)—with declining misdemeanor-arrest rates.[25]

These two studies have, not surprisingly, been challenged. Harcourt and Ludwig, for example, reanalyzed the New York City evidence at the precinct level and proffered an alternative explanation for declining crime rates. Harcourt and Ludwig argue that the dramatic decline in violent crimes that Kelling and Sousa attribute to order-maintenance tactics might reflect what social scientists call "mean-reversion"—the phenomenon known colloquially as "what goes up, must come down." They note that cities with the greatest increases in crime during the 1980s experienced the sharpest declines during the 1990s. The same phenomenon holds true for New York City police precincts: Crime declined most precipitously in precincts with the highest crime rates during the previous decade. Not surprisingly, broken windows policing (measured by misdemeanor arrests) also was conducted most intensively in New York City's most violent neighborhoods. Thus, Harcourt and Ludwig conclude that at best the case for the broken windows hypothesis "leaves us with a Scottish verdict—'not proven.'" In a separate article, Harcourt and Ludwig use data from New York to bolster the argument that order-maintenance practices continue to threaten the civil liberties of racial minorities, finding that the aggressive misdemeanor-arrest policies were disproportionately enforced in African American and Latino precincts.[26]

Beyond the Broken Windows Hypothesis

The evidence supporting Wilson and Kelling's assertion that disorder breeds serious crime (and, therefore, that curbing disorder will reduce serious crime) is mixed and subject to multiple interpretations. This book's goal is not to enter the empirical debate, but rather to expand upon it. As chapter 6 discusses in more detail, there are many reasons to believe that disorder imposes serious costs on a community even if it is not criminogenic. Thus, order-maintenance policies may benefit cities in numerous ways other than crime reduction. Moreover, order-maintenance policies may also act to *directly* reduce crime. For example, order-maintenance tactics tend to be labor intensive: They usually increase the total number of police officers and maximize officer presence on the street. This is one reason that civil libertarians worry about order-maintenance tactics: They increase the frequency and intimacy of police-citizen interactions. While some skeptics cite the evidence suggesting that disorder and crime are not causally linked to question the wisdom of allocating scarce policing resources in such a labor-intensive way, there is evidence that hiring more police officers tends to reduce crime. For example, Steven Levitt has argued that positive crime trends during the 1990s are more likely to be attributable to increases in the size of police forces (along with rising rates of incarceration, the waning of the crack epidemic, and the legalization of abortion) than to changes in policing tactics. Order-maintenance tactics also may directly reduce serious crime because many of them directly target serious crimes. As Sampson and Raudenbush suggest, one of the reasons that disorder may appear to "cause" crime is that the elements of disorder (or some manifestations of disorder) may be "part and parcel of crime itself." This is one of Harcourt's principal complaints about Skogan's research: Skogan's measure of "disorder" in a community included serious crimes, such as drug trafficking and gang activities, rendering parts of his analysis "tautological." Of course, to the extent that order-maintenance policies directly target serious crimes and dangerous criminals, they can be expected to reduce serious crimes directly, rather than by mediating social norms.[27]*

---

*Interestingly, Corman and Mocan found that neither the effects of incapacitation resulting from misdemeanor arrests nor police-force increases substantially affected felony crime rates. Corman and Mocan, "Carrots, Sticks, and Broken Windows," 251–54.

2

Ordering the City

Largely missing from the academic debate about the order-maintenance revolution is a discussion of the complex and important role of property regulations in order-maintenance efforts. To be fair, broken windows scholarship concentrates primarily on policing strategies that are, in a sense, property regulations: They seek to restore order by regulating public places—streets, parks, and so on. For example, the anti-gang-loitering law invalidated by the Supreme Court in *City of Chicago v. Morales* had "zoning" characteristics. It was enforced only in "areas in which the presence of gang members ha[d] a demonstrable effect on the activities of law abiding persons in the surrounding community," and, in its brief before the Supreme Court, Chicago used zoning analogies to defend this practice. And, as discussed in more detail in chapter 5, other communities have explicitly applied zoning principles to public streets. But the tools and goals of "traditional" property regulation also shape order-maintenance efforts in important and understudied ways.[1]

As highlighted in the introduction, property regulations shape the order of American cities in two very different ways. Some property regulations, such as housing and building codes and nuisance laws, serve a *disorder-suppression* function. They target the physical (and related social) disorders that signal, and contribute to, urban decline, and cities regularly include them in their order-maintenance toolkits. American property regulations, however, do far more than suppress disorder. Our dominant form of land-use regulation, Euclidean zoning, serves an *order-construction* function. Zoning puts "everything in its place." It reflects a long-standing value judgment that the appropriate way to order different land uses is to separate them from one another into single-use zones. Reasoning from first principles, there is no particular reason to equate the disorder-suppression and order-construction functions of property regulations. That is, the "order" constructed by American zoning laws is not necessarily the same thing as the absence of the physical and social disorders targeted by order-maintenance-policing efforts. For example, zoning laws might declare a nonconforming use, such as a corner grocery store in an older residential neighborhood, as a "disorder," but surely few city officials would see the store, which is likely to provide a valuable service to nearby residents, as the same kind of disorder as chronic street nuisances such as aggressive panhandlers or the "squeegee men" famously targeted by Mayor Giuliani in New York City. Nor is there any self-evident reason why segregating different land uses from one another will suppress disorder. As Jane Jacobs influentially argued, mixed-use environments might be safer and more orderly than single-use ones because a diversity of land uses helps guarantee an around-the-clock presence of a people to provide "eyes upon the street" and to enforce the social norms that the order-maintenance literature suggests are critical to disorder suppression.[2]

Nevertheless, a foundational premise of the order-construction enterprise is that government intervention to order land uses does, in fact, suppress disorder. This chapter explores the role that the order-construction ideal has played in shaping the regulation and development of American cities. In short, urban policymakers have long seen order-construction regulations as forming an important bulwark against social disorder. The Progressive-era reformers who championed zoning were avowed "positive environmentalists," who firmly believed that the chaos of the industrial city was morally corrupting, and, moreover, that order-construction regulations—that is, zoning rules that segregated commercial and industrial establishments from residences, and, importantly, single-family homes from all other uses—would curb the social disorders plaguing those cities. Those Progressives inherited from earlier generations of reformers hostility toward urban life and skepticism of commercial activity. As the discussion below highlights, they not only believed that mixed-use environments were disorderly but also that commercial activity was itself a disorder (albeit in some cases a necessary one that should be carefully controlled). Zoning was seen as a means of shielding residents from the corrupting influences of the city, including commercial activity. In the second half of the twentieth century, other land-use reformers—the modernist planners championing the "renewal" of our "obsolete" urban cores—used bulldozers to accomplish what the Progressives could not, imposing single-use patterns on pre-zoning, mixed-land-use neighborhoods.[3]

Spheres of Human Activity

For most people, for most of human history, work and home were inextricably intertwined. Practically everyone—from the farmer to the city dweller—worked at home. Houses and apartments were not only dwelling places, but also centers of commercial activity. As historian Kenneth Jackson has observed, in the pre-industrial world, "each household was a business." Physicians treated patients, and attorneys served clients from offices located in their homes; butchers, bakers, and candlestick makers lived above, below, or behind their shops. Tailors and seamstresses greeted customers in their living rooms and altered clothes in their bedrooms. Blacksmiths and carpenters plied their trades in backyard workshops. Families regularly rented out a room or two to make ends meet. Households were the basic units of production, and all members of the household contributed. In 1795, for example, when Martha Moore Ballard wrote "a woman's work is never done," she was referring not simply to her domestic duties as wife and mother; to the contrary, the sixty-year-old matron of a working farm also contributed to her household's finances by serving as a trusted midwife throughout her community and by manufacturing and selling domestic crafts to her neighbors.[4]

The phenomenon of leaving home to *go to work* became commonplace only after the Industrial Revolution changed the rhythm of daily life. Historians describe how the physical separation of work and home affected societal views of the home (and, importantly, of women within the home), culminating in the long-enduring "separate spheres" ideology. Through the transformation from pre-industrial to modern economic organization, men left home for work, and commerce and industry left the home with them. Economic and domestic roles became highly gender segregated, giving rise to a "cult of domesticity." Throughout the pre-industrial period, women like Ballard were celebrated for their industriousness. Consider, for example, the biblical poet's celebration of the "good wife" in Proverbs:

> A good wife who can find?
>> She is far more precious than jewels. . . .
> She seeks wool and flax,
>> and works with willing hands. . . .
> She considers a field and buys it;
>> with the fruit of her hands she plants a vineyard. . . .
> She perceives that her merchandise is profitable. . . .
> She makes linen garments and sells them;
>> she delivers girdles to the merchant.
> Strength and dignity are her clothing,
>> and she laughs at the time to come. . . .
> Her children rise up and call her blessed;
>> her husband also, and he praises her:
> "Many women have done excellently,
>> but you surpass them all."

By the middle of the nineteenth century, this ancient ideal had given way to hazy Victorian images of the wife as a cloistered nurturer who shunned the world for domestic pursuits. Work, at least work for pecuniary gain, came to be seen not as a virtue but as a "contagion" that endangered women and children.[5]

The home—long the productive building block of society—became the rarified "domestic sphere," which stood in sharp contrast to the grueling, cutthroat "world." In the Victorian era, the idealized home became commerce-free (although many women continued to bring piecemeal work into their homes). The home was "both a shelter *from* the anxieties of modern life . . . and a shelter *for* those values which the commercial spirit and critical spirit were threatening to destroy." The home was seen as an oasis, a place where women and children were shielded from the dangers of competitive modern economic forces, and a place of respite for a weary husband returning from work each night. As a New Hampshire minister urged in 1827, "It is at home, where man seeks a refuge from the vexations and embarrassments of business, an enchanting repose from exertion, a relaxation from care by the interchange of affection where some of his finest sympathies, tastes, and moral and religious feelings are formed and nourished; where is the treasury of pure disinterested love, such as is seldom found in the busy walks of a selfish and calculating world."[6]

The Industrial Revolution also dramatically altered residential housing patterns, leading to an explosion in suburban growth that continues today. While all cities, throughout history, have spawned suburbs, the suburbs of pre-industrial cities developed primarily to accommodate noxious land uses (the Talmud provides, for example, that "a dump for animal waste, and a cemetery, and a tannery must be kept at least 50 cubits distant from the city") and to house the very poor. American development reflected similar historical patterns. Colonial-era suburbs tended to house those too poor to live near the city center and to provide pastoral retreats for the very wealthy. The social and economic dislocations of the Industrial Revolution, however, reversed this trend. Industrialization led to previously unknown population densities in urban centers but also caused development to spill out beyond city boundaries. Just as city densities peaked, our cities began decanting rapidly, as residents abandoned them for new suburbs developed expressly for the wealthy and, in due course, for middle- and working-class families as well.[7]

There were, of course, very good reasons for those with the financial means to do so to move away from urban cores. The health and safety threats posed by rapidly industrializing cities were real and substantial: Overcrowding, disease, substandard city services, and poor public infrastructure made cities unpleasant and dangerous places to live. But post-industrial suburbs proliferated for philosophical as well as practical reasons: Those who came to see the home as a sanctuary from the harshness of modern commercial life also came to desire distance between the two "spheres" of human existence. After all, how could the home serve as a retreat from the realities of the urban work-a-day world unless it was physically set apart from them? As Frederick Law Olmsted, the visionary planner and landscape architect who designed New York's Central Park, observed in 1868, "we may safely assume that the general division of all the parts of every considerable town under the two great classifications of commercial and domestic . . . will not only continue, but will become more and more distinct." Olmsted reasoned that the intensity of the intellectual activity demanded by modern commerce made the "tranquilizing recreation" provided by this separation of work and home "more essential to continued health and strength than until lately it has generally been."[8]

Kenneth Jackson's insightful history of the American suburbs chronicles the ties between the development and the promotion of early suburbs and the separate-spheres ideology. He notes, for example, that while earlier peripheral cities self-consciously patterned themselves after their compact urban neighbors, late nineteenth-century "suburbs" featured detached, single-family homes set in a semi-pastoral setting. The single-family dwelling came to embody the do-mestic sphere, and the isolated suburban household became the American ideal. Boosters touted this model of development as the perfect family environment—a true sanctuary purged of the chaos, filth, and degradation associated with the industrial cities. As Jackson observes, "[t]he suburban ideal offered the promise of retreat from commercialism and industry," and every suburban home—from the Victorian mansion to the working man's cottage—"seemed immune to the dislo-cations of an industrializing society and cut off from the toil and turbulence of emerging immigrant ghettos." Thus, one advertisement for a new suburban development featured "Lady Justice" promising an industrious working man a home on an inexpensive payment plan. "Where All Was Darkness, Now Is Light," she proclaims as she points to a tidy suburban cottage.[9]

Thanks to abundant land, increasingly efficient transportation, and the de-velopment of cheaper construction methods (especially the "balloon frame" house), the dreams of "ruralizing all of our population," shared by suburban visionaries such as Olmsted and Andrew Jackson Downing, had begun to be realized by the early twentieth century. As suburban houses became more af-fordable, more "common men" could afford to live in them. The suburban "ideal" was becoming a reality for larger numbers of American families by the time that zoning exploded onto the American scene during the first decades of the twentieth century.[10]

Positive Environmentalism

The reformers who promoted zoning in the early decades of the twentieth century were driven by a complex set of motives—from a faith in the "scien-tific management" of economic life, to revulsion at the condition of immi-grant workers' tenements (combined with an ugly dose of nativism), to the desire to protect property values (especially of single-family homes). However, as Richard Chused has persuasively argued, the Progressive-era proponents of zoning were, first and foremost, "positive environmentalists," who firmly be-lieved that "changing surroundings would change behavior." Specifically, they believed that low-density, single-use suburban developments featuring single-family homes were the best way to advance the important goal of promoting social capital. Many of these men were "internal immigrants" who had moved from the country to the city, and like their antebellum predecessors who de-veloped the first intentional suburbs, they viewed the rural life as an antidote to the harsh realities of the post-industrial world. Zoning offered a legal mechanism for promoting and protecting their ideal. Benjamin Marsh, an early and vigorous proponent of zoning, provided a colorful example of this sentiment in his 1909 defense of city planning. Among the causes of city congestion, Marsh argued, "gregariousness . . . has been a most important factor, particularly in a country which has received so many millions of foreigners within the past few decades." Marsh allowed that "gregariousness" was "not peculiar to the immigrant" but rather also reflected "a serious lapse of our people, who used to prefer the hazards of frontier life to the pleasures and excitements of concentrated populations." In the zoning context, such views translated into the argument that carefully ordering land uses into more "rural" patterns—by mandating open spaces, separating commercial and industrial establishments from residences, and, most importantly, separating single-family homes from all other uses—would curb the social disorders plaguing crowded American cities.[11]

Although zoning is, in most respects, a peculiarly American institution, early twentieth-century reformers imported the idea from Germany, where relatively strong city governments combined with relatively weak private property rights to enable centralized urban planning. Despite their admiration for German planning, many American land-use reformers expressed skepticism that it could be replicated in the United States, where revulsion and distrust of city government was almost as firmly ingrained as atavistic attachment to private property. Nevertheless, in 1916, a coalition of wealthy developers and Progressive-era reformers combined to secure the enactment of the first comprehensive zoning ordinance in New York City. (Los Angeles had adopted a less ambitious ordinance, which segregated heavy industry from residential and commercial uses, in 1909.) While proponents touted New York's zoning scheme as a means of rationalizing and curbing the excesses of commercial development in the city (especially the rapid proliferation of skyscrapers), the immediate motivation for many was a desire to prevent the further "invasion" of sweatshops and their immigrant laborers into respectable communities. Over the previous decade, increasing numbers of garment manufacturers had come to occupy lofts along Fifth Avenue, alarming owners concerned about property values and, importantly, merchants who believed that the appearance of large numbers of immigrant workers on posh city streets frightened away their paying customers. Following an intensive public relations campaign spearheaded by the "Save New York" coalition—made up primarily of wealthy property owners—zoning was enacted into law on July 25, 1916.[12]

What followed, as Seymour Toll has observed, was "one of the most remarkable legislative campaigns in American history." New York quickly became a

"Mecca for pilgrimages of citizens and officials who would have their cities profit by her example." By the end of 1916, eight cities had followed New York's example and enacted zoning controls; by the end of the 1920s, 800 cities had, with a total population of 37 million people. While some of the particulars of New York's zoning story are as unique as the great city where the story unfolded, others repeated themselves many thousands of times over the decade that followed, as zoning swept the nation like wildfire. In 1921, then-Secretary of Commerce Herbert Hoover appointed an advisory committee on zoning, comprised primarily of men who had been intimately involved in the urban reform movement. Within a year, the committee had drafted and issued the Standard State Zoning Enabling Act, which continues to serve as the template for zoning enabling legislation. The purpose of the effort was to provide a model for states that wished to adopt laws empowering local governments to enact zoning legislation. Such state enabling legislation was regarded as a prerequisite to any local zoning activity because, as a matter of legal theory, local governments lack inherent authority to act. Instead, they must draw upon the state's police power, granted to them through enabling legislation or a more general grant of "home rule" authority. The first printed edition of the Standard State Zoning Enabling Act, issued in 1924, sold more than fifty thousand copies. A year later, nearly one-quarter of the states had passed enabling acts modeled substantially on the Standard Act; by the end of the decade, only six states had cities without zoning ordinances. By 1936, 1,322 cities (or 85 percent of the total), had zoning laws. Today, 97 percent of cities with a population greater than 5,000 employ zoning; Houston, Texas, is the only city larger than 250,000 that has not enacted a zoning ordinance.[13]

A variety of overlapping factors explain why zoning proved so attractive to local governments. One common thread in the early zoning movement was the shifting focus from the theoretical to the practical. While the intellectual energy behind zoning remained with planning idealists, zoning "sold" in wholesale political terms by empowering local governments to exclude unwanted land uses and to protect desired ones. For example, in a 2004 article, William Fischel observed that residents of early twentieth-century suburbs were anxious about the invasion of unwanted land uses, especially industrial uses, into their communities. By protecting them from these invasions, zoning guaranteed stable property values and tax revenues. As a result of zoning, suburban communities no longer viewed industrial or urban development as inevitable. Once they could control their land-use densities, suburbs no longer needed access to city services and infrastructure. Instead, they could affordably pro-

vide the less intense services demanded by a residential and commercial citizenry, either alone or in cooperation with other suburban governments.
Moreover, zoning also provided local officials with a legal tool—namely the
power to restrict the locations available for affordable, multifamily housing—
to exclude unwanted residents. As the trial judge opined in his decision invalidating the Euclid, Ohio, zoning ordinance (which would three years later be
overturned by the Supreme Court in the landmark opinion clearing the constitutional path for zoning): "The plain truth is . . . the result to be accomplished is to classify the population and segregate them according to their
income or situation in life." By segregating single-family and multi-family
housing, zoning had the effect of shielding "respectable" Americans from an
influx of less fortunate neighbors, an exclusionary tendency that continues to
plague affordable-housing advocates to this day. Early zoning practices also
accelerated the practice of defensive incorporation. Increasingly, suburban
communities sought to avoid annexation and guarantee long-term legal control over land uses by incorporating as separate municipalities, thus anticipat-
ing current debates about the proper structure of local regulatory authority
within metropolitan areas.[14]

Zoning therefore allowed suburban governments to create, preserve, and enhance the value of the kinds of neighborhoods—low-density communities of
detached, single-family homes—that most Americans preferred. Zoning created a hierarchical pyramid of preferred uses. Industrial uses were at the bot-
tom of the pyramid, followed by commercial, then multi-family housing, and
finally single-family homes. At least until the Second World War, this scheme
was "cumulative," so that favored uses were permitted in, but protected from,
uses permitted in "lower" zones. Sitting at the peak of the zoning pyramid, the
talismanic "home" was thereby absolutely protected from all less-favored uses.*
A separate curiosity of particular relevance to this book, however, is why zoning
universally shielded single-family homes so completely from all elements of
economic life, with most going so far as to prohibit all but a few home occupations. Standard explanations for exclusively residential communities focus on
the noise and congestion associated with commercial activity. For example, in
Village of Euclid v. Ambler Realty Company, Justice Sutherland expressed concern about "the disturbing noises incident to increased traffic and business . . .

---

* By the second decade of the twentieth century, private deed restrictions, perfected by
Kansas City developer J. C. Nichols, provided additional, perpetual protection for single-
family communities.

depriving children of the privilege of quiet and open spaces for play." His opinion echoed those of dozens of lower-court judges considering constitutional challenges to zoning in the decade leading up to *Euclid*. As Justice Owen of the Louisiana Supreme Court warned a few years earlier, "Places of business are noisy; they are apt to be disturbing at night; some of them are malodorous; some are apt to breed rats, mice, flies, ants, etc."[15]

But two other, more theoretical, objections to the mixing of residential and commercial life also shaped zoning patterns. The first echoed the separate-spheres ideology of the previous century, suggesting that single-family residential development promoted social capital. As the California Supreme Court observed in 1925, "Residential zoning may, in the last analysis, be rested upon the protection of the civic and social values of the American home. . . . The home and its intrinsic influences are the very foundation of good citizenship, and any factor contributing to the establishment of homes and fostering of home life doubtless tends to the enhancement not only of community life but of the life of the nation as a whole." To zoning proponents who endorsed this view, the physical separation of work and home, through the segregation of homes into "exclusively residential" districts, was desirable not simply because commercial activity was noisy and disruptive but also because it was *disordered*. Economic life, early zoners argued, endangered the mental and physical health of women and children. These objections can be found both in the writings of early zoning proponents and in pre-*Euclid* lower-court decisions passing on the constitutionality of zoning laws. Both the judges considering challenges to zoning before the Supreme Court and the reformers promoting and defending it voiced two overlapping objections to mixing residential and commercial uses. For example, the New York Court of Appeals wrote in 1925 that the establishment of exclusively residential zones was sound policy because"[t]he primary purpose of such a district is safe, healthful, and comfortable family life rather than the development of commercial instincts and the pursuit of pecuniary profits." The influential *amicus curiae* brief submitted by Alfred Bettman on behalf of the National Conference of City Planning in the *Euclid* case relied upon a similar argument. For example, Bettman included in an appendix a report of the Public Health Federation of Cincinnati suggesting that "men and women are better able to withstand the strain of present-day life when they may enjoy rest and quiet in their homes."[16]

Zoning advocates and judges in early zoning decisions also articulated a case for exclusively residential zoning that parallels in many ways the standard social-influence arguments in favor of order-maintenance policies. That is, many contemporary observers argued that traditional urban, mixed-use environments were themselves disorders that should be suppressed (or prevented *ex ante*). As Lawrence Veiller, secretary of the National Housing Association and a man intimately involved with the early zoning movement, observed at the 1914 National Conference on City Planning, "It is only in very recent years that we have been conscious of the necessity of doing something to protect our citizens in the enjoyment of the right to lead a quiet, contented, rational existence. . . . Heretofore we have gone along in a truly American fashion of mixing up in a haphazard way business and residential districts without regard to the rights of others or the welfare of the community." His words were echoed a decade later by the Ohio Supreme Court, which observed that "Family life is promoted by the separation of families, and by their residence in districts where . . . the freedom from the society which presses around one in a partial business and tenement district, make for health through recreation and peace of mind."[17]

Reformers' endorsement of these arguments was hardly novel. Housing advocates' belief that urban design could and should serve as a means of social control had long been evident in the tenement reform movement. For example, "model" tenements frequently incorporated internal courtyards in an effort to break what Jacob Riis called the "street habit" of tenement dwellers—the bustling activity on the front stoops, sidewalks, and back alleys—by isolating residents from the corrupting influence of their neighborhood. It is hardly surprising, therefore, that Frederick Law Olmsted Jr., in presenting a city plan to New Haven, Connecticut, extolled the civilizing influence of good planning. After observing that "[p]eople of the old New England stock still to a large extent control the city," Olmsted warned, "and if they want New Haven to be a fit and worthy place for their descendants it behooves them to establish conditions about the lives of *all* the people that will make the best fellow-citizens of them and of their children." As Daniel Burnham, the principal architect of the 1896 Chicago World's Fair Exhibit and a central figure in the "City Beautiful" movement that influenced many early zoning proponents, once asserted, "After all has been said, good citizenship is the prime object of good city planning."[18]

During the early decades of the twentieth century courts and policy advocates expressed two overlapping social-norms justifications for single-use zoning. First, they asserted that zoning was necessary because the mixing of residential and commercial uses tended to incubate disorder. As the Louisiana Supreme Court observed in 1923, "A place of business in a residence neighborhood furnishes an excuse for any criminal to go into the neighborhood where, otherwise, a stranger would be under the ban of suspicion. Besides, open shops invite loiterers and idlers to congregate." Similarly, the Ohio Supreme Court warned in 1920 that "[t]he number of people passing in and out [of mixed-use districts], render immoral practices therein more difficult of detection and suppression." It reemphasized in a decision five years later that "[t]he entrance of business blocks into a residence district tends to 'blight' the district and gradually invite therein hazards, both physical and moral, which exist in the sections which combine business and home life."[19]

Zoning advocates also urged that mixed-use neighborhoods had a negative effect on their residents' mental and physical well-being. As Benjamin Marsh argued in his influential 1909 treatise, the "fruits of congestion" included a "high insanity rate . . . loss of physical vigor . . . loss of privacy" and a "low morality rate." Zoning would serve to minimize these effects in two ways. First, it would prevent the kind of mixed-use environments that generated them. And second, by shoring up property values, it would encourage investment in single-family homes, not just by the wealthy but by those of moderate means. The proceedings of the 1919 Conference on City Planning, for example, included an extensive discussion suggesting that industry benefited from zoning by encouraging workers to invest in homes in suburban settings. Without zoning, conference speakers urged, workers fearful that the incursion of commercial establishments would undermine property values would be reluctant to purchase single-family homes. Industry would suffer as a result, if laborers remained in urban settings instead of relocating to "contented home settings."[20]

And when the Supreme Court considered the constitutionality of zoning a few years later, the concern that city planning generally—and the preservation and single-use zoning in particular—was critical to the moral development of young people formed a centerpiece of planners' defense of zoning. In his influential *amicus* brief, Alfred Bettman reminded the Court:

[T]he man who seeks . . . an orderly neighborhood . . . assum[es] that his children are likely to grow mentally, physically and morally more healthful in such a neighborhood than in a disorderly, noisy, slovenly, blighted and slum-like district. This assumption is indubitably correct. The researches of physicians and public health students have demonstrated the importance of our physical environment as a factor in our physical health, mental sanity and moral strength; and the records of hospitals and criminal courts amply support these conclusions. . . . Disorderliness in the environment has as detrimental an effect upon health and character as disorderliness within the house itself.

By referring to "blighted and slum-like district[s]," Bettman drew upon the well-accepted stereotypes of the immigrant ghettos—places where *urban* living conditions were widely assumed to impede the development of solid American citizens. Bettman reminded the Court that by segregating residential and commercial land uses, zoning could minimize what social norms scholars call the "negative social-influence effects" of urban life. In the end, as Seymour Toll suggests, "it may well be that the laurel wreath for the *Euclid* decision should have gone not to . . . the small zealous group of men who made zoning one of the important progressive missions of this century . . . [but to] Herbert Spencer," the father of Social Darwinism and the quest for social engineering that flowed from it.[21]

Order Construction in the Post-*Euclid* World

After *Euclid* cleared the constitutional path, zoning became unstoppable, but it affected development in cities and suburbs quite differently. In older communities, which were built up prior to the enactment of zoning laws, zoning rules tended to map onto preexisting development patterns. Where preexisting patterns departed from new zoning-use restrictions, older, established land uses were grandfathered (at least temporarily) by "nonconforming use" provisions. Zoning restrictions affected all new construction in cities, when, for example, nonconforming uses were abandoned (as regulators anticipated and hoped). New buildings also had to satisfy the height, bulk, and setback requirements of the city's zoning codes and, as automobile usage increased, provide for generous amounts of off-street parking. All of these regulations, in keeping with their intent, tended over time to give city neighborhoods a more "suburban" flavor. In new suburbs, however, zoning provided the blueprint for development. While urban governments might hope that their communities would evolve to become more "orderly," reflecting over time the order constructed by zoning maps, suburban governments could mandate that order *ex ante*. The careful segregation of land uses—the elimination of traditional, mixed-use "urban" neighborhoods and the elevation of single-family homes above all other land uses—became the American norm. Indeed, in retrospect, it is hardly surprising that then-Secretary of Commerce Herbert Hoover promoted suburbs as havens of "normalcy," in large part by encouraging the rapid proliferation of zoning codes.[22]

The expansion of this orderly, suburban pattern of development accelerated in the late 1920s, when the decentralization of American urbanized areas began to peak. The Great Depression slowed the urban exodus, as the economic downturn brought the housing boom to a halt. (Between 1928 and 1933, both new residential construction and expenditures on home repairs declined by 90 percent.) Changes in government housing policy that occurred during the Great Depression did, however, set the stage for the explosion in suburban development—and the replication on a grand scale of the order constructed by zoning laws. In the early 1930s, desperate to stem the tide of home foreclosures—which had reached the rate of more than one thousand per day by the spring of 1933—the federal government embarked on an unprecedented path of intervening in the housing industry. In 1932, the Federal Home Loan Bank Act established a credit reserve for mortgage lenders. The following year, Congress created the Home Owners' Loan Corporation, or HOLC, which refinanced tens of thousands of mortgages in danger of foreclosure. The HOLC had an immediate short-term impact; assisting 40 percent of eligible homeowners nationwide. But its lasting influence came from its perfection of the long-term, self-amortizing mortgage. Previous practice favored short-term (during the 1920s, for example, five-to-ten-year terms) renewable mortgages requiring large deposits. HOLC mortgages were longer— the payment period extended to about twenty years—and fully amortized, meaning that houses were fully paid off when the final payment was due. Therefore, HOLC loans not only saved many thousands of families from losing existing homes but also enabled future homeowners to secure affordable, stable financing for new homes.

HOLC practices also influenced urban design. Because all Depression-era loans were risky—more than 40 percent of HOLC loans were foreclosed even after refinancing—the agency perfected the art of property appraisal. The agency devised a system of rating neighborhoods designed to predict the marketability and useful life of housing. The system used a color-coded letter-grading scale to rate neighborhoods. "A," or "green," neighborhoods were new, ethnically homogenous communities that would be "in demand as residential locations in good times and in bad." "B," or "blue," neighborhoods were those that had "reached their peak" but were predicted to remain desirable for some years to come. "C," or "yellow," ratings went to "declining" communities. Finally, neighborhoods "in which the things taking place in C areas have already occurred" were rated "D," or "red." Homes within a "redlined" community were ineligible for refinancing. These ratings systematically disadvantaged older urban neighborhoods for a number of reasons: Newer homes were preferred over older ones; ethnically homogeneous neighborhoods over diverse ones; and single-use, suburban land-use patterns over mixed-use, urban ones. The HOLC assessment of a white, working-class neighborhood in St. Louis, for example, complained, "Lots are small, houses are only slightly set back from the sidewalks, and there is a general appearance of congestion. . . . Age of properties, general mixture or type, proximity to industrial section on northeast and much less desirable areas to the south makes this a good fourth grade area."[23]

After the Great Depression, these appraisal practices were embraced by the two federal agencies—the Federal Housing Administration, or FHA, and the Veterans Administration—that exerted the greatest influence on postwar housing policies. The FHA, created in 1934, insures long-term mortgage loans for home construction and sale. The FHA revolutionized the practice of residential financing—reducing the down payment required for a home loan from at least 30 percent to 10 percent or less; extending the loan repayment period to thirty years; insisting that home loans be fully paid at the time of the last payment; and establishing uniform standards for home construction. These four changes—along with the mortgage-interest tax deduction—make it cheaper for many Americans to buy than to rent a home. Although the FHA's role as mortgage guarantor has diminished over the past few decades, these reforms have been widely adopted, and have helped us to become a nation of homeowners: In 2005, nearly 68 percent of Americans—nearly 75 percent of whites and 50 percent of African Americans and Hispanics—owned their own homes. Evidence suggesting that the subprime mortgage crisis has disproportionately affected owners in the latter two groups, however, suggests that the promising rise in rates of minority home ownership may have been inflated by overexuberant lending practices.[24]

The extent to which the FHA influenced the decline of urban centers in the postwar period has sometimes been overstated. Suburbanization was well under way long before the Second World War, and FHA lending practices arguably did little more than reinforce these trends. The FHA did, however, do much to shape postwar suburbia, especially by promoting monolithic, single-use development patterns. Importantly, the availability of government-insured loans enabled residential developers to finance large-scale residential developments. Prior to the Second World War, large-scale residential developments were rare. The relative paucity of financing options meant that prewar subdividers tended to purchase developable land and then sell lots to individual builders. Federal intervention in the housing lending market enabled subdividers to become full-fledged housing developers, not only purchasing and improving land, but building and selling completed homes as well. The FHA also worked hand in hand with developers to strengthen both private and public land-use regulations. Private developers had, since the inception of the earliest Victorian suburbs, influenced public planning policies by shaping American conceptions of desirable communities. Indeed, as Marc Weiss has argued, developer-implemented private deed restrictions, which were eagerly accepted by homeowners, "opened the wedge for the introduction and extension of public land-use controls," serving as "both the physical and political model for zoning laws and subdivision regulations."[25]

Many of the largest developers, such as Kansas City's J. C. Nichols, were staunch advocates of public land-use regulations, believing that "municipal assistance" (both financial and regulatory) was a necessary component of their community-building efforts. During the 1930s and 1940s, developers worked with the FHA to shape and promote uniform subdivision standards and more restrictive zoning practices. As Gwendolyn Wright has observed, postwar housing policies were "designed to stabilize the nuclear family and perpetuate an 'orderly'—that is, use-segregated and zoned—pattern of development." The FHA not only made zoning and subdivision regulation a prerequisite for insuring a home mortgage, but also exerted direct pressure on local governments to eliminate zoning practices that supported denser, mixed-use developments, such as "overzoning" to promote property speculation and apartment construction and "spot zoning" to authorize small commercial incursions in residential neighborhoods. In 1940 alone, the FHA's Land Planning Division held 221 conferences to assist local officials in the "preparation of city plans and zoning ordinances." These efforts had their intended effect—namely, the cementing of single-use-development patterns. Not only did the favored zoning practices preclude more "urban" land-use patterns, but the FHA's regulatory policies also put the piecemeal builders who dominated the prewar suburban housing market out of business. These builders, known derisively as "jerrybuilders" or "curbstoners," found it difficult to satisfy the FHA's development standards and therefore were unable to secure mortgage insurance. As a result, large developments of relatively homogeneous homes became the norm.[26]

The FHA, like the HOLC before it, also used the power of the purse to encourage suburban development over urban redevelopment. The vast majority of FHA-backed loans supported new construction in the suburbs. The FHA required an "unbiased professional estimate" as a prerequisite to any loan guarantee, and appraisal practices systematically disfavored older, urban communities. The factors given the most weight in FHA consideration—"relative economic stability" and "protection from adverse influences"—were distinctly anti-urban. For example, the FHA's 1939 *Underwriting Manual* directed appraisers that "crowded neighborhoods" and that "older properties . . . have a tendency to lessen desirability." The FHA also sought to control the design and construction of suburban homes in an effort to achieve "neighborhood stability." The agency not only endorsed zoning but insisted that no single-family home have facilities that could be used as a shop, office, preschool, or rental unit; it also encouraged the use of restrictive covenants to further guarantee residential homogeneity. The FHA disfavored multifamily residential construction. Although the FHA had a division devoted to the promotion of large-scale rental construction in big cities, loans for apartment buildings were approved far less frequently and on much less desirable terms. And while the FHA did insure loans for home repair and improvement, the loans were relatively small and short term, making it more affordable for many families to purchase new homes rather than renovate old ones. Well into the postwar period, the FHA also refused to insure loans in racially mixed neighborhoods, expressly indicating a concern that "inharmonious racial groups" led to neighborhood instability. It was not until the mid-1960s—when the Civil Rights movement began to raise awareness of the negative effects of discriminatory redlining on urban communities—that the FHA began to insure more loans in city neighborhoods.[27]

Order Construction with a Bulldozer

The widespread condemnation of the two postwar federal programs that did exert profound influence on the order of our urban centers—urban renewal and public housing—stands in sharp contrast to the remarkable success of the FHA's efforts to encourage suburban home ownership. Both of these programs also strongly favored single-use development, although the type of development funded—high density residential and commercial construction—diverged sharply from the single-family residential neighborhoods underwritten by the FHA. The methods chosen by planners to shape postwar cities also contrast sharply with the FHA's indirect role. The FHA undoubtedly encouraged suburbanization by favoring new suburban neighborhoods and shunning older urban ones. But urban renewal and public housing programs armed local officials with the tools needed to forcibly reorder our cities quickly—money, the power of eminent domain, and bulldozers. The result was the elimination of traditional multiple-use urban communities and their replacement with single-use commercial and residential developments.

Urban Renewal

The "urban renewal" ideal emerged conceptually during the 1930s and 1940s among planning intellectuals convinced that virtually all of the largest American cities, as well as many smaller urban centers, were in a state of rapid deterioration. City planners and municipal leaders recognized urban problems in fundamentally material, not sociological, terms. As such, they hoped to rectify the problem of urban "blight" primarily through the wholesale destruction and reconstruction of existing neighborhoods. "If we are to build houses and cities adequate to the needs of the twentieth century," social critic Catherine Bauer observed in a 1934 essay, "we must start over again from the ground up." After the war, the Housing Act of 1949 provided substantial funds for slum clearance and urban development, financing both urban renewal and public housing. The urban renewal program underwrote the widespread exercise of eminent domain by local governments to condemn "blighted" areas and sell the properties to private investors at bargain-basement prices. As a result, "city renewal directors were searching for 'blight that's right'—places just bad enough to clear but good enough to attract developers." In their quest to eliminate "blight," officials razed homes and displaced hundreds of thousands of families and tens of thousands of businesses. Thousands more businesses and several hundred thousand more families were displaced during the same period to make way for the interstate highway system.[28]

Like their Progressive-era ancestors, urban renewal enthusiasts believed that reordering our cities would solve urban problems. Thus, "slum-removal" efforts reflected a desire not simply to eliminate unsafe and unsanitary conditions—by the actual demolition of substandard buildings—but also a conviction that the mixed-use, prezoning form of many urban neighborhoods was hopelessly antiquated. As Louis Justement argued in 1946, "The time has come to rebuild our cities. The mere redevelopment of blighted areas will not provide the inspiration that we shall need to achieve . . . the goal of further arresting urban decay." Advocates believed that the only way to save cities was to transform, according to a rational plan, mixed-use, prezoning neighborhoods. Thus, the urban renewal bulldozers were not overly discerning. The good had to go in order to redeem the bad; nearly 40 percent of dwellings demolished for urban renewal projects were classified as structurally sound. The goal, in the words of one slum-clearance proponent, was not to be "destructive," but rather "to reconstruct the city . . . building everything in its proper place" according to a plan that "thinks about the city as a whole . . . and tries to conceive of the needs and function of the city as an entity." Renewal projects sought to "modernize" the city by replacing mixed-use neighborhoods with projects designed to carefully segregate different zones of human activity. Planners also were enamored of modernist architecture and favored unadorned, sterile buildings, set apart from areas in the surrounding community that survived the bulldozers.[29]

The wisdom of the massive land grab that enabled the interstate highway system, constructed during this same period, remains the subject of substantial debate—although efforts (discussed at length in chapter 7) to tear down elevated highways, redevelop the land beneath them, and reconnect the communities that they divided suggest at least some projects were ill-conceived. Urban renewal, however, has been widely condemned, on both humanitarian and planning grounds. Jane Jacobs colorfully captured the humanitarian critique when she observed during the height of the urban renewal period:

> [P]eople who get marked with the planners' hex signs are pushed about, expropriated, and uprooted much as if they were the subject of a conquering power. Thousands upon thousands of small businesses are destroyed, their proprietors ruined, with hardly a gesture at compensation. Whole communities torn apart and sown to the winds, with a reaping of cynicism, resentment, and despair that must be heard and seen to be believed. . . .
>
>> Could Job have been thinking of Chicago when he wrote:
>> Here are the men that alter their neighbor's landmark . . .
>> shoulder the poor aside, conspire to oppress the friendless.
>> Reap they the field that is none of theirs, strip the vine-
>> yard wrongfully seized from its owner . . .
>> A cry goes up from the city streets, where wounded men lie groaning . . .
>
> If so, he was also thinking of New York, Philadelphia, Boston, Washington, St. Louis, San Francisco and a number of other places. The economic rationale of current city rebuilding is a hoax. The economics of city rebuilding do not rest soundly on reasoned investment of public tax subsidies, as urban renewal theory proclaims, but also on vast, involuntary subsidies wrung out of helpless site victims.

Jacobs's words proved prophetic. Long-term studies of urban renewal projects found that urban-renewal-era planners were mistaken to disregard the high social-capital costs of destroying poor but socially cohesive urban communities. There is ample evidence that the forced displacements destroyed many close-knit urban communities and "created nothing less than a life crisis" for residents. As Bernard Friedan and Lynne Sagalyn have noted, "planners had a knack for picking low-income neighborhoods where residents held deep attachments to friends, relatives, neighbors, churches, schools, and local businesses." One study of the long-term psychological effects on residents displaced by the demolition of Boston's West End in the late 1950s found that 46 percent of women and 38 percent of men suffered "fairly severe grief." Displaced residents in Southwest Washington, D.C.— the renewal effort at issue in *Berman v. Parker* (and discussed at greater length in chapter 7)—reported similar emotional losses.[30]

Unfortunately, despite the enthusiasm of "slum clearance" proponents, the physical and economic results of urban renewal were profoundly disappointing. In many places, urban renewal likely made things worse. After bulldozers destroyed communities and scattered residents to the winds, many residents had difficulty even locating a new place to live. This was especially true of black families, for whom the post-displacement situation was "close to desperate." Continued migration from the rural South led to overcrowding in the remaining black neighborhoods, and systematic housing discrimination made white areas off-limits even for those who could afford them. Most of those displaced during the period eventually found replacement housing, but many ended up paying more for living arrangements that were not appreciably better than those they left behind. The typical resident displaced by urban renewal paid 20 percent more rent after being relocated. Subsequent studies found that from one-fourth to one-half of displaced families were living in substandard housing despite a substantial rent increase.[31]

Adding insult to injury, redevelopment efforts tended to proceed at an excruciatingly slow pace. On average, it took three years for the local government even to sell the condemned land to a private developer. In its report to Congress and President Johnson, the National Commission on Urban Problems deplored the "unconscionable amount of time consumed" by the urban renewal process. Writing in 1959, Lyman Brownfield, general counsel for the U.S. Housing and Home Finance Agency, complained that cities had disposed of only 30 percent of the land acquired through urban renewal programs. Local officials only made matters worse by creating "land banks" (that is, by condemning and stockpiling land until needed). Even more depressing, "many cities saw nothing at all rise from the ground." As of 1965, the Kosciusko Project in St. Louis, the Southwest Temple Project in Philadelphia, and the Camden Industrial Park in Baltimore had been vacant since 1956, and the Ellicott District Project in Buffalo and the Lake Meadows Project in Chicago, since 1952. Rubble-strewn wastelands in St. Louis and St. Paul earned such less-than-affectionate nicknames as "Hiroshima Flats" and "Superhole." Many never-renewed plots of vacant land continue to haunt cities, depressing values of adjacent property and plaguing communities with concomitant ills, such as crime, vandalism, fire hazards, and worry about unsafe and unsanitary conditions. Although much of the land condemned for urban renewal purposes was eventually developed, renewers' hopes that urban renewal would accomplish one of the three land-use goals set forth in the introductory pages of this book—namely, to promote city-suburb competitiveness—never materialized. As Michael Schill has observed, "[t]he numbers of jobs created and the amount of private sector investment generated by the program were below hopes and expectations of its proponents [and] the human toll caused by displacement and the destabilization of nearby residential communities casts doubt upon the efficacy of subsidized site assembly." It is therefore ironic, but perhaps not surprising, that many cities now seek to advance the goal of city-suburb competitiveness by replacing *successful* urban renewal projects with new communities that look like the ones destroyed by bulldozers to pave the path to a modern city.[37]

Public Housing

Unfortunately, federal intervention in urban housing policy during the same period makes urban renewal look like a resounding success. After the war, the Housing Act of 1949, which also funded urban renewal efforts, authorized the construction of 810,000 new public housing units. In order to accommodate the concerns of private developers, who were worried that a massive influx of new subsidized housing units would reduce overall housing prices, the Housing Act included an "equivalent elimination" or "one-up–one-down" provision. This provision required the demolition of one unit of substandard housing for every new unit of public housing constructed. Since the Housing Act also authorized only the demolition of "blighted" or "slum" properties, the provision effectively precluded suburbs from participating in the public housing program; they lacked substandard housing that qualified for demolition. As a result, almost all postwar public housing projects were constructed in poor urban communities. The equivalent elimination provision also affected the design of public housing. Because developable space was at a premium in cities and developers were eager to claim most cleared properties for profit-generating urban renewal efforts, dense high-rise construction was attractive. But ideology also drove public housing authorities, in the postwar years, to shift away from smaller projects and toward massive high rises. Public housing advocates, like their urban renewal brethren, were both enamored of modernist architecture—especially the writings of architect Le Corbusier—and thoroughly soured on the design of traditional cities. They favored the large-scale demolition of existing neighborhoods of low-rise townhomes and apartment buildings aligned along traditional grid-pattern streets and their replacement with "superblocks" of high rises on reconfigured limited-access streets. Such efforts were undertaken in part to situate families within an ideal environment that would break the slum habits associated with urban life. As the Chicago Housing Authority's Elizabeth Wood proclaimed at the time, planning for public housing "must be bold and comprehensive—or it is useless and wasted. If it is not bold, the result will be a series of small projects in a wilderness of slums."

Wood later withdrew her endorsement of large-scale high-rise projects, but her realization, and that of others, came too late to avoid consigning tens of thousands of families to the ravages of a failed social experiment. Using the three policy goals articulated in the introduction as yardsticks against which to measure success, postwar public housing policy was an abysmal failure. Bulldozers destroyed whatever social capital existed in the communities cleared to make space for the high rises. These communities were replaced with developments that could hardly have been more ill-suited to rebuilding what was lost. Not only were the physical designs of the high rise projects antithetical to community building—as Oscar Newman devastatingly demonstrated in his classic *Defensible Space*—but, moreover, the dense concentrations of very poor people living in them proved to foster and amplify social disorder. By the end of the 1960s, the effort to order the lives of America's poor by cramming them into "orderly" high rise developments had already come to be seen by many as a monumental failure. In 1968, the National Commission on Urban Problems condemned public housing as "anticommunity," in large part because of the dominance of high-rise, single-use design. Today, the projects are disappearing, along with their urban renewal cousins, in favor of new mixed-use projects designed to mimic the very neighborhoods that previous generations of planners scorned.[33]

3

A Four-Category
Taxonomy of Disorder

At the same time that urban policy has become intensely focused on curbing urban disorder, many policymakers, land-use scholars, and urban planners have come to question the wisdom of the order-construction enterprise *on order-maintenance grounds.* This new generation of zoning skeptics, especially those who endorse the "new urbanism," worry that the separation of urban land uses might contribute to, rather than suppress, urban disorder. This view can be traced to Jane Jacobs's insight—repeated quite often these days in law reviews, architectural magazines, and planning journals—that *people* make city streets feel safe and vibrant. Jacobs argued that the busyness generated by mixed-land-use environments might bolster, rather than suppress, the social norms needed to keep harmful disorder in check. If so, the law can help ensure healthy urban communities by fostering, or at the very least permitting, a diversity of land uses. Mixed-use environments, Jacobs argued, give *people* more reasons to be present in a community—publicly present, that is, on streets and sidewalks—throughout the day and night. If Jacobs was correct, in other words, zoning is an urban villain: By separating economic and noneconomic activities, zoning may devastate city neighborhoods by precluding the diversity that gives them both security and life. According to this view, city officials make a serious mistake when they embrace the traditional assumption that ordered land uses suppress disorder.[1]

My initial ruminations about the intersections between land-use policies and order-maintenance policies were sparked by a conversation in my urban development seminar several years ago. The semester's material begins with zoning—and Jacobs's critique of zoning—and ends with the order-maintenance debate. At the end of the semester, a student asked whether the increasingly widespread endorsement of Jacobs's ideas, or at least that version (or some would argue perversion) of it promoted by today's "new urbanists," conflicted with the even-more-widespread embrace of the broken windows hypothesis. After all, the broken windows hypothesis emphasizes the need for government intervention to impose order in our urban environments, and local officials have long assumed that zoning is precisely such an intervention. On the other hand, as Wesley Skogan has observed, Jacobs believed that "a measure of disorder is actually *good* for us." Is it not the case, my student asked, that urban policymakers are coming to demand less disorder *and* more disorder?[2]

This chapter considers this excellent question. The chapter begins by highlighting the confusion about what disorder is and the paucity of careful thinking about how manifestations of disorder interact with one another. The central purpose of this discussion is not to articulate an all-encompassing definition of disorder, but rather to highlight how this confusion hinders systematic analysis of the myriad policies seeking to address the many different manifestations of disorder in our cities. Confusion over what disorder *is* poses a particular impediment to sorting through a puzzle at the heart of this book—namely, the connections (if any) between commercial activity, land-use patterns, disorder, and crime in urban communities. As discussed in greater detail in chapter 2, early zoning proponents proceeded on the assumption that commercial activity needed to be limited, controlled, and contained for many of the same reasons that order-maintenance proponents seek to suppress disorder: They believed that commercial activity was either itself disorder or that commercial activity in residential communities undermined the social capital associated with healthy, orderly homes. Today, although city officials acting as *developers* increasingly promote projects that incorporate mixed-use urban designs, city officials acting as *regulators* continue to act as if they share these early reformers' belief that ordered land uses suppress disorder. For example, they treat zoning rules as a helpful disorder-suppression device and consider commercial activity (or at least unauthorized commercial activity) in residential neighborhoods as a "disorder" to be suppressed.

It might be that these city officials are right. Perhaps commercial activity either is itself "disorder" or, alternatively, it generates disorder (and perhaps also crime). Or it might be that they are making a category mistake. Current thinking about urban policy exhibits the apparent schizophrenia identified by my student only if the mixed-land-use environments championed by Jacobs (and by new urbanists today) are in fact disorderly—or, put slightly differently, only if commercial activity is, or causes, disorder. The fact that an environment is not "ordered" according to a certain principle—for example, Euclidean zoning—does not (necessarily) make it "disordered." Zoning laws provide one mechanism by which regulators order our cities, but neighborhoods that fail to conform to the single-use ideal are not necessarily disorderly ones. Regulators schooled in the traditional arguments against the integration of commercial and residential land uses may fail to see that such neighborhoods are *differently ordered*, according to another regulatory mechanism (for example, the form-based coding promoted by new urbanists or the informal norms championed by Jacobs). If the apparent disorder of mixed-use environments generated by economic life is actually something else—busyness, perhaps, or vitality—reflecting a healthy organic order, then the contradiction in demands for less disorder, and more, vanishes. If this is the case, policymakers who mistake healthy busyness for unhealthy disorder may cling to the order-construction enterprise with tragic results. As Jacobs asserted, "There is a quality even meaner than outright ugliness or disorder, and this meaner quality is the dishonest mask of pretended order, achieved by ignoring or suppressing the real order that is struggling to exist and to be served."[3]

This chapter explores the connections between commercial activity, crime, and disorder in two contexts. The first is the long-standing debate over the regulation of street vending in New York City, which reemerged as a major legal and political issue during the early 1990s. The second is the asserted connection between mixed-use urban neighborhoods and crime and disorder, which is the subject of a surprisingly extensive (but relatively rarely cited, at least in the legal literature) empirical literature. Analyzing the possibility of a commerce-disorder nexus in these specific contexts helps overcome some of the definitional confusion that plagues the order-maintenance literature; it may also shed light on how other manifestations of disorder affect urban health.

The Disorder Muddle

"Disorder" is neither well defined nor well understood. Despite the fact that disorder-suppression efforts have taken center stage in urban policy in recent years, systematic efforts to define "disorder" are in short supply. Both the order-maintenance and land-use literatures tend to gloss over important first-order questions, including what disorder *is* and whether all "disorders" are harmful, or—as Jacobs suggested—whether some manifestations of disorder actually are healthy, enlivening, and even able to suppress bad disorder. The failure to carefully consider these questions carries with it the risk of overinclusion: Any urban environment that is not "orderly" becomes "disorderly," and urban policymakers set their sights on imposing order without carefully considering the potential unintended consequences of their order-promotion efforts.

Two-Column Laundry Lists

Most discussions of order-maintenance policies begin by dividing the universe of disorder into two categories—social disorder and physical disorder. According to Wesley Skogan, "Social disorder is a matter of behavior," and "physical disorder involves visual signs of negligence and unchecked decay." Beyond this familiar distinction between physical and social disorder, many scholars' approach to defining disorder parallels Justice Potter Stewart's approach to defining obscenity: "I know it when I see it." Consider, for example, the description provided by Skogan in the introduction to *Disorder and Decline*: "Disorder is evident in the widespread appearance of junk and trash in vacant lots; it is evident, too, in decaying homes, boarded-up buildings, the vandalism of public and private property, graffiti, and stripped and abandoned cars in streets and alleys. It is signaled by bands of teenagers congregating on street corners, by the presence of prostitutes and panhandlers, by public drinking, the verbal harassment of women, and open gambling and drug use." Skogan's laundry-list approach pervades the order-maintenance literature. For example, Debra Livingston has identified panhandling (especially around ATM machines), public urination, sleeping in parks, loitering (by drug dealers as well as teens), public intoxication, playing loud music, "hanging out," vandalism, fire-damaged buildings, littering, "cruising," fighting, drug trafficking, gambling on public streets, prostitution, homelessness, and underage drinking as chief targets of order-maintenance efforts. After defining disorder as "incivility, boorish and threatening behavior that disturbs life, especially urban life," George Kelling and Catherine Coles provide a similar list of disorders, adding the "obstruction of streets and public spaces," "menacing behavior," "unlicensed vending and peddling," "squeegeeing" car windows, and "other such acts."[4]

Empirical studies of disorder similarly tend to measure the presence and effects of selected manifestations of disorder, rather than attempt a careful definition of the term. For example, Robert Sampson and Stephen Raudenbush's effort to systematically observe and record disorder in Chicago neighborhoods sought to measure the presence of nine "physical disorders" ("cigarettes in the street, garbage/litter in the street, empty beer bottles, graffiti painted over, gang graffiti, abandoned cars, condoms on sidewalks, needles/syringes on sidewalks, and graffiti") and seven "social disorders" ("adults loitering or congregating, drinking alcohol in public, peer group with gang indicators present, adults fighting or arguing in a hostile manner, selling drugs, prostitutes on the street, [and] drunken intoxicated people on the street.") The authors provided little by way of explanation about why they selected these particular manifestations of disorder, other than to suggest that some were "less serious indicators of disorder in public spaces" and others "more serious." The failure to account for the complex nature of disorder—especially the underexplored connections between different kinds of disorder and between order and disorder—impedes systematic evaluation of when, where, and what kinds of disorder should be suppressed.[5]

Four Overlapping Categories

This traditional approach to defining disorder is flawed for a number of related reasons. As an initial matter, the seriousness of the alleged "disorders" included on disorder laundry lists varies dramatically. There is a vast gulf of deviancy between cigarettes on the street and prostitutes on the street. Robert Sampson and Stephen Raudenbush have observed that one of the reasons that disorder may appear to "cause" crime is that the elements of disorder (or some manifestations of disorder) may be "part and parcel of crime itself." Indeed, many things traditionally characterized as *disorder* are *crimes* rather than precursors to crimes. Consider, for example, the California Supreme Court's decision, in *State ex rel. Gallo v. Acuna.* The case concerned an effort of the City of San Jose, California, to enjoin members of a violent street gang from terrorizing the city's Rocksprings neighborhood. San Jose's complaint described Rocksprings as "an urban war zone":

> Gang members . . . display a casual contempt for notions of law, order, and decency—
> openly drinking, smoking dope, sniffing toluene, and even snorting cocaine laid out

in neat lines on the hoods of residents' cars. The people who live in Rocksprings are subjected to loud talk, loud music, vulgarity, profanity, brutality, fistfights and the sound of gunfire echoing in the streets. . . . Murder, attempted murder, drive-by shootings, assault and battery, vandalism, arson, and theft are commonplace. . . . Area residents have had their garages used as urinals; their homes commandeered as escape routes; their walls, fences, garage doors, sidewalks, and even their vehicles turned into a sullen canvas of gang graffiti. The people of this community are prisoners in their own homes. Violence and the threat of violence are constant.

Although most of these activities are criminal, many of them major felonies, the city opted to file a public-nuisance action—a classic antidisorder device—against gang members, rather than to prosecute them. The trial court entered an order enjoining the defendants from engaging in a host of criminal activities, including those listed above, as well as the fear-inducing behaviors targeted by the gang-loitering ordinance invalidated in *City of Chicago v. Morales*—"standing, sitting, walking, driving, gathering or appearing anywhere in public view with any . . . [other gang] member." The California Supreme Court ultimately approved this course of action, reasoning that the city could choose to address the problem of gang criminality either *ex ante* through a civil injunction or *ex post* through criminal prosecution.[6]

Environmental psychologist Ralph Taylor's "continuum of disorder" better captures the progressive nature of disorder. Taylor groups disorders into three categories—conditions, street hassles, and crime—and arrays different manifestations of disorder falling into each category on a continuum (figure 3.1). Taylor's continuum remedies a central defect in the laundry-list approach by seeking to capture the progressive severity of different manifestations of disorder. But it falls short of addressing a second shortcoming in standard disorder discussions, that is, the significant overlap between different categories of activities categorized as "disorder": Loitering, commonly categorized as a "social disorder," historically was regulated through the criminal law; it remains a crime—or has been recriminalized as part of order-maintenance efforts, as *Morales* indicates—in many jurisdictions. Vandalism is a crime; the results of vandalism—broken windows, graffiti, and so on—represent physical disorder. Many criminal activities are also economic ones, including prostitution and drug trafficking. (In some neighborhoods, these crimes may be the most prevalent economic activities.) Moreover, conducting otherwise licit economic activities without required regulatory approvals frequently is subject to criminal penalties.[7]

Taylor's continuum also overlooks that the activities and conditions commonly described above as disorder fall into at least four, not three, categories.

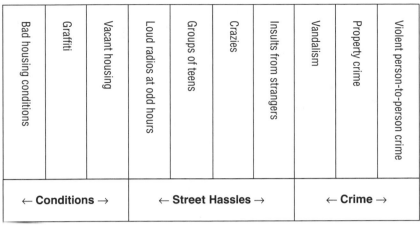

Bad housing conditions	Graffiti	Vacant housing	Loud radios at odd hours	Groups of teens	Crazies	Insults from strangers	Vandalism	Property crime	Violent person-to-person crime
← **Conditions** →			← **Street Hassles** →				← **Crime** →		

← **Least Serious**   **Most Serious** →

Figure 3.1. Ralph Taylor's "Continuum of Disorder." Reprinted from the *Handbook of Environmental Psychology* (New York: Wiley, 1987).

(1) The term *physical disorder* is used to describe various background environmental conditions frequently associated with urban decay, such as abandoned buildings, broken windows, litter, and graffiti. (2) The term *social disorder* usually describes the disfavored behaviors thought to signal a breakdown in healthy social norms in struggling communities. It is important to note, however, that many behaviors grouped as "social disorders," such as prostitution and drug trafficking, are also (3) *crimes*. Finally, some (4) *economic activities* are labeled as "disorders" when conducted in the wrong place or without the required regulatory approvals. This fourth category is the focus of this chapter, which explores whether and under what circumstances economic activity belongs in the taxonomy of disorder.

Commercial Activity as Disorder

The remainder of this chapter explores the intersection between commercial activity and the other activities commonly grouped as "disorder." It examines two related questions: First, whether commercial activity belongs in the taxonomy of disorder at all (that is, whether commercial activity is itself disorder—and if so, where and when); second, how commercial activity interacts with—either generating or suppressing—the other behaviors and conditions in the taxonomy of disorder. In order to unpack those questions,

I examine two categories of economic activity that are legally permissible under certain circumstances but that are categorized as "disorders" or even
"crimes" when conducted in the wrong place or without the required regulatory approvals.

The chapter begins with a case study of Mayor Rudolph Giuliani's efforts
to enforce and strengthen regulations restricting the operation of street vendors on New York City sidewalks. These efforts, which comprised one episode
in a century-long struggle between the city and vendors, yield insights into
both of the questions articulated above—why economic activity comes to be
considered "disorder" and whether such activity fosters or suppresses other
kinds of disorder. A discussion of street vending as disorder is valuable, in my
view, for two reasons. First, the prospect of earning a livelihood by vending
undoubtedly is most attractive to individuals of limited means and education.
Therefore, it is a kind of economic activity that is likely to appear—whether
sanctioned by law or not—in poor neighborhoods. Second, because vendors
operate in a commons—the public sidewalk—cost-internalization is particularly problematic. To the extent that economic activity is, or generates, disorder, vending will manifest that disorder more acutely than commercial activity
on or in private property.

The discussion then turns to a puzzle at the heart of the order-construction
enterprise—the effects of mixing commercial and residential land uses in urban neighborhoods. One of the central, animating themes of American property regulation is the belief that economic activity is, or contributes to, other
kinds of disorder. One of the reasons that zoning segregates residential land
uses from commercial ones is because Progressive-era "positive environmentalists" believed that this segregation would produce healthier, better citizens,
that is, that protecting single-family homes from economic life would build
social capital. Jacobs (and today's new urbanists) challenge this assumption,
arguing that the Progressives got it exactly backward—that economic activity
represents a healthy urban *order,* not *disorder,* and that, furthermore, it suppresses, rather than fosters, other kinds of disorder. Despite this challenge, the
idea that economic and commercial activity is *disorderly* continues to influence the regulation of public and private spaces in our cities. A relatively sizable empirical literature supports this traditional assumption—finding that
mixed-land-use communities have higher levels of social, physical, and criminal disorder than exclusively residential ones. This literature poses a particular
challenge to those scholars and policymakers, including myself, who intuitively endorse Jacobs's view that mixed-used urban environments are likely

to be more healthy and vibrant than single-use ones. The final pages of this chapter begin to sort through that challenge, offering three lessons about the categorization of economic activity as disorder that will guide discussion of disorder in the remainder of the book.

A word about the terminology used in this chapter: As the discussion above highlights, the behaviors and conditions commonly labeled as "disorder" overlap significantly and unavoidably. As Sudhir Venkatesh's ethnography of the underground economy in one poor Chicago neighborhood illustrates, the line between legality and illegality in inner-city communities is frequently blurred. For example, drug trafficking is economic activity that is also a crime; vending hot dogs without a license is economic activity and, in many jurisdictions, also a crime. With full recognition of the obvious grounds for objection, the following discussion uses the terms *commercial* and *economic* as shorthand for describing the kinds of economic activities that Venkatesh refers to as "licit" (as opposed to "illicit"). That is, they are likely to be found in mixed-use urban environments (street vendors, retail establishments, restaurants, and other small businesses) and are, at least under some circumstances, legally permissible. The definition of the term *legally permissible* has both subjective and objective components: Subjectively, common sense dictates that ordinary people draw normative distinctions between different kinds of "economic" activities. We do not equate drug trafficking and prostitution with illegal home businesses—except, of course, if the resident-proprietor is operating a brothel or a drug den—even if all of these activities are sanctioned by the criminal law. Objectively, the discussion is concerned with the effects of "economic" activities that are legally permissible, given compliance with applicable regulations. For example, it is legally permissible to sell hot dogs from a pushcart in New York City, provided that the vendor secures a license and operates on a street where vending is permitted. Hairstylists with cosmetology licenses can operate beauty salons in commercial zones but, in most cities, not in their living rooms. The regulations governing these kinds of commercial activities are, to borrow from First Amendment parlance, the "time, place, and manner" restrictions of economic life. Although many result from naked interest-group politics, the effort to draw lines between permissibility and impermissibility—even if the line drawn is mistaken—signals that lawmakers have concluded that the regulated activities are, at least under certain circumstances, socially beneficial.[8]

Street Vending in New York City

New York City, like most local governments, tightly regulates street vending. The city licenses 3,000 food vendors, but prohibits them from operating on many of the city's busiest streets, especially in midtown and downtown Manhattan. Only 850 licenses are available for "peddlers" selling merchandise other than food. As a result of these restrictions, many thousands of street vendors in New York City operate illegally. Most merchandise vendors operate without a license: The waiting list for peddling licenses exceeds 5,000 applicants, and city officials estimate that as many as 10,000 unlicensed merchandise vendors operate on any given day. Food vendors are more likely to be licensed, because vending licenses are more plentiful, but many operate illegally on streets that are off-limits to all vendors.

When the time came for Rudolph Giuliani to bow out as mayor of New York City, several retrospectives highlighted his abandoned effort to clear food vendors from midtown sidewalks—both by enforcing existing vending restrictions and by implementing new ones (in particular, by expanding the number of vendor-free streets). For Giuliani, the vendors represented another obstacle to his vision of a more livable New York. They threatened New Yorkers' quality of life, he argued, by clogging already crowded sidewalks with unsightly pushcarts and stands. To the New Yorkers who said "enough" to their mayor, the vendors represented something very different—part of the fabric of a healthy street life, a place to get a cheap lunch, and a step onto the first rung of the economic ladder. After weeks of protests and derisive editorials, Giuliani blinked. The vendors stayed.[9]

At one level, it seems odd—even petty—for these retrospectives to highlight the street-vending dispute. After all, many credit Giuliani's leadership generally, and his quality-of-life agenda in particular, for New York City's widely celebrated, and somewhat unexpected, renaissance during the 1990s. And certainly Giuliani's quality-of-life policies have been indicted on more serious grounds than unfairness to hot-dog vendors. (Objections, discussed in chapter 1, include that New York's order-maintenance efforts raised serious civil-liberties concerns and promoted uneven enforcement and even police brutality.) What's more, the restrictions that Giuliani sought to enforce and strengthen were not appreciably harsher than other cities' vending regulations. On the contrary, many cities impose harsher restrictions on vending; some prohibit it outright.[10]

One reason why the street-vending dispute may have captured New Yorkers' imaginations, however, is that it is emblematic of the tension between the pursuit of order and promotion of diversity and vitality in urban policy. The latter—that is, the promotion of vitality—ultimately carried the day in the Giuliani–food-vendor controversy: Removal of the vendors to promote more orderly sidewalks, many believed, would simply be antithetical to "New York-ness." Yet Giuliani successfully evicted vendors from the stalls that lined 125th Street, arguing that they had created chaos along the neighborhood's main thoroughfare. Giuliani's two enforcement efforts, one successful and one abandoned, provide an opportunity to explore whether and when one form of commercial activity prevalent in urban environments, especially in poor communities—vending—belongs in the taxonomy of disorder.

A Short History of New York's
Vending "Problem"

Street vendors—and urban governments' efforts to control them—are nothing new. Throughout urban history, many individuals operating at the economic margins have sought to eke out a living by selling their wares on busy streets and sidewalks, and urban governments have attempted (often unsuccessfully) to regulate them. New York's efforts to control street vending during the 1990s followed a pattern reflected throughout the city's history: frustration over the proliferation of illegal vendors, formal efforts to control and contain them, and the eventual abandonment of enforcement efforts when the containment efforts fail and vendors return to the streets. And the motivations for the enforcement effort also sounded familiar themes: In the 1990s, as in the 1890s and before, city officials cracked down on vending under pressure from established merchants, who expressed concerns about both the "disorder" and "unfair competition" generated by vendors.

Regulation of street vending in New York City dates to a 1691 ordinance prohibiting street selling by "hucksters" until two hours after the public markets opened. In 1707, the city prohibited all street hawking. These efforts sought to protect the public market system, which served the important function of pairing city dwellers with rural provisioners. As commercial activity increasingly moved inside fixed shops in the nineteenth century, the city's interest in protecting the old regulated public marketplaces disappeared, but street vendors did not. On the contrary, during the late nineteenth and early twentieth centuries, not only did the number of itinerant peddlers grow rapidly, but informal, semipermanent street markets began to emerge. These markets, like the busy street bazaars that Giuliani sought to suppress a century later, emerged largely as a result of immigration. Newcomers were poor, familiar with street markets in Europe, and eager to buy cheap goods; the markets provided safe cultural space and, importantly, economic opportunity. "For those who had no handicraft," an observer noted in 1899, "there was but one resource—peddling." A survey of Jewish families in the Lower East Side, dating from the same time, found that peddling was the second largest occupation, after tailoring.

To some early twentieth-century New Yorkers, pushcart markets were an integral and picturesque part of urban life. Elite opinion, however, strongly disfavored them. As middle- and upper-class residents ceased their patronage of street markets, vending increasingly became identified with the poverty of the immigrant ghetto. It came to be viewed as a lesser form of commerce, which stood in sharp and disfavored contrast to "modern" urbanism, exemplified by enclosed shops and skyscrapers. By the turn of the twentieth century, pressure to further restrict or even ban street vending intensified. Regulatory efforts ostensibly aimed to control the "congestion" problems caused by pushcarts, but vending opponents clearly had other motives as well. The strongest opposition to pushcarts came from established merchants seeking to limit (or eliminate) competition from vendors operating without overhead. Moreover, as immigrants moved out of the ghettos, the vendors moved with them—dispersing throughout the city and "invading" wealthier neighborhoods. This phenomenon was particularly troubling for development interests and property owners, who worried that pushcart markets drove down property values: Not only were pushcarts associated in the popular imagination with poverty and urban decline, but crowded streets curtailed development opportunities by limiting owners' ability to intensify land uses.

In 1906, the city convened an official "Pushcart Commission" to study approaches to vending—from banning pushcarts outright to limiting them to designated areas.* The Commission's recommendation—to limit the number of carts on a block to four—was derailed when pushcart operators staged a massive protest. Ultimately, the city opted instead to establish official pushcart "markets," but these containment efforts failed. By the 1930s, the pressure to ban pushcarts outright gained steam. Mayor Fiorello La Guardia, who viewed vending as "unworthy of the reputation of this great City," closed many push-

---

* The deliberations preceding the enactment of New York's 1916 zoning law also included an open critique of pushcarts, including their contribution to street congestion and neighborhood deterioration.

cart markets, drastically limited the number of peddling licenses, and increased enforcement against vendors operating illegally. By the 1940s, only a vestige of the old pushcart system remained on New York sidewalks. Fifty years later, Mayor Giuliani inherited it.[11]

The 125th Street Bazaar

For reasons that are not entirely clear, the number of street vendors hawking their wares on New York sidewalks increased dramatically during the summer of 1990. Contemporary observers credited various factors for the upswing—an economic downturn, rising rents, and, especially, immigration from countries (particularly in Africa) where street vending is commonplace. Although the trend was citywide, it was felt acutely along 125th Street, Harlem's main thoroughfare, where as many as one thousand unlicensed peddlers a day crowded the sidewalks in competition with shop owners. (The Harlem experience is hardly unique. As Gregg Kettles has observed, immigrant vendors appeared in large numbers in many American cities during the same time period.) In Harlem, almost immediately, local merchants demanded that the city crack down on the vendors. The merchants' arguments echoed those made in opposition to pushcart commerce during the early twentieth century. In 1911, a petition submitted by Greenwich Village shopkeepers voiced two complaints. The pushcarts were disorderly: "It is impossible for the ordinary customer to pass by our stores without being molested by the push-cart peddlers as well as hundreds of hawkers," the petition charged. And, the pushcarts engaged in unfair competition, "selling practically the same kind of merchandise that we have in our stores thus working great hardship upon us." Similarly, the bulk of opposition to Harlem vendors came from established businesses upset about competition and development interests worried about the image conveyed by the vending bazaar. As a spokeswoman for the 125th Street Business Improvement District observed, "[t]he businesses in the area have come to the conclusion that store owners and the vendors do not mix well with one another." Disorder generated by unlicensed vendors was one reason cited for this conflict. One attorney with an office on 125th Street complained, "You can't walk the sidewalk because the vendors crowd them. . . . They leave the place filthy." But merchants' most frequent complaint was that the vendors sold similar goods at lower prices; one called them a "massive tax swindle."[12]

As with the debate over pushcart commerce a century before, it is difficult to sort through the extent to which enforcement efforts were actually motivated by a desire to suppress the disorder generated by the 125th Street vendors, as opposed to outright protectionism. Some of the complaints about the vending-related disorder undoubtedly were true. As one editorialist observed during the controversy, "Even the vendors concede that 125th Street is out of control." Indeed, some vending might be better described as a manifestation of social, rather than economic, disorder. In his ethnographic account of street vendors on New York's Lower East Side, Mitchell Dunier describes vendors, many of whom are mentally ill, who "lay shit out," placing miscellaneous items on pieces of corrugated cardboard or directly on the sidewalk, thus making the "streets feel *less safe* and *less vital.*" Vendors also occasionally are associated with crime. They are vulnerable to pressure by organized crime, just as the pushcart operators participated in late nineteenth-century graft and corruption, and may sell merchandise of questionable origin and/or knock-off merchandise that infringes intellectual property rights. Giuliani, for example, also cracked down on the practice described in Dunier's work—called by one commentator "Alphabet City's version of a garage sale"—at least in part because some of the peddlers were trafficking in stolen goods. Certainly not a recipe for social capital.[13]

This reality does not mean, of course, that all—or even most—125th Street vendors were disorderly. On the contrary, there is evidence that the rise of the busy street marketplace may have helped to suppress preexisting disorder in Harlem. The 125th Street vendors attracted thousands of tourists, who arrived daily in tour buses and generated substantial foot traffic in the previously struggling commercial corridor. Some merchants therefore sided with the vendors, citing the tourism boom. Many merchants and vendors coexisted peacefully, with vendors paying shop owners to store their goods overnight—and in some cases even agreeing not to sell the same merchandise as an adjacent store. When the vendors were driven from the street in late 1994, some merchants worried their businesses would suffer as the tour buses stopped coming. The fact that many at the economic margins—especially poor African immigrants—depended upon street vending for their livelihood also led some observers to worry about the social and economic consequences of displacing them.[14]

Giuliani, unmoved by these concerns, made a crackdown against unlicensed vendors one of his "quality of life" priorities. The mayor complained that the situation on 125th Street was "out of control" and resolved to eliminate the vendors altogether. As had his early twentieth-century predecessors, Giuliani's policy incorporated tough law-enforcement and official containment efforts: He used the police to clear the vendors from 125th Street and established an official marketplace, several blocks away, as a vending safe haven. While an organized protest derailed similar enforcement efforts undertaken by his predecessor, David Dinkins, Giuliani initially succeeded in relocating the vendors. Yet vendors viewed the new marketplace as a poor substitute for their lucrative 125th Street location; it was set apart from foot traffic and, the vendors argued, poorly lit and dangerous. A new market, operated by a local mosque, achieved modest success, but many vendors found it difficult to eke out a living after paying the fee to operate there. Similar efforts to relocate vendors to official "marketplaces" in other parts of the city also floundered. Ultimately, the city's effort to impose order on New York City's sidewalks—or at least to contain vendors in an out-of-the-way location—failed. A 2004 *Business Week* profile described 125th Street as "street vendor territory with table after table of books, posters, incense, and CDs."[15]

Manhattan Food Vendors

Mayor Giuliani's quest to impose "order" on New York's sidewalks also included an effort to close most of the streets in midtown and the financial district to food vendors. Many of these streets were already officially off-limits to food vendors, largely as a result of restrictions imposed by former Mayor Ed Koch, who—like Dinkins—had abandoned his enforcement effort in the face of massive protest by vendors and their patrons. In 1994—the same year that he swept vendors from 125th Street—Giuliani sought to begin enforcing existing regulations. And in an effort to broaden the scope of the vending ban, Giuliani also established a Sidewalk Vendor Review Panel to consider requests for additional street closures. Over the next several years, city officials—backed by restaurant owners and, as in Harlem, the pro-development Business Improvement Districts—engaged in a tug-of-war with vendors and their supporters. As in Harlem, arguments against the vendors focused both on the disorder generated by vending (in the case of food vendors, the most common complaint was that they created sidewalk "congestion," rather than disorder *per se*) and on the vendors' "unfair competition" with merchants and restaurant owners. In 1998, Mayor Giuliani unveiled a plan to close 144 streets in Manhattan to food vending. He argued that this plan would impose "a rational distribution of street vendors throughout the city of New York, so that they can have a good business, so they can lend something to the quality of life in the city. It's a rule of reason," Giuliani insisted. "That's part of living in a civilized city, as opposed to a place that is chaotic." Other, privately filed petitions brought the number of requested street closures to nearly 300.[16]

Giuliani's campaign against vendors generated vehement protest. A *New York Times* editorialist worried, for example, whether Giuliani had "lost a sense of proportion about his civility campaign." The editorialist continued:

> There is a difference between making the streets safer . . . and making war on the New Yorkness of New York City. In his zeal for order and obedience, he must not destroy the lively street scene that is part of the city's historic flavor. No one misses the squeegee men, but do we really want to outlaw the corner hot-dog stand? . . . Any new system will never—and should never—totally eradicate the hurly-burly nature of the city's pushcart trade. There must be a better way for the city to hear the voices of hot-dog vendors and their customers, not just those who sell sandwiches and real estate nearby.

When vendors protested the new restrictions, "Secretaries and stockbrokers alike came to their defense." In interviews, New Yorkers expressed alarm that Giuliani had gone too far in his effort to sanitize the city, with some characterizing Giuliani's vending plan as "ridiculous." Giuliani relented, opening negotiations with vendors (a group that Mayor Koch had called "a hydra-headed monster"). In a rare admission of misjudgment, Giuliani acknowledged that his plan "may have been broader than necessary." Ultimately, the review panel passed a compromise plan, restricting vending on 100 additional blocks and rejecting the requests for 300 additional block closures.[17]

Mixing Private Land Uses

As discussed in chapter 2, concern about the inherent disorderliness of commercial life heavily influenced the development of American land-use regulation. The Progressives' concern about economic disorder tracked the broken windows hypothesis in important ways: Order-maintenance proponents link social, physical, and sometimes economic disorder to a breakdown in social norms that leads to serious crime. Progressives believed that single-land-use patterns would foster a healthier—physically and morally—citizenry. By enacting zoning rules that sought to suppress and contain commercial activity, they hoped to minimize its negative secondary effects. This view of economic activity—that it is itself disorderly, even dangerous, that it fosters social disorder, and that it degrades human character—has influenced thinking about land use in the United States for more than a century.

The view received its sharpest and most influential challenge in Jane Jacobs's classic work *The Death and Life of Great American Cities.* Jacobs vehemently challenged the prevailing wisdom that mixing commercial and residential land uses would not only expose residents to economic disorder but would also foster social disorder. The prevailing view, Jacobs countered, had it exactly backward: Commercial activity suppresses, rather than fosters, disorder and crime. Jacobs reasoned that while busy city street life may appear disorderly, the vitality generated by mixing land uses is necessary for urban health. A diversity of land uses, she argued, gives people a diversity of reasons to be present in a community throughout the day and night. Therefore, mixing residential and commercial uses helps guarantee private "eyes upon the street" to monitor and suppress disorder and crime. Moreover, she predicted that retail enterprises—the corner shop, the neighborhood tavern—would provide needed opportunities for informal social interaction among relative strangers in a community. These kinds of establishments help build social capital— including the social capital necessary to curb disorder and crime—by, to borrow Robert Putnam's formulation, bridging different groups of people.[18]

Today, almost fifty years after the publication of her important book, Jacobs's ideas may be at the peak of their influence. In particular, her views about the value of mixing land uses in urban communities, now popularized by the self-styled new urbanists, are shaping both suburban design and urban redevelopment efforts, especially the federal HOPE VI program, which funds the demolition and redevelopment of distressed public housing projects. Furthermore, and importantly, Jacobs's influence is beginning to be reflected in incremental changes to long-standing land-use policies and regulations, especially in the planning and design of urban redevelopment projects and, to a lesser extent, in a gradual trend toward the adoption of mixed-use zoning. Communities embracing these practices are not necessarily doing so on order-maintenance grounds. Rather, they may well be seeking to achieve some other policy goal, such as revitalizing moribund central-city neighborhoods and/or drawing the attention of younger professionals who are attracted to a more "urban lifestyle." Yet all of these efforts implicitly endorse Jacobs's argument that mixed-land-use environments are, at least under some circumstances, socially beneficial.[19]

The popular and academic commentary on Jacobs's work, however, frequently overlooks the empirical literature testing her hypothesis that mixed land uses suppress, rather than foster, disorder and crime. In a number of studies, criminologists, sociologists, and environmental psychologists have sought to examine the connection between different land-use patterns (that is, exclusively residential versus mixed-use) and disorder and crime. The relative neglect of this work in the literature on land-use policy is unfortunate. These studies mount a serious challenge to Jacobs's now-popular hypothesis that proponents of mixed-land-use urban environments (including myself) must confront. In fact, most of the researchers conducting these studies reject Jacobs's hypothesis as intuitively appealing but empirically unsustainable. They find instead that mixed-land-use patterns are connected to observable physical, social, and criminal disorder. While many such studies focus on specific land uses thought to be criminal "hot spots" (such as bars),* other researchers have found that the introduction of any commercial uses results in a substantial increase in the risk of disorder and crime, including violent victimization.

A common method for testing the effects of commercial land uses on neighborhood stability is comparing neighborhood pairs. Researchers compare the crime rates (and in some studies the presence of observable physical disorder) in two neighborhoods with similar demographic profiles but different land-use patterns. These studies generally find that exclusively residential neighborhoods have lower crime rates and less disorder than mixed residential-and-commercial neighborhoods. For example, a study of one hundred neighborhoods in Seattle, Washington, found that the introduction of a single commercial enterprise was correlated with a 31-percent increase in crime. Researchers conducting these studies link their findings to the "routine activities" theory of crime. Routine-activities theory builds on the insight that most predatory crime is opportunistic. That is, as Sampson and Raudenbush summarize, crime "involves the intersection of . . . motivated offenders, suitable targets, and the absence of capable guardians." Land-use patterns are relevant to this thesis for two reasons: First, because they are quasi-public, commercial land uses may serve to invite strangers—including would-be offenders—into a neighborhood. By providing places for neighbors to congregate, commercial land uses may also generate a larger pool of potential victims than residential ones do. Thus, while Jacobs may have been right that commercial uses increase the number of individuals present in an urban neighborhood at any given time, the routine-activities theory suggests that higher numbers of "eyes upon the street" actually may raise the number of potential offenders, rather than opportunities for informal surveillance.[20]

---

* Jacobs argued that even a neighborhood tavern might reduce crime by ensuring the presence of people on the sidewalks in the evening hours. It is fair to say that this empirical literature does not bear out her hypothesis.

Second, contrary to Jacobs's intuition, commercial uses may decrease private surveillance efforts. This argument flows from Oscar Newman's important work on "defensible space." Newman argued that architectural and urban design can decrease crime by increasing opportunities for residents to exercise "ownership" over public spaces. Proponents of routine-activities theory suggest that the desire to exercise control over our environment is strongest closer to our homes. Events occurring in one's yard are more important than those occurring on the sidewalk; sidewalk events are more important than neighborhood events; and so on. According to this theory, by introducing strangers into a community, commercial uses create "holes in the resident-based territorial fabric" or "valleys in the topography of territorial control." Resident surveys conducted for these studies suggest that nonresidential land uses reduce informal monitoring by residents, in large part because increased traffic makes it more difficult to discern who "belongs" in a community. In one study, for example, residents on blocks with nonresidential land uses reported that they recognized other block residents less well, felt that they had less control over events in the neighborhood, and were less likely to count on a neighbor to monitor suspicious activity than residents of exclusively residential blocks were.[21]

Disorder, Vibrancy, and Social Capital

The studies linking commercial land uses to disorder and crime and the debate over street vending in New York both yield important insights into the question posed early in this chapter—whether and when economic activity belongs in the taxonomy of disorder. Some of this evidence is contrary to my own intuitions. Street vendors undoubtedly generate physical disorder—for example, in Harlem, merchants complained about the trash left each evening. Sudhir Venkatesh's ethnography of one poor Chicago neighborhood chronicles residents' frustration with "hustlers" that hawk wares and leave litter, some of it dangerous, in public spaces. Vendors also are vulnerable to exploitation by, and participate to varying degrees in the activities of, serious criminals. It is reasonable to assume that much vending-related disorder flows from the fact that vendors do not internalize the costs of their activities because they use a commons resource (the public sidewalk). Still, the studies of mixed-use communities discussed above also suggest that commercial activity can generate disorder even when private property rights are clearly demarcated. These studies also suggest that commercial land uses may increase opportunities for crime by drawing perpetrators and victims together and that they sometimes reduce social capital by undermining residents' ability and incentives to informally monitor their neighborhood.[22]

There remains the important question about how regulators should address these realities. One alternative is the strict enforcement, and perhaps enhancement, of regulations restricting commercial activity in urban environments, including bans on vending and zoning rules segregating commercial and residential land uses. Ralph Taylor, an environmental psychologist and the author of a number of studies of the land-use/disorder nexus, has made this suggestion. After reviewing the evidence linking commercial land uses to crime and disorder, he proposes that city officials "may wish to carefully monitor zoning variance requests, business license requests, and code enforcement in neighborhoods at risk of increased crime . . . because of the implications such decisions may have for informal social control and crime."[23]

On the other hand, city officials might worry about the broad implications of Taylor's recommendation. Even if single-use zoning correlates with lower levels of disorder, urban policymakers have reason to question whether limits on commercial land uses are really the best way to reverse city fortunes, especially in struggling urban communities. First, it is likely that the crime statistics—measured on a per-resident basis—overstate the correlation between commercial land uses and victimization. More crimes may well occur in mixed-use areas, but crime statistics do not control for the fact that there often are more *people* present in a mixed-use area. Crimes-per-persons-present is difficult to gauge. Moreover, for reasons elaborated in chapter 6, a rise in crime rates in mixed-use areas may actually reflect an increase, rather than a decrease, in social capital. That is, more crime may result from the fact that the activity in such areas makes people *feel safer* and therefore take fewer steps to avoid victimization. It is hardly cause for celebration if residents avoid being victimized by remaining inside behind locked doors.

Second, it is important to remember that many cities gained population in the 1990s, following years of precipitous decline. This apparent "urban rebound" occurred in a decade during which urban redevelopment efforts began to focus on increasing the diversity of urban land-use patterns. Even some cities that lost population during the last decade of the twentieth century experienced a "downtown rebound," gaining population in the neighborhoods where commercial uses are likely to be most common. Both trends suggest a possible correlation between "urban" land-use patterns and city competitiveness vis-à-vis their suburban neighbors, a theme explored in greater detail in subsequent chapters. Moreover, and importantly, in the poorest city neighborhoods, city officials might worry that restrictions on commercial land uses could impede efforts to reverse the precipitous *decline* in economic activity in inner-city neighborhoods, which is frequently cited as a primary contributor to the social disorders plaguing our cities. Neighborhood-level retail establishments may also be particularly important in poor neighborhoods, as residents of these communities are less likely to travel distances for shopping than wealthier individuals are.[24]

There are no clear answers to these questions. If the answers were clear, debates about order-maintenance policies in general—and the extent to which land-use policies serve order-maintenance functions in particular—would undoubtedly generate less controversy. Rather than seeking to articulate a one-size-fits-all policy prescription, the remaining discussion draws three general lessons about whether and when commercial activity belongs in the taxonomy of disorder. These lessons will inform further discussion of the importance of land-use diversity in the remainder of this book, but they also have broader implications, by and large outside the book's purview, for the order-maintenance debate generally.

Disorder Is Contextual

First, the nature, causes, and consequences of disorder must be considered contextually. Chapter 5 explores one reason why disorder must be analyzed in context: When disorder is concentrated, its harmful effects may be amplified. One possible reason why the 125th Street merchandise vendors were (or were perceived to be) more disorderly than midtown and downtown food vendors was their intense geographic concentration: During the period when enforcement efforts peaked, approximately three thousand food vendors were dispersed throughout the city (albeit primarily in lower Manhattan), but as many as one thousand vendors crowded a few blocks of Harlem's main thoroughfare each day. It is reasonable to assume that concentrating large numbers of vendors in a relatively small area amplified the negative effects of any disorder generated by individual vendors.

Another reason why disorder should be considered contextually is that certain manifestations of disorder may be harmful in some communities but benign or even beneficial in others. Consider, for example, the important questions posed by Bernard Harcourt. Harcourt observes, "In some neighborhoods, residents sit on the steps of their houses and chat," he observes. "They hang out. They are idle. . . . Kids make chalk markings on the street, play ball, kick empty Coke cans, tussle, chase after and scream at one another. . . . What makes some of these acts disorderly and others not? And where is the line between absent-mindedness, laziness, bad manners, and disorder?" These observations lead Harcourt to worry that our perceptions of *disorder* become too intertwined with our perceptions of the *disorderly.* George Kelling and Catherine Coles observe, for example: "Many more of us than would perhaps like to admit doing so have urinated in public, been drunk, asked someone for money when in a jam . . . , bought goods or services from illegal vendors, used prostitutes, obstructed auto traffic or pedestrians on a sidewalk, committed minor acts of vandalism, or carried out other such minor offenses constituting 'disorderly behavior.' " Harcourt and other scholars worry that the order-maintenance agenda targets these behaviors only when they are committed by poor minorities who live in poor urban neighborhoods. Dorothy Roberts, for example, warns that the order-maintenance agenda reinforces stereotypes about black criminality, a concern at least partially confirmed by Sampson and Raudenbush's findings linking perceptions of disorder to the racial composition of a neighborhood.[25]

These findings are disturbing, to be sure, but they do not necessarily mean that policymakers should ignore the reality that certain behaviors and conditions may be more harmful in some communities than others. This reality is reflected in community policing efforts inviting residents to help establish order-maintenance priorities; perceptions of which behaviors and conditions are "disorder" may vary by community. Harcourt's examples highlight that some activities that appear to be disorderly to outsiders might reflect healthy social capital. For example, "stoop sitting" might be a manifestation of social disorder if the "sitters" are gang members asserting territorial authority and terrorizing neighbors. But adults sitting on stoops to monitor the behavior of young people or to strategize about how to best address neighborhood problems are engaged in the very activities that social scientists use to measure collective efficacy and social capital. Perceptions of the "harmfulness" of commercial activity may be particularly susceptible to community variation. Consider, for example, the dramatic gulf between elite and immigrant perceptions of pushcart commerce in early twentieth-century New York City. Today, immigrants accustomed to high levels of street commerce also may be less likely to perceive economic activities as "disorderly" than native-born Americans accustomed to zoning's segregation of land uses. This dynamic clearly affects the perceptions of street vending. As Gregg Kettles observes, immigrant vendors "come from a culture where sidewalk vending is widely accepted . . . and express[] bewilderment as to why sidewalk vending is illegal."[26]

More broadly, the effect of economic activity in poor communities deserves nuanced consideration. The literature linking commercial land uses to crime and disorder could be interpreted to suggest that economic activity should be minimized in the poorest urban neighborhoods. Given the high levels of crime and disorder already plaguing these communities, why introduce land uses that might exacerbate the situation? Interestingly, however, at least one study (of the neighborhood-pair variety discussed above) found that nonresidential land uses were detrimental in relatively stable neighborhoods but *beneficial* in unstable ones. In other words, nonresidential land uses appeared to increase crime and disorder in a relatively stable, middle-class community and to decrease crime and disorder in a relatively poor community. The researchers had predicted the opposite effect—that "Jacobs's notion of pubic land use providing supervisory 'eyes on the street' (and thus leading to lower crime) might be more operative in advantaged, stable neighborhoods." The fact that the data conflicted with their intuitions led the researchers to reject the assumption that "busy" places generate crime and disorder as "overly simple." Venkatesh's study of the informal economy on Chicago's South Side similarly suggests that those engaged in economic activity serve important norm- and law-enforcement functions. Even "hustlers" operating illegally monitor the behavior of social deviants in public spaces—at times receiving compensation from shop owners to do so—and provide valuable information to law-enforcement officers.[77]

Chapter 4 highlights several reasons why Jacobs's prediction about the positive effects of "busy" places might be most operative in poor, unstable neighborhoods (where, it is safe to assume, the disorder levels are high). Economic stagnation and chronic unemployment have wreaked havoc in many inner-city communities. Current land-use restrictions may impede the development of the neighborhood-level commercial activity that a number of leading social scientists believe is critical to reversing these trends. Economic activity in poor communities might also reverse the physical decline that is closely connected to social and criminal disorder (as discussed in greater detail in chapter 4 of this book). Indeed, while studies testing Jacobs's hypothesis usually find some connection between *viable* commercial land uses and other manifestations of disorder, most suggest that the crime and disorder are most strongly correlated with *vacant commercial property* (for example, boarded storefronts). Efforts to fill these storefronts might do more to check disorder and crime than limits on commercial land uses.[28]

Perceptions of Disorder Are Political

The second lesson is that perceptions of disorder, perhaps especially perceptions of economic activity as disorder, frequently are political. Consider, for

example, Mayor Giuliani's two efforts to control vending. One plausible explanation why one succeeded (at least temporarily) and the other was abandoned
is that Harlem's vendors actually were more disorderly than lower-Manhattan
food vendors. Such comparisons were made during the food vending dispute,
with some commentators arguing that food vendors were in fact less problematic than merchandise peddlers. A second possibility, however, is that the food
vendors were able to wield political power more effectively than the 125th
Street peddlers. While unlicensed vendors on 125th Street were primarily immigrants (some of them undocumented aliens) who operated independently, a large
consortium with the resources to threaten legal action owned many available
food vending permits. The arguments of food vendors' clientele—professional
and paraprofessional New Yorkers eager for an inexpensive meal—also resonated
with city officials. The tourists who patronized the 125th Street bazaar undoubtedly had less influence over political leaders than Harlem merchants did. Not
only is it likely that most of the tourists who patronized the 125th Street vending
bazaar lived outside of the city, but the merchants opposing Harlem's vendors
were well organized and situated in a community that the city has long been desperate to renew.

    While Giuliani himself may have viewed the vendors as disorderly, there is
significant evidence that vending opponents' primary motivation for supporting Giuliani's efforts was a desire to eliminate competitors selling similar
products for less money. As deputy mayor Rudy Washington noted at the
time, "When I hear people yelling, 'They're putting us out of business,' that
gets my ears up and I pay attention." After admitting that his food vending
proposal "may have gone too far," Giuliani himself reflected on the "ongoing
process of trying to balance the need for the street vendors to make a living
and the need for the businesses that are affected by the street vendors to make
a living." In Harlem, the vendors offered one means of city-suburb competition: The daily tour buses showed that some consumers enjoyed the alternative to the suburban commercial offerings. But development interest in Harlem
in the early decades of the twenty-first century, as in the early decades of the
twentieth, saw vending as antithetical to the type of competition that they
sought to foster—higher end, tailored to wealthier professional residents, not
poor people in search of inexpensive consumer goods or tourists out to "slum
it" for a day.

    Perceptions about the "disorder" associated with mixed-use environments
also are highly politicized, as every student of land-use policy knows. In some
cities (as discussed in greater detail in chapter 4), zoning enforcement efforts

have become centerpieces of mayoral campaigns. In the same cities, planners promote new, mixed-use, relatively dense developments—especially, but not exclusively, in the public-housing context—as an "antidote" to urban decline, while at the same time expressing concern about "teardowns" and other efforts to intensify land-use patterns. My own city, South Bend, Indiana, which has long sought to stem the tide of suburban sprawl to outlying areas, recently saw a bitter political battle over the construction of a new "college town," featuring a mixed-use new-urbanist design near my own university-district home. Some of my neighbors opposed the project (which the city ultimately approved), arguing that it would introduce disorder—especially student-related disorder—into our quiet community.[29]

Disorder and Vibrancy

Finally, there may be a tension between the desire to control commercial activity and the need for vibrancy in the urban core. This tension is nothing new: During the debates over vending in New York City at both the opening and closing of the twentieth century, supporters argued that street vendors were an integral and essential component of a vibrant street life. In Harlem supporters went further, arguing that the vending bazaar was helping restore economic health to the poor community by attracting busloads of tourists to the previously moribund 125th Street corridor. Street vending—even those vendors operating illegally (as most do)—also represents both an important source of cheap consumer goods and financial resources for those living at the economic margins in poor and immigrant communities. It might be that vending supporters were simply wrong—that the vending is a manifestation of economic disorder, which contributes to criminal and social disorder—and that Giuliani (as others before him) was right to limit it. Alternatively, perhaps some kinds of economic activities associated with traditional urban life—from street vendors to the corner store—are not disorder at all. Rather, as Jacobs argued, these activities, which may look disorderly to the naked eye, might instead reflect a healthy, organic order. The appearance of disorder masks this organic order, and efforts to suppress it ultimately deprive urban communities of much-needed vibrancy. Or, finally, it might be that economic activity sometimes *is* disorder—or causes disorder (as the empirical studies on mixed land uses discussed above suggest)—but that certain manifestations of disorder, especially economic disorder, are essential to city life.

If either of the latter possibilities is true, policymakers must carefully consider what Richard Sennett has called the "uses of disorder" (or activities that appear to be disorderly) in our cities. Perhaps, as suggested by Sennett and Gerald Frug, some kinds of disorder—and perhaps especially "economic disorder"—build social capital by forcing (sometimes uncomfortable) social interactions that draw strangers together. Perhaps (as discussed in more detail in chapters 4 and 7) the vitality fostered by economic "disorder" can help cities compete with suburbs. For example, Edward Glaeser and Joshua Gottlieb have argued that while city amenities, including mixed-land-use patterns, are not correlated with social capital, the apparent resurgence in city fortunes during the 1990s is attributable to an increase in the demand for the informal social interactions that cities facilitate and, moreover, that this demand was fueled by dramatic decline in crime that previously precluded these social interactions. In either case, the decline, and perhaps also the overregulation, of economic activity in urban communities may be inconsistent with the cultural and economic units known as "cities."[30]

Measuring What Matters

These observations—that perceptions of disorder are contextual and political and that some disorder-suppression efforts may conflict with the goal of fostering needed urban vitality—hardly provide a useful yardstick for measuring urban policy success. City leaders might well throw up their hands and ask, "When is stoop sitting good and vending bad, and when is it the other way around?" Or, "When, exactly, does neighborhood economic activity cross the line between vibrancy and disorder?" The final pages of this chapter offer two ways that officials might begin to answer these important questions, and the many others raised by the discussion thus far.

First, the market matters. City officials acting as developers promote mixed-use urban environments in order to compete with suburban life by offering an alternative to it. In other words, when city officials act as economic actors, they behave as if they believe that mixed-use neighborhoods sell. The widespread endorsement of this idea will enable, over the course of the years to come, economists to measure whether this assumption is correct. It may be that property values reflect my intuition—that there is a "right" amount of economic activity in a community—although that optimum mix is likely to vary by community. For example, in a well-known study of the effects of different suburban land-use patterns on property values, published three decades ago, Ronald Lafferty and H. E. Frech found that housing prices increased when commercial land uses were present in a community but concentrated in commercial districts, rather than dispersed throughout residential areas. Lafferty and Frech's findings, therefore, tend to support the traditional assumptions underlying zoning regulations. Their study is not only dated, however, but also focused on single-family housing prices in suburban communities. It might be that urban real estate values reflect different patterns, especially three decades later, when cities appear to be on the rebound and new-urbanism planning is in ascendancy. Perhaps urban real estate value patterns are different today. Perhaps for city neighborhoods to thrive—and it is my view that "thriving" requires successful competition with their suburban counterparts— they cannot look like suburban neighborhoods. But too much economic activity, at least in some communities, ultimately decreases the attractiveness of the urban ideal. This observation is a logical corollary to the common-sense proposition that different residents have different tolerance thresholds for the background noise of urban life. My parents, who both grew up in rural Kansas, are likely to have lower thresholds than someone who grew up on Manhattan's Upper East Side.[31]

There are more informal ways of gauging whether the city-qua-developer's "bet" on the traditional urban form is correct: Condos will either sell or they won't; new merchants will fill in the storefronts or they won't. There are, of course, complications—including tough economic times and, as discussed in greater detail elsewhere in the book, regulatory compliance costs (including the new urbanists' "form-based" alternative to zoning). It is also important, in my view, to learn over time more about the "life cycle" of mixed-use developments, old or new. Successful neighborhoods hopefully will do more than simply attract young and unattached professionals, but retain them as they age and develop attachments to spouses and children.

Second, ask the neighbors. Community policing policy efforts are the progeny of the order-maintenance revolution, but they are not focused solely on disorder. Rather, the central animating feature of community policing policies is that the neighbors frequently know better than city officials what disorder *is* in their community. The need to consider disorder contextually weighs in favor of devolving certain land-use decisions—especially about those activities, such as street vending and perhaps some home businesses, closest to the disorder line—to the neighborhood level, either through community policing discussions or other more formal mechanisms. These community-level discussions would lend themselves to a more nuanced evaluation of how efforts to balance disorder and vibrancy are faring than reliance on, for example, crime statistics, which might mask the benefits of increased economic activity, including especially an uptick in the number of people declining to take precautions against crimes. Various mechanisms that might be used to implement the devolution of land-use decisions are discussed in greater detail in the book's concluding chapter, but for now it is sufficient to note that a one-size-fits-all disorder-suppression policy may be no more appropriate in the land-use context than it is in the policing context.

4

Order Construction as Disorder Suppression

Several years ago, a *Washington Post Magazine* cover story featured James Delgado, a "building inspector with a bulletproof vest," engaged in a one-man crusade to use property regulations to restore order in the poorest, most chaotic communities in the nation's capital. For his efforts, Delgado earned the gratitude of D.C. residents. "Thank God Mr. Delgado works for the city and thank God he was able to help us," wrote one resident after Delgado closed down a crack house in his neighborhood. But Delgado's unorthodox, aggressive approach—especially his willingness to "creatively push . . . the outer limits of laws and regulations"—also raised more than a few eyebrows. The story provided a fascinating window into the promise and perils of the order-maintenance agenda: It told the tale of an honorable public servant determined to improve the lives of his city's most vulnerable residents, and willing, when necessary, to abuse his authority to accomplish that goal.[1]

Delgado's tale also illustrates the on-the-ground confusion over the different functions of property regulations illustrated in the first three chapters of this book. To recap: Some property regulations—housing

and building codes—serve a disorder-suppression function; they empower government officials to remediate physical (and related social) disorders associated with private property. Others—zoning laws—serve an
order-construction function; they define the geographic order of urban land
uses by separating them from one another. James Delgado clearly did not dis-
tinguish between order-construction and disorder-suppression regulations.
When it was expedient, he aggressively enforced all of the regulatory tools
at his disposal. This chapter seeks to better differentiate those two different
functions and to challenge the many government officials who, like James
Delgado, assume that order-construction and disorder-suppression are one
and the same.

Property Regulation as Disorder Suppression

The order-maintenance revolution has produced thousands of pages of academic commentary, much of which focuses on the questions raised by police
efforts to curb disorder in public places. This debate about the appropriate
scope of police authority frequently fails to take sufficient account of other
weapons in the order-maintenance arsenal. Importantly, much of the order-
maintenance literature disregards how property regulations can be—and
are—used to suppress physical disorder and the social disorders associated
with it.

Social scientists have long considered abandoned or deteriorating property
to be a sign of serious neighborhood decline. Blighted properties contribute to
a city's economic problems by discouraging neighborhood investment, depriving the city of tax revenue, lowering market values of neighboring property, and increasing insurance costs. Furthermore, blight has a "multiplier"
effect: Deferred maintenance of one building reduces the incentives for neighbors to continue upkeep efforts, as Wilson and Kelling tacitly acknowledged
in the title of their essay. Property decline also is linked to social and criminal
disorder. For example, abandoned buildings are "magnets for crime," places
that serve as criminals' hangouts or staging areas. One study conducted in
Austin, Texas, found evidence of illegal activities in 83 percent of unsecured
abandoned buildings. Local governments and city officials alike understand
the seriousness of the problems associated with physical property disorder.
Wesley Skogan's study of the crime-disorder nexus found that inner city residents consistently cite physical decay as one of the most significant "disorders" plaguing their communities. And in a survey of the two hundred most

populous American cities several years ago, 69 percent of respondents rated abandoned property as a significant problem for their cities. The number was even higher—95 percent—for northeastern cities.[2]

Not surprisingly, therefore, a number of cities consider aggressive enforcement of disorder-suppression regulations to be an important order-maintenance priority. Cities use property regulations to remediate physical disorder in a variety of ways. Some cities engage in the widespread demolition of abandoned buildings. Detroit demolished more than twenty-eight thousand homes between 1989 and 2002 and has since turned its sights on abandoned downtown skyscrapers. In fact, Detroit's zeal for demolition landed "Historic Buildings of Downtown Detroit" on the National Trust for Historic Preservation's list of "11 Most Endangered Places" in 2005. A handful of cities have also reformed tax-foreclosure laws and established "land banks" to streamline the disposition of abandoned and vacant buildings. It is hardly surprising, therefore, that cities' governments consider the wave of foreclosures attending the current economic downturn to be a crisis.[3]

Many cities have also stepped up regulatory inspections of private property in an effort to address disorder related to property decline, with some reforming building-code-enforcement procedures to permit local governments to undertake repairs or demolish buildings even when the owner cannot be located. The most ambitious of such efforts are multiagency enforcement "sweeps" of struggling neighborhoods, which include property inspections among a range of disorder-suppression devices. One sweep in Tampa, Florida, netted seven felony arrests and 122 code violations. Other recent enforcement sweeps targeted crime-ridden neighborhoods in Atlanta, Houston, Omaha, and San Antonio. Sweeps are so popular that candidates in recent mayoral elections in Dallas, Detroit, and Indianapolis, citing the importance of suppressing disorder, made election promises to step up enforcement sweeps if elected.[4]

The housing and building inspectors included in these sweeps—and the codes that they enforce—are not well regarded. Inspectors have long been condemned as corrupt and ineffective. The handful of available studies conclude that code enforcement is spotty, complaint-driven, and arbitrary, and that inspectors are not up to their appointed tasks of combating urban blight and guaranteeing minimal housing standards. Furthermore, a substantial economic literature indicts the costs imposed by building and housing codes for contributing to the property-abandonment problem and for reducing the stock of affordable housing. But when housing codes are treated as only one of the various weapons in the order-maintenance arsenal, some of the perceived "weaknesses" of the code-enforcement system begin to look like strengths. While it is true that inspection regimes are primarily complaint-driven (and necessarily so, because many code violations are not visible from the outside of a building), community-policing theory encourages citizen input into law-enforcement efforts, especially to identify problems that government officials may overlook. Aggressive code enforcement fits neatly into this "problem solving" approach to identifying and addressing disorder. For example, a number of cities have incorporated programs asking citizens to identify problem properties into community policing efforts.

Previous code-enforcement studies have also criticized the "thickness" of the regulatory code book. Lawrence Ross observed, for example, "the inspector's quandary is created by the fact that the housing code is both voluminous and ideal." A housing inspector, however, may like the "thickness" of the code. "Thickness" gives inspectors the significant bargaining power that comes with the authority to issue citations carrying significant fines at virtually any time and with little fear of judicial interference. Thus, inspections often represent the first step toward nuisance remediation. Inspectors may encourage owners to make cosmetic improvements that enhance a neighborhood's appearance and deter crime, or, in more-serious cases, may close a building that fails to pass inspection until it is code-compliant. When buildings are simply beyond repair—or the cost of compliance too high—they may be demolished, sometimes with the "consent" of a property owner desperate to avoid tens of thousands of dollars in ongoing fines.[5]

Public officials in some cities have also turned to the courts, using public-nuisance suits to suppress disorder. The public-nuisance cause of action, which empowers a court to award equitable relief for "an unreasonable interference with a right common to the general public," has proven to be a remarkably flexible one. Flexible enough, as discussed previously, to permit San Jose, California, to use it as a means of controlling disorderly and deviant individuals, an action that further blurs the lines between crime and disorder. More commonly, however, cities aggressively pursue public-nuisance actions against problem properties. Many have established public-nuisance task forces, which solicit citizen input about property problems, have dedicated one or more prosecutors solely to public-nuisance cases, and have even created "problem properties courts." Some cities have also taken steps to encourage community groups to *privately* prosecute public-nuisance actions, a few going so far as to eliminate legislatively the primary obstacle to these private prosecutions, namely, the standing requirement that a private individual suffer a "special injury," distinct from the public's injury, to seek injunctive relief against a public nuisance. Many public-nuisance efforts target properties used for criminal activities, particularly drug trafficking and prostitution. In January 2008, the City of Cleveland took the unusual and aggressive step of filing a public-nuisance suit against twenty-one of the nation's largest banks and financial institutions, arguing that subprime foreclosures were devastating city neighborhoods.[6]

The Case(s) against the Order-Construction/
Disorder-Suppression Equation

As discussed in chapter 2, urban policymakers have long believed that order-construction regulations also suppress disorder. Progressive-era proponents of zoning were "positive environmentalists," who firmly believed that "changing surroundings would change behavior." These beliefs translated into the argument that carefully ordered land uses—the separation of commercial and industrial establishments from residences, and, importantly, the segregation of single-family homes from all other uses—would curb the social disorders plaguing crowded American cities. Included among the many reasons for zoning's stubborn persistence over the past century is city officials' continued endorsement of the view that ordered land uses suppress disorder. Anecdotal evidence suggests that the current focus on disorder suppression reinforces this traditional view in the minds of many city officials. For example, a number of cities include zoning violations among the "disorders" targeted during code-enforcement sweeps.[7]

Herein lies a danger: City officials who reflexively view property regulation as a convenient weapon against disorder may tend to discount the significant economic and social costs that order-construction policies impose. The renewed emphasis on curbing disorder, including property-related disorder, comes at the same time that many land-use scholars and urban planners are of the view that order-construction regulations may contribute to urban decline. And while the available empirical evidence challenges Jacobs's assertion that mixed-use environments will be more "orderly" than single-use ones, there also are reasons—historical, theoretical, and economic—to ask whether order-construction policies sometimes hinder, rather than help, disorder-suppression efforts.

"Non-Plan": The (Almost) Forgotten Case
for a Deregulatory Urban Policy

The assertion that overly burdensome regulations impede the social and economic prospects of poor people has become standard fare in moderate-left
to libertarian-right circles. This claim is an attractive one—indeed, one that I
have endorsed—both because it rings true (everyone has heard a red-tape hor-
ror story) and because it suggests that government can renew our urban cores
and empower our poorest citizens simply by stepping aside. Perhaps the most
comprehensive case for a deregulatory urban policy was made in the early
1980s by proponents of so-called "enterprise zones." Enterprise zones have a
diverse intellectual pedigree, having been proposed by a socialist, almost immediately championed by a luminary of the British Conservative Party, and
imported to the United States by a scholar at a conservative think tank. The
idea originated with Peter Hall, a professor of geography at Great Britain's
Reading University and an avowed socialist. Hall returned from a visit to Asia
in the late 1970s impressed with the level of industry generated by the free-
market economies of Hong Kong and Singapore and convinced that economic deregulation might work similar miracles in Britain's depressed areas.
Hall therefore proposed that Britain establish a limited number of "freeports":
"Small, selected areas of inner cities would simply be thrown open to all kinds
of initiatives, with minimal control." He described his policy as "an essay in
non-plan," based upon "fairly shameless free enterprise" where "government
regulation would be reduced to the absolute minimum."[8]

Soon after Hall unveiled his proposal in 1977, leading spokesmen of the
then-opposition British Conservative Party began to champion it. These Conservatives outlined a bold plan for limited zones within which "the Queen's
writ shall not run." Within these zones, planning laws and rent and wage controls would be virtually eliminated (save for basic health and safety standards),
local and national governments would be required to sell all of the land that
they owned, entrepreneurs would enjoy significant tax relief, and, finally, government subsidies would be eliminated. When the Conservatives swept into
power in 1979, the new leadership quickly established a watered-down version
of these enterprise zones, which, as in the United States, incorporated the tax
incentives but eschewed sweeping deregulation. Interestingly, within British
enterprise zones, deregulation actually took the form of use-based zoning
principles to eliminate the project-by-project regulatory approval required in
non-enterprise-zone areas.[9]

The enterprise zone idea soon struck the fancy of American economist Stuart Butler, who used his post at the conservative Heritage Foundation to spread the free-market gospel on this side of the Atlantic. Butler's case for enterprise zones relied heavily on the works of Jane Jacobs and David Birch. From Jacobs, Butler drew the idea of the successful urban neighborhood as an organic entity bound together by complex economic and social relationships. From Birch, an MIT economist, he found support for his claim that small businesses would fuel any successful renewal effort. The goal of enterprise zones, Butler asserted, was "[t]he creation of employment for inner city residents" generally and a new entrepreneurial class of residents in particular. To accomplish this goal, Butler argued that the federal government should offer federal tax relief in exchange for state and local regulatory concessions.

Butler's indictment of the regulatory status quo was a sweeping one, but he singled out zoning rules as "very costly in social and employment terms." He argued that zoning harms poor communities in two ways. First, zoning laws preclude mixed-use patterns of development that are "an essential element in the stability and vitality" of poor neighborhoods; and second, they impose unnecessary compliance costs on small businesses and providers of low-cost housing. In asserting that the elimination of zoning laws could fuel inner-city renewal, Butler relied upon Bernard Siegan's study of land-use patterns in Houston, Texas— the only large U.S. city without zoning laws. Siegan argued that the lack of zoning in Houston helped to create an entrepreneurial class in low-income neighborhoods. Siegan quoted, for example, Houston's planning director for the proposition that: "The mixed land use pattern that is found in some sections of the city [because of the absence of zoning] should, therefore, not be viewed as bad. In a lower income area, the availability of car-repair services, eating establishments, bars and such service outlets makes for an "attractive" neighborhood in the sense of convenience for a group that has low mobility. The ability to establish a business in one's garage or home contributes to easy entry of individuals into the economic system." The idea implicit in this statement—that zoning rules would impede low-income individuals' efforts to start businesses—was therefore at the heart of the original enterprise-zone proposal. Although the idea garnered early bipartisan support and the strong endorsement of President Ronald Reagan (who made enterprise zones the centerpiece of his urban agenda), enterprise zones did not become a part of federal policy until Congress enacted the Empowerment Zone and Enterprise Communities Act in 1993.[10]

Despite federal legislative inaction (or perhaps because of it), state and local governments quickly seized upon the idea and within a decade established literally hundreds of enterprise zones across the nation. Along the way, however, the deregulatory aspects of the early enterprise zones fell by the wayside. Although both the Reagan administration and model legislation circulated by the American Legislative Exchange Council recommended that state and local governments minimize regulatory barriers to low-income entrepreneurs, including price and rent controls, minimum-wage provisions, and zoning and building codes, these reforms were rarely enacted into law. Instead, state and local—and until very recently federal—efforts have concentrated almost exclusively on providing fiscal incentives to locate new businesses within enterprise zones. Rare examples of regulatory relief tend to be procedural. For example, "one-stop permit shops" or "regulatory ombudsmen" seek to reduce red tape and field questions from frustrated permit applicants.[11]

Similarly, the federal "Empowerment Zone" legislation ultimately enacted in 1993 demands no regulatory concessions from local governments, but instead relies upon a combination of tax incentives and government subsidies to spur investment in inner cities. It was not until the creation of federal "Renewal Communities" in 2001 that Congress incorporated *deregulation* into an enterprise-zone-type policy. The federal law creates forty geographically based Renewal Communities within which significant federal tax incentives are available. To qualify for these incentives, state and local governments must agree to waive or reduce at least four of the following regulations—occupational licensing requirements, zoning restrictions on home-based businesses and/or childcare centers or schools, permit requirements for street vendors, and franchises or other restrictions on competition for businesses providing public services, including taxicabs, jitneys, cable television, or trash hauling.

Even considering the regulatory relief mandated by this new federal policy, however, the enterprise-zone concept has strayed far from its laissez-faire roots. Indeed, the progeny of Butler's enterprise-zone proposal frequently result in more government intervention in economic affairs, not less. For example, the competitive application process for coveted Empowerment Zone status requires local governments to submit a "Strategic Plan" reflecting four principles—"strategic vision for change," "community based partnerships," "economic opportunity," and "sustainable community development"—and incorporating five elements—"vision and values," "community assessment," "goals," an "implementation plan," and a "strategic planning process." Moreover, most Empowerment Zones are managed by elaborate administrative structures. These mini-bureaucracies are usually, in keeping with current trends, "public-private partnerships," which administer zone funds, provide loans and venture capital, facilitate land assembly for new projects, and provide a forum that enables the "public participation" mandated by federal and state laws. The economic literature on the success of enterprise zones is mixed in both the United States and Britain; if anything, British scholars are more inclined to attribute urban success stories to enterprise-zone designations. It is unclear whether legislative failure to incorporate deregulation contributed to the tepid results. While some studies suggest that interventionist management strategies correlate positively with enterprise-zone success, the current zones are certainly a far cry from Peter Hall's "essay in non-plan."[12]

The New Urbanism: Planning
for Diversity?

While enterprise-zone enthusiasts' calls for land-use deregulation in inner cities are all but forgotten, a growing number of scholars, planners, and architects have rediscovered Jane Jacobs's objection to the segregation of land uses. These self-styled new urbanists claim to advance Jacobs's ideas, although their claim is complicated by the fact that, unlike Jacobs, new urbanists are in no way proponents of an "organic" order. Rather, the new urbanists insist upon a carefully constructed land-use scheme, albeit one that differs dramatically from the order constructed by Euclidean zoning. The new urbanists are today's positive environmentalists. Progressive reformers linked the geographic segregation of the family home from commerce and industry to the cultivation of a correct moral constitution; new urbanists believe that single-use zoning corrupts our souls and hearts. New urbanists assert that heterogeneity of city life, not the homogeneity of suburbs, is conducive to true community life. The new urbanists champion dense, "mixed-use" neighborhoods, where homes are situated within walking distance of stores, restaurants, and parks. They assert that commercial establishments enhance a neighborhood by giving residents a place to go on foot and ensuring that people will be outside, mingling among each other. As Philip Langdon observes, "[T]he tavern, the cafe, the coffee shop, the neighborhood store . . . have been zoned out of residential areas. . . . As informal gathering places have been banished, many opportunities for making friendships and pursuing common interests have disappeared."[13]

The new urbanists' ideal is the pre–World War II American city—a place with a "traditional" main street and city center. And indeed they are best known for their attempts to re-create these communities from scratch, in places like Celebration and Seaside, Florida. As a result, new urbanists face accusations that they are nothing more than developers of high-end, cutesy (or creepy) suburban enclaves. Indeed, in contrast to the new urbanists, Jacobs herself took care to limit her critique of modern planning to large cities, not to suburbs. Jacobs viewed the segregation of uses as particularly problematic for urban communities because they are so dependent on a healthy street life. Anyone who has ever visited the downtown areas of many major American cities after business hours has observed her insight in action. Because they are places where people work but do not live, the downtown areas of cities like Kansas City (my hometown) are eerily deserted as soon as the clock strikes five. This is one reason (as discussed in greater detail in chapter 7) that many city redevelopment policies seek to promote a more vibrant downtown nightlife by encouraging both residential infill projects and higher concentrations of entertainment venues.[14]

Streets in other parts of major cities are similarly deserted for another reason: Many poor communities are places where people live but no longer where they work. A crisis of economic stagnation deprives our poorest neighborhoods of the commercial activity that might promote a healthy street life. In his comprehensive study of Chicago's "Black Belt," sociologist William Julius Wilson illustrates this problem with poignant interviews. One former resident recalls, "[There were all kinds] of stores up and down Sixty-third Street, and it was, you know, a fun place. Then when I came back in the seventies, it was like . . . barren." A current resident, an elderly woman, similarly worried, "It's not safe anymore. . . . When all the black businesses and shows closed down, the economy went to the dogs. The stores, the businesses, the shows, everywhere was lighted." Wilson notes that the number of businesses in the South Side neighborhood of Woodlawn, immediately to the south of the University of Chicago, declined from more than eight hundred to fewer than one hundred, and that most of the remaining businesses are "tiny catering places, barber shops, and thrift stores." As the economic decline has progressed, public spaces once filled with busy shoppers have become the "turf" for gang members and drug dealers, a reality that forces law-abiding citizens to choose between moving (if economically possible) and remaining behind closed doors.[15]

While curbing disorder may be a necessary prerequisite to economic renewal in many urban communities, the indirect economic benefits of order-maintenance policies are by no means guaranteed. The new urbanists, however, argue that their version of comprehensive land-use reforms can simultaneously promote economic vitality and stifle harmful disorder. First, to the extent current land-use regulations prohibit the mixed-use environments that foster healthy street life, "zoning for diversity" (to again borrow a term from Jacobs) can help reinvigorate the economic and social climate of poor communities. Encouraging the coexistence of residential and commercial land uses may give people reason to leave their homes and mingle on the sidewalks. And increasing the number of law-abiding users of the sidewalks may check the disorder caused by the criminal element that currently controls too many urban public spaces. Second, the new urbanists argue that, in addition to prohibiting mixed-use urban environments, current land-use regulations frequently favor building designs that are antithetical to public safety. For example, many zoning laws require buildings to be set back away from streets and fronted with significant numbers of parking spaces, thus precluding the development of an attractive "street wall" and limiting the opportunity for informal surveillance of the street by building occupants. Modern planning codes also favor wide residential streets without sidewalks, discouraging pedestrian uses of public spaces. These and other factors encourage people to remain inside their homes or—if they are not residents—to drive through, rather than linger in, a neighborhood. When this occurs, would-be informal monitors of disorder are converted to disinterested passersby, much as the reform-era reliance on patrol cars extricated the "beat" officer from intimate involvement in community life. Thus, new-urbanist-favored design standards—especially sidewalks, on-street parking or rear parking lots, shallow building setbacks, and front porches—may minimize crime. Moreover, these "traditional" designs may themselves encourage informal social interaction that fosters urban vitality and a healthy community life.[16]

A Test Case in East Harlem

New York City has aggressively embraced zoning reforms as integral to redevelopment. This chapter focuses on one of many such efforts, which aimed to improve the area of Manhattan known as East or "Spanish" Harlem. Before these reforms, East Harlem's zoning had not been comprehensively changed since 1961. For more than a decade, Community Board Eleven, which represents East Harlem—a primarily Latino community and one of the city's poorest—examined economic development and land-use policy in the area. As the board's final report demonstrated, the community's land-use problems were immediately apparent. Located in a city with a perpetual housing crisis, East Harlem was a primarily residential community that lost more than half of its residents and many thousands of its residences (more than six-teen thousand housing units) in the latter half of the twentieth century. The rate of housing loss in East Harlem outpaced that of New York City gen-erally, which has a higher rate of loss than other major cities. Moreover, in large part because East Harlem was the "beneficiary" of a great deal of urban renewal attention, the area had the highest concentration of public housing units in the city. High-rise public housing units comprised one-third of the total block area of the community, and 40 percent of residents lived in pub-lic housing, most in now-discredited "towers-in-a-park"–style projects on "super-blocks." An additional 22 percent of the residential units were in pri-vate, government-subsidized buildings. Home ownership rates were among the lowest in a city of renters. And despite a citywide housing crunch, East Harlem had a higher concentration of vacant housing than the rest of New York City.

The second-most-prevalent land use in East Harlem (after public housing) was vacant property. In 1995, nearly 25 percent of East Harlem was classified as "vacant land" by the Department of City Planning. As with public housing, many vacant lots were a hangover from the urban renewal era: More than eighty thousand square feet (two acres) of property was officially categorized as "urban renewal property," meaning that it had been vacant since it was con-demned some thirty-odd years before for urban renewal projects that never materialized. The City of New York itself owned nearly one hundred vacant properties in the area, most obtained either for urban renewal or in tax fore-closures. Less than 9 percent of East Harlem property was used for commer-cial enterprises, and street level commercial activity was hindered by the prevailing land uses: The high-rise public housing projects on "superblocks" discouraged foot traffic, in part because developers eliminated cross streets to create public housing sites. And the flow of commercial traffic was further dis-rupted by a number of large health-care facilities in the community. Not sur-prisingly, East Harlem could hardly be described as a "vibrant" community. Community board member Debby Quinones recently quipped that "when you get off the subway in East Harlem, it's like you're in the Stone Age."

The community board's decade-long process culminated in a formal rezon-ing proposal, which the City Planning Commission endorsed and the city council approved, with a few minor changes, on June 24, 2003. The new zon-ing scheme sought to increase community vitality in three ways. First, most of East Harlem previously was zoned "R7-2," a designation that requires rela-tively deep setbacks and significant amounts of off-street parking. As the community board's formal request noted, this designation is consistent with the area's "tower-in-the-park" projects, but it discourages commercial activity and prevents the creation of a "street wall" appropriate for an urban area. The City Planning Commission thus recommended a new residential zoning designation that permitted shallower setbacks to encourage the development of a physical infrastructure that enlivens the community. Second, the rezoning eliminated most off-street parking requirements in the area's "commercial overlays," where limited commercial activity is permitted in residential zones. As the planning commission acknowledged, these requirements imposed a regulatory burden on small businesses; they also resulted in the dedication of large sections of the community to unsightly (and potentially dangerous) parking facilities. Third, the rezoning added a new commercial overlay along one block of 116th Street.[17]

The rezoning may work. Central Harlem is said to be undergoing a "second renaissance," with high-end retail establishments opening weekly along West 125th Street and professionals renovating old brownstones and building new ones. Community leaders clearly hope that the zoning changes will help East Harlem join the renaissance. The zoning reforms are hardly a purist's dream, however. The new scheme actually *increases* the number of different zoning designations from eleven to fourteen. With the important exception of eliminating off-street parking requirements in commercial overlays, no effort was made to eliminate regulatory barriers to entrepreneurial activities by area residents. Those who seek to start a business must run a daunting regulatory gauntlet that begins with the headache-inducing task of deciphering which activities are permitted in the different overlay zones. For example, property on some streets is zoned C1-5 but on others, C2-5. And on others, C1-5 and C2-5 designations occur on opposite sides of the same street. This is actually an improvement; previously, there were five different overlay designations in the area. Commercial activity continues to be prohibited on most east–west streets. The most significant change—the adoption of a new residential zoning classification for much of the area—takes advantage of the planning code's provision for "contextual" zones (that is, special classifications suited for the "context" of a neighborhood). Such neighborhood-specific zoning classifications have themselves been criticized for impeding development efforts.[18]

That said, the public-choice factors discussed in greater detail in the closing chapter are likely to make the kinds of comprehensive deregulation advocated by Stuart Butler in the 1980s a near impossibility. Local governments have demonstrated a particularly strong attachment to zoning despite decades of criticism from all sides. Not only does local officials' significant interest in maintaining their broad authority over land-use regulation make them resistant to change, but the number of politically powerful groups with similarly strong interests in the regulatory status quo suggests that any proposal of comprehensive land-use reform would open up a Pandora's Box of interest-group politics. East Harlem's rezoning success, in other words, may represent a textbook example of the "second best" principle in action.

Challenges and Responses

These public-choice impediments to comprehensive regulatory reform undoubtedly are reinforced by the traditional assumption that order-construction regulations suppress disorder. The theoretical foundations of order-maintenance policies would seem to support this assumption. Social-norms scholars argue that *government intervention* is a key to order restoration. They posit that public efforts are necessary first steps toward reinvigorating the informal social controls that check disorder and crime. Thus, it is easy to see why city officials would assume that code-enforcement sweeps fit within a broken windows policy manual. By using regulatory enforcement to remediate property blight, government officials seek to signal that property neglect and abandonment will not be tolerated in a community, no matter how poor.

But the claims supporting changes in order-construction regulations, made by the early enterprise-zone proponents and to a lesser extent by today's new urbanists, do not mesh neatly with standard broken windows theory. On the contrary, they rest on the assumption that government intervention to promote order is a *problem,* not a solution, in our cities. A similar argument was made about police efforts around the time that Wilson and Kelling articulated the broken windows hypothesis. Proponents of "depolicing" advocated *decreasing* police presence. Depolicers argued that many communities had become too dependent upon official police protection and ceased to engage in private policing measures, including "preventive surveillance," local dispute settlement, and similar forms of self-help. Depolicing theory is in keeping with the standard law and economics literature on deterrence, which suggests that high levels of law enforcement create a moral-hazard problem. That is, police protection reduces private citizens' incentives to deter and condemn crime and disorder. Just as depolicing proponents argued that public efforts to control crime and disorder backfire, advocates of "deconstructing" the order of city land uses assert that government intervention to impose order stands in the way of organic forces that help check disorder.

The perceived success of order-maintenance policies would seem to suggest that depolicing theory was wrong and that social-norms scholars correctly emphasize the importance of relatively vigorous government disorder-suppression policies. Perhaps it follows, therefore, that relaxing order-construction regulations might lead to more disorder, not less. As Wesley Skogan has observed, while Jane Jacobs offered an order-maintenance justification for favoring mixed-use environments, the premise of her work actually is that we have a taste for *disorder* in urban environments. (The empirical evidence discussed in chapter 3 tends to support Skogan's observation.) Moreover, some land-use scholars cite the lack of (or laxly enforced) rules segregating land uses in poor minority neighborhoods as evidence of "environmental racism." Jon Dubin asserts, "Residents deprived of zoning protection are vulnerable to assaults on the safety, quality, and integrity of their communities, ranging from dangerous and environmentally toxic hazards to more-commonplace hazards, such as vile odors, loud noises, blighting appearances, and traffic congestion." Other scholars have argued that the lack of zoning in Houston—and its underenforcement elsewhere—harms, rather than helps, the poor by depriving them of an important legal means of minimizing disorder. (And, in fact, the City of Houston's enforcement of private covenants provides wealthier residents with an alternative means of disorder suppression.) Scholars critical of the deregulatory approach argue that the best way to protect the poor is to strengthen, not abandon, the enforcement of order-construction regulations in poor neighborhoods.[19]

These critiques are worthy of serious consideration. Obviously, regulatory reforms that abandon or relax the order constructed by zoning rules, inviting these questions, entail risks. Perhaps the regulatory reforms proposed in this book's closing chapter—for example, expanding mixed-use zoning and deregulating home businesses—might lead some low-income entrepreneurs to establish the types of businesses equated with urban decay. These businesses—auto repair shops, pawn shops, "hole-in-the-wall" restaurants, hair salons, and so forth—are likely to be attractive to individuals with limited formal education and training. Still when confronted with a lone run-down bodega, policymakers must ask whether this kind of establishment signals hopelessness or, on the contrary, shows that *at least someone* is making a go of it. The remaining pages of this chapter weigh some of the risks against the possible upsides of regulatory reforms that seek to partially deconstruct our urban land-use patterns, such as those proposed in this book's final chapter. These reforms can, I believe, be reconciled with the social-norms justifications for the order-maintenance agenda. Indeed, for the reasons discussed below, deconstructing our cities may prove crucial to its success.

City-Suburb Competition

First, any effort to weigh the relative costs and benefits of reforming land-use laws to encourage diversity of uses must include the reality of city-suburb competition. Jacobs may have been right that *some* Americans have a taste for urban life, but it is indisputable that most Americans with financial options choose to live a suburban one. Over the past half century, major cities have declined as first residents and then businesses left for greener suburban pastures. Although there are many reasons for this decline, a major culprit is the structure of local government law, which encourages the development of "metropolitan areas," with major cities ringed by many dozens, if not hundreds, of independent municipalities. Economist Charles Tiebout influentially predicted that within this system, municipalities will compete for residents by offering attractive packages of goods and services. Central-city governments recognize this fact, and have long tried to compete with suburbs for development and investment. For example, the new empowerment/enterprise-zone strategies discussed above are just the tip of the competition iceberg. The current economic development landscape is characterized by a dizzying array of subsidized financing, tax abatements, infrastructure improvements, and other "goodies." Regulatory concessions are sometimes included in a "package" of incentives, especially to encourage the redevelopment of contaminated "brownfields." The available empirical evidence, however, suggests that fierce intergovernmental competition renders these strategies—which seek to attract larger employers to a city—ineffective.[20]

If cities are to compete successfully, their leaders must do more than offer economic incentives. Importantly, they must recognize the role that land-use policy—a local government's "most important local regulatory power"—plays in city-suburb competition. The standard account of city-suburb competition provides that local-government power over land use leads inevitably to a tragedy of the commons situation within a metropolitan area. Each suburban government, viewed as co-equal in the eyes of the law, jealously guards its authority to regulate land use so as to maximize local tax revenues (and resident satisfaction). More-affluent suburbs tend to accomplish these goals with exclusionary zoning techniques that freeze out new development, pushing it to the urban fringe. Communities located on that fringe, recognizing their competitive advantage, encourage development by relaxing zoning laws. Increased sprawl—and urban disinvestment—result inevitably from this pattern of exclusion and invitation.[21]

Unfortunately, many city officials fail to consider whether order-construction policies hamstring their ability to compete. In order to compete effectively, city governments must play to their land-use strengths. To the extent that city neighborhoods have *any* competitive land-use advantage over suburban ones, it is likely that some Americans do in fact have a taste for diverse urban environments. For this reason, city governments should hope that Jacobs was right and that policies designed to make *urban* land uses more orderly and *suburban* were their downfall. (And, indeed, many redevelopment efforts, including those discussed in chapter 7, appear to embrace such a hope.) That is not, however, to say that cities find it easy to sell urban life. Public opinion polls consistently find that a majority of Americans, regardless of race or class, prefer to live in a single-family home in the suburbs. The off-site amenities offered by a suburban home are substantial—good schools, safer neighborhoods, more-efficient and "cleaner" governments, wealthier neighbors, and so on. For all of these reasons, even residents who enjoy the urban aesthetic might prefer to live in a new-urbanist suburban development over an older, urban one. For the same reasons, newer developments in cities may also have a competitive edge over older buildings, many of which need substantial renovations.

Moreover, it is important to come to terms with the aesthetic and cultural consequences of the fact that the United States has been a suburban nation for decades: By the 1960s, more Americans lived in suburbs than central cities; the employment balance shifted to the suburbs by the mid-1970s. By 1990, a solid majority of all Americans resided in the suburbs, and by 2000 roughly three out of five jobs in American metropolitan areas were located in suburbs, with only 22 percent of people working within three miles of the center city. One result of these demographic realities is that most Americans' vision of the "good life" is entirely formed by suburbs that have long been decidedly, and intentionally, anti-urban places. The ubiquitous order-construction regulations (that is, zoning laws and subdivision regulations) summarized in chapter 2 mandate "conventional" suburban design—commercial land uses on major arterial roads, separated from residences tucked away on cul-de-sacs and curvilinear streets—may make the physical and economic layout of the urban core seem foreign, odd, and incorrect. This is no less true—and in fact may be more true—of the young people in Richard Florida's "creative class," upon whom many cities (as discussed in chapter 6) are pinning their hopes for renewal. Ultimately, these native suburbanites may prove more creative than hip.[22]

Changing suburban land-use patterns ultimately may foster an affinity for urban life among native suburbanites. Contrary to conventional wisdom, the decentralization of urban areas in the United States peaked between the 1920s and the 1950s, and many suburbs are now becoming denser. Not only are bigger houses being built on smaller lots, but suburban development is increasingly characterized by a diversity of housing types. Manufactured housing, condominiums, and multifamily apartments are becoming more common. And land recycling efforts—including commercial "infill" projects and residential "teardowns"—are intensifying suburban land uses. Joel Kotkin recently argued that "we need to look at current suburbia not as a finished product, but something beginning to evolve from its Deadwood phase." Kotkin expressed his hope that our suburbs can learn from "our ancient sense of the city . . . about the need for community, identity, the creation of 'sacred space,' and a closer relation between workplace and home life." For reasons practical and perhaps philosophical, many suburbs are beginning to incorporate more "urban" features. Moreover, the growing influence of new urbanism is "changing the look, if not the underlying character, of sprawl." Even in the most far-flung entrance points, suburbia has begun to assume a more-urban flavor.[23]

Whatever the competitive obstacles facing cities, there is one overriding reason why cities should concentrate on being urban: A city is better at being urban than suburban. This conclusion is somewhat analogous to the economic theory of comparative advantage, which holds that weaker international trading partners should focus on doing the things at which they are least bad. Some cities continue to pin their hopes on large-scale projects that incorporate "suburban-office-park" developments into their urban environments, but it seems unlikely that downtown sites will prove attractive for these kinds of land uses. The problem of assembling a parcel of land large enough for even a modest development is itself enough to deter new entrants, unless the local government is willing to exercise the fiscally and politically costly power of eminent domain. Indeed, it was the need to assemble land for a major redevelopment project in New London, Connecticut, that led to the infamous *Kelo v. New London* case in 2005. And while the Supreme Court signaled in that case that the Constitution permits the use of eminent domain for redevelopment, the public outcry over the decision likely makes eminent domain a politically unfavorable option.

Thankfully, the 1990s was the best postwar decade for those American cities that previously suffered the most devastating population losses. Moreover, the population growth of many downtowns—the most "urban" areas—outpaced overall population growth in many cities. Some cities saw their *downtown* population grow despite city population losses. The increased preference for urban living is also reflected in the fact that many downtown areas have been gaining white residents, even in cities that continue to lose them. And the 1990s happily saw many urban success stories: Central Harlem, once a symbol of urban despair, is now undergoing a "second renaissance," attributed in large part to the federal Empowerment Zones Initiative; Chicago's notorious high-rise public housing projects are being replaced with attractive, upscale condominiums; and the tech boom is transforming San Francisco's Mission District.[24]

It remains a cold hard reality that many of the communities that have suffered the most from the spiral of urban decline may never see this kind of a boom. Consider, for example, the development prospects of Chicago's Englewood neighborhood. Englewood was one of the communities featured in William Julius Wilson's comprehensive study of Chicago's "Black Belt," discussed above. It also earned a stop on former President Clinton's "New Markets" tour, which sought to highlight communities that had not shared in the prosperity of the 1990s. The population of Englewood is 98 percent African American, and 43 percent of residents fall below the federal poverty line. Crime is a problem, although rates fell steadily in the 1990s, after Chicago began the comprehensive community policing discussed in chapter 6. The Englewood community made national headlines a few years ago when two young boys, ages seven and eight, were charged with the first-degree murder of another child. The charges were subsequently dropped.[25]

In places like Englewood, the need to reconsider long-standing order-construction policy is imperative. Chicago has invested substantial resources toward redeveloping Englewood, and parts of the community fall within a federal empowerment zone as well as a state enterprise zone. One major retail development project—complete with a new-urbanist design—is under way on the area's main thoroughfare, and the local Kennedy-King College campus is expanding to incorporate new retail development as well. Government intervention might succeed in attracting a few projects like this retail center, which is located on land that the city acquired and donated to the developer. But these projects alone probably cannot turn around a community, especially in the face of difficult financial times. Furthermore, the prospect of being "saved" by an outsider may spawn resentment by residents. Indeed, the Englewood project has generated precisely such a controversy. Moreover, successful redevelopment projects frequently raise concerns about the displacement that accompanies gentrification. For example, the University of Chicago is expanding south into the Woodlawn community, mentioned above. While the expansion provides anecdotal evidence that Woodlawn's fortunes are improving—at least in terms of security—neighborhood residents fear that the new construction by both the university and private developers may price them out of their community. More serious are the claims of some observers that the revival of downtown Cincinnati—spurred on by two new professional sports stadiums—and the city's concerted efforts to redevelop the black neighborhood known as Over-the-Rhine fueled racial tensions that led to race riots in 2001. An economic renewal promoted by land-use reforms that seek to unleash the entrepreneurial energies of local residents is not only the most realistic hope for places like Englewood, it might prove to be a more organic and sustainable one as well.[26]

The Norms of Work

Second, order-maintenance proponents argue that government must take steps to reinvigorate the social norms that check physical and social disorder. Many local government officials apparently believe that the best way to accomplish that important goal is to vigorously enforce any order-promoting regulation, regardless of whether the regulation constructs order or suppresses disorder. A more nuanced approach to the problem of disorder might yield a very different conclusion. Indeed, regulatory changes that *deconstruct* the order of urban land uses might do far more to reinvigorate civil society by eliminating regulatory barriers to entrepreneurial economic activity in poor communities.

While social-norms scholars blame the chaos plaguing inner-city communities on the government's failure to enforce basic standards of decency through the criminal law, other social scientists connect the persistent poverty, crime, and disorder in poor urban neighborhoods with the lack of a "culture of work." For example, most inner-city residents endorse the importance of individual initiative and hard work. But people's faith in the efficacy of such initiative may be undermined unless it is based on an observable reality. As a result of chronic joblessness, in other words, inner-city residents develop what psychologists would term negative self-efficacy; they wish to achieve success through work, but become so discouraged by the reality of their community that they cease to believe that it is possible to do so. The economic effects of this phenomenon parallel the social-influence effects of urban disorder. Just as visible disorder discourages law-abiders by signaling that a community tolerates lawlessness, widespread unemployment signals that economic prospects are dim and disheartens job seekers.[27]

The lack of a "culture of work" resulting from chronic joblessness contributes to social disorder. As Wilson observes, work "constitutes a framework for daily behavior and patterns of interaction because it imposes disciplines and regularities." But "where jobs are scarce . . . many people eventually lose their connection to work in the formal economy; they no longer expect work to be a regular, and regulating, force in their lives." Work determines where we are going to be and when we are going to be there. The lives of those without regular employment become less coherent, not just economically, but socially as well. In one of the earliest studies of the effects of long-term unemployment, Marie Jahoda, Paul F. Lazarsfeld, and Hans Zeisel chronicled how Depression-era unemployment affected the small industrial community of Marienthal, Austria. The study demonstrated that prolonged and overwhelming unemployment devastated the cultural life of the community. Residents who once participated wholeheartedly in community and political life "lost the material and moral incentives to make use of their time" and "drift[ed] gradually out of an ordered existence into one that is undisciplined and empty." The same phenomenon occurs in inner-city communities. The study that formed the basis of Wilson's work in Chicago found that unemployed men and women "were consistently less likely to participate in local institutions and have mainstream friends [that is, friends who are working, have some college education, and are married] than people in other classes."[28]

Furthermore, sociological and psychological evidence suggests that persistent unemployment makes it more difficult for parents to reinforce norms favoring law-abiding behavior. This story is a familiar one. When a community lacks appropriate "role models"—when children observe that drug dealing and gang membership are the easiest paths to success and respect—parents find it more difficult to inculcate mainstream values. This is particularly true if the parents themselves are jobless. As Wilson observes, "The more often certain behavior such as the pursuit of illegal income is manifested in a community, the greater will be the readiness on the part of some residents of the community to find that behavior 'not only convenient but morally appropriate.' They may endorse mainstream norms against this behavior in the abstract, but then find compelling reasons and justifications for this behavior, given the circumstances in their community." Chronic joblessness has also been linked with the breakdown of the family, which itself correlates with self-destructive behavior among young people.[29]

Many social scientists, moreover, argue that suburbanization has resulted in a "spatial mismatch" problem: Many of the low-skilled jobs appropriate for low-income inner-city residents are now located in the suburbs. Because city residents lack information about suburban jobs—as well as a reliable way to get to them—these jobs are, as a practical matter, unavailable. Thus, Wilson and others have suggested that neighborhood jobs and businesses are critical to re-establishing the "culture of work" that reinforces public order. The recollections of older inner-city residents about their neighborhoods' better days support this conclusion. These residents tend to connect the loss of social *order* in their communities to the decline of economic activity. They recall a time when their community was safe and healthy, precisely because local businesses made them—as Jacobs would predict—vibrant. Rethinking how land-use regulations may reduce the availability of *legitimate* alternatives to criminal entrepreneurism may serve, in other words, a function similar to dispersing loitering gang members and excluding drug dealers from troubled communities—that is, to enhance the social norms that keep disorder in check.[30]

The Social-Influence Effects of Law Avoidance

Third, order-construction regulations, like all land-use regulations, are routinely disregarded; enforcement usually is sporadic and complaint-driven. In poor neighborhoods, where the cost of complying with order-construction regulations is particularly burdensome, it is reasonable to expect high levels of law avoidance and low levels of enforcement. Local entrepreneurs may be unable to afford to comply. Neighbors, sympathetic to their plight, or sharing in it, might refrain from reporting known violations. It is important to consider this probability in light of the negative social-influence effects of widespread, visible law avoidance. As explained in chapter 1, the term *social influence* describes a commonplace phenomenon—that our behavior is shaped by, and frequently conforms to, our perceptions of others' behavior. Put simply, people will be law-abiding when they perceive that their neighbors are obeying the law. This is one way in which "depolicing" advocates may have erred; the private deterrence measures that they advocated—neighborhood watch groups, bars on windows, and so on—may signal the prevalence of crime and thus "erode deterrence by emboldening law-breakers and demoralizing law-abiders." Similarly, widespread regulatory avoidance may send mixed signals about community members' attitude toward complying with the law generally. The broken windows hypothesis itself suggests that relatively minor legal infractions (for example, vandalism and public drunkenness) can create an environment that fosters serious crime.[31]

The broken windows hypothesis also suggests that law avoidance alone may not warrant legal reforms. After all, order-maintenance proponents argue that the decriminalization of minor (and probably prevalent) public-order offenses, like public drunkenness, contributed to the disorder plaguing many urban communities. This difficulty only serves to highlight the importance of more-fine-grained thinking about the different kinds of disorder discussed in chapter 3: It is critical to understand when and where different kinds of disorder are harmful. To the extent that zoning laws suppress disorder, their target is *economic* disorder, although in suburban communities, and perhaps wealthier urban ones as well, an unfortunate reality is also that zoning laws seek to suppress disorder by excluding poor residents. Given the dire need for economic energy in many city neighborhoods, there is reason to think that city officials are mistaken to suppress economic activity in the name of maintaining order. When the negatives of regulatory avoidance are considered together with the economic realities in many poor communities, the case for legal reform deconstructing city land uses becomes quite strong. The goal of these reforms is not simply to legalize disorder, but rather to stimulate the social and economic activity necessary for healthy and orderly community life. Thus, changing the law to recognize the land-use realities of poor neighborhoods (for example, many women are paid to care for children in their homes) might actually do more to reinforce norms favoring law-abiding behavior than the regulatory status quo.

Diffusing the "Us versus Them" Perception

Finally, and importantly, order-maintenance proponents repeatedly confront the argument that broken windows tactics unfairly single out minority communities and their residents. While it is likely to be true that poor minority communities have the most to gain from order-restoration efforts, it is also true that minorities continue to be more distrustful of police efforts in their communities than white Americans are. For this reason, order-maintenance proponents caution against policing tactics that single out minority communities for extreme measures, such as law-enforcement "crackdowns" that send

" 'warriors to intervene . . . as strangers" into a community on a one-time basis. Such efforts may backfire by alienating those whom they seek to assist.
One order-maintenance tactic—community policing—seeks to diffuse those
tensions by encouraging residents to work with police to identify and prioritize community problems. As Debra Livingston observes, "The police look to
the community in formulating police initiatives; broad authorization, at the
neighborhood level, is deemed essential to involving the police significantly in
efforts to lessen disorder problems." It remains the case, however, that order-
maintenance policies resulting from these programs occasionally place police
officers in an adversarial position with members of the very community identifying the targeted disorders. Land-use reforms that seek to bolster social
norms not by criminalizing disorder, but rather by eliminating regulations
that may stand in the way of a healthier economic and social climate in our
poorest communities, represent another opportunity to dispel these tensions.
This richer, more constructive understanding of the public-order puzzle—one
that includes more than efforts to crack down on disorder—could further
broaden community support for, and therefore improve the success of, order-
restoration efforts generally.[32]

Asking the Right Questions, Now

Urban policymakers' current focus on disorder makes the task of unpacking
the difference between property regulations' order-construction and disorder-
suppression functions critically important. City leaders are eager for order-
maintenance efforts to succeed; they are also worried about the legal
vulnerability of order-maintenance-policing tactics. As discussed in greater
detail in the following chapter, these legal concerns increase the probability
that local governments will turn to the tools of land-use regulation to control
disorder. Indeed, so great is the discretion afforded the government-qua-
property regulator, that Debra Livingston, a community policing expert, cites
regulatory measures (like closing abandoned buildings) as evidence of the proposition that many order-maintenance policies do not raise *legal* issues at all. Yet,
the reality is that property regulations are laws that local officials can enforce
without fear of legal repercussions. This reality places the onus on political actors to examine how property regulations shape efforts to restore order, and
life, in urban communities.[33]

5

Relocating Disorder

Maricopa County, Arizona, is re-creating skid row. Several years ago, the county acquired several square blocks of property south of downtown Phoenix for a "human services campus" and has begun to relocate governmental, nonprofit, and religious organizations that serve the homeless to new facilities there. County officials hail the project as a cutting-edge, "collaborative effort among faith-based, private, governmental and community organizations" that will integrate dispersed providers, enabling them to better serve the area's large homeless population "in an environment of compassion and dignity." But the county's motives are not solely humanitarian. As many as one thousand homeless people congregate on Phoenix's downtown streets each night. Many of these individuals suffer from substance abuse, serious mental illness, or both. Their presence also may impede efforts to woo professionals downtown to live, work, and play. Relocating the organizations that serve the homeless may encourage their clients to spend time on the campus, rather than on the downtown streets. As the county's promotional material asserts, "downtown Phoenix needs a campus so the current service providers can better serve the persons who need assistance while providing greater security and safety for them as well as the community."[1]

Maricopa County is not the only local government seeking to use land-use policy to relocate the disorderly. Many other communities have built, or are considering, homeless campuses. Other cities have targeted inner-city neighborhoods for aggressive property inspections, hoping to address physical decay and to relocate those individuals responsible for social disorder. At least two major cities—Portland, Oregon, and Cincinnati, Ohio—and numerous public housing authorities have adopted "neighborhood exclusion-zone" policies. Exclusion-zone policies, which incorporate elements of both zoning and trespass law, empower local officials to exclude particularly disorderly individuals from struggling communities. All of these tactics employ different management techniques—some concentrate disorder and others disperse it—but they have the same goal: Homeless campuses, exclusion zones, and regulatory sweeps all seek to relocate urban disorder from one place (where it is perceived to be harmful) to another (where policymakers hope it will be more benign).

As the previous chapters have outlined, policies seeking to curb urban disorder have become central to city renewal efforts. The disorder-relocation strategies outlined above contribute to the rich debate over the wisdom and efficacy of those policies in an important way. While the vast majority of order-maintenance scholarship treats the control of disorder as a *policing* question, it is also a *land-management* problem. For many generations, police officers regulated the level of disorder in our cities' public (and, to a lesser extent, private) spaces, usually informally, but also by enforcing laws criminalizing public-order offenses, such as vagrancy, loitering, and public drunkenness. The criminal procedure revolution of the 1960s and 1970s rendered many public-order offenses unenforceable, and cases from this era now haunt officials struggling to restore order in America's cities.

Legal challenges have sent local lawmakers scrambling to find order-maintenance policies that will survive judicial scrutiny. In this environment, some city officials apparently have come to view land-management strategies as legally "safer" alternatives to order-maintenance policing. As in Phoenix, local governments are increasingly adapting the tools of property regulation to a task traditionally reserved for the police, that is, the control of disorderly people. This development is not surprising. As Bob Ellickson has argued, "federal constitutional law is indirectly encouraging cities to bring back Skid Rows, but in a form far more official than the 1950s version." As chapter 2 makes clear, not only have urban policymakers long assumed that regulations ordering land uses effectively curb disorder, but the broad deference granted to the government qua regulator makes land-use policy a particularly attractive disorder-suppression tool. Thus, these new disorder-relocation policies may create what Dan Kahan has called a "cost of rights" problem: In an effort to avoid constitutional challenges, local governments are turning to land-use policies that may impose costs at least as significant as their order-maintenance-policing substitutes.[2]

The institutional shift effected by contemporary disorder-relocation strategies—transferring authority to control the disorderly from police to planners—has profound and understudied implications. These strategies change more than the identity of the regulator; they also change the nature of the regulation. When police informally manage disorder, officers exercise discretion to make *ex post* determinations about what behaviors and which individuals threaten the public order. Disorder-relocation strategies require *ex ante* determinations of who the disorderly are and where disorder is most harmful. City officials then rely upon these decisions to determine whether the individuals responsible for disorder should be concentrated or dispersed. A number of legal scholars have criticized American land-use policy precisely because it relies upon such predictive decision making. *Ex ante* decisions designed to minimize disorder often impose high "prevention costs" because the predictions enshrined in land-use policy are inevitably overbroad, and sometimes they are simply wrong. The costs of integrating these predictions into formal policies are worthy of more in-depth consideration than they have received to date.

Building upon the background review of the order-maintenance revolution and its connection to traditional property regulation set forth previously, this chapter examines three disorder-relocation policies adopted, at least in part, to respond to cases invalidating order-maintenance-policing innovations. Each of these three mechanisms—homeless campuses, neighborhood exclusion zones, and regulatory "sweeps"—employs traditional property-regulation tools to manage urban disorder. After a brief evaluation of how well these strategies respond to the legal objections to order-maintenance policing, the discussion turns again to history, exploring past efforts to treat urban disorder as a land-management problem, including "skid rows" and "red-light districts." This historical record reveals that the disorder-relocation efforts are nothing new. Urban policy has long wavered between disorder concentration and disorder dispersal, and past experience with these strategies provides important insight into how well new disorder-relocation efforts respond to the concerns of order-maintenance opponents. Unfortunately, the history also suggests that disorder-relocation policies raise serious concerns about economic and racial justice and may prove less efficacious than their order-maintenance-policing alternatives. "Disorder zones"—such as skid rows and red-light districts—may shield other areas of a city from urban problems. These zones, however, previously have proven so problematic that policymakers have consistently sought to disperse the disorder within them, a decision that in turn exposed more neighborhoods to disorder. Furthermore, the competing disorder-management techniques advance different and possibly inconsistent urban policy goals: Concentration strategies are used to clean up downtown by containing the disorderly in less-desirable, poorer neighborhoods; dispersal strategies aim to protect poorer neighborhoods from disorder and the disorderly.

Three Contemporary Disorder-Relocation Strategies

Faced with judicial skepticism of new order-maintenance policies, local officials seeking to implement new policing strategies have learned to ask, "[W]ill we get sued?" This concern has prompted Tracey Meares and Dan Kahan to warn of a "coming crisis" in criminal procedure, but lawsuit-weary officials may seek to avert this crisis by turning to other strategies, including land-use policies, that are likely to escape judicial review. In this environment, the three land-management strategies discussed below—homeless campuses, regulatory "sweeps," and "neighborhood exclusion zones"—are attractive. They permit officials to take advantage of the traditional deference granted regulators of private property.[3]

Disorder Concentration: The Example of the Homeless Campus

Phoenix's "human services campus" may be the most ambitious effort to centralize homelessness services, but it is not the only one. Maricopa County's project is modeled upon a smaller campus in Orlando, Florida, which features an outdoor covered pavilion providing sleeping accommodations (essentially, and somewhat disturbingly, human parking spaces), meals, and showers for 375 men, a smaller indoor residential treatment facility, and a residential facility for homeless women and children. Smaller homeless campuses exist in Anchorage, Atlanta, Sacramento, San Antonio, Jacksonville, Ft. Lauderdale, Miami, Las Vegas, New Orleans, and Washington, D.C. Campuses have also been considered in Dayton, Chicago, Colorado Springs, Honolulu, Salt Lake City, and even Hyannis, Massachusetts.[4]

In an age of tight budgets and "compassion fatigue," why would cities build expensive homeless campuses? While city officials cite the need to coordinate services, homeless advocates argue that campuses warehouse the homeless out of sight. A proposal to create a "compassion zone" in Kansas City, Missouri, supports the latter hypothesis. Within the compassion zone, a new daytime drop-in shelter would provide an alternative to wandering the thirteen blocks between existing shelters and a large downtown soup kitchen. The director of the Downtown Community Improvement District calls these blocks "kind of a trail of tears." That the "compassion zone" is viewed as a way to "shoo undesirables out of the central business district" is made apparent when it is coupled with other city land-use plans. Officials anticipate establishing a "security zone" around the city's new main library and excluding all individuals with criminal records from it. Homeless advocates assert that the policy is designed to prevent the new library branch from becoming a de facto daytime shelter—a role that the existing main library currently serves.[5]

Campuses also avoid constitutional concerns raised by the use of order-maintenance-policing techniques against the homeless. Importantly, the chance for a successful legal challenge to a local government's decision to establish a campus is exceedingly small. While the constitutionality of criminalizing behaviors linked with homelessness remains an open question, the constitutionality of most local land-use policies does not. As a matter of federal constitutional law, nonconfiscatory land-use regulations are subject to rational basis review—that is, they will be upheld if some *conceivable* government interest justifies them. This is certainly the case for homeless campuses. A campus serves at least two "conceivable" policy goals—improving homeless services and aiding downtown redevelopment. Nor could the neighbors who might suffer a reduction in property values because of a campus raise successful regulatory takings challenges, requiring the government to compensate them for their financial losses. Any government action resulting in less than a total deprivation of all property value is subject to ad hoc judicial review, which strongly favors the government. Moreover, a reduction in property values attributable to a homeless campus probably would not warrant even this deferential, pro-government scrutiny. Under certain narrow circumstances, "inverse condemnation" claims are available to remedy economic damages that result indirectly from government actions. Unless it can be shown that the physical invasion of a plaintiff's property was the foreseeable result of campus construction, however, the owner would be likely to suffer what Abraham Bell and Gideon Parchomovsky have called a noncognizable "derivative taking."[6]

In some states, even a nuisance remedy would not be available to remedy disorder caused by shelters operated by local governments: A few states do not permit nuisance suits against local governments at all; others preclude injunctive relief. Where shelters are operated by private, not-for-profit entities, or where nuisance relief is available against local governments, neighbors harmed by campus-related disorder can seek nuisance relief, but such relief would be available only after the campus was constructed and the property owners injured. And that damage may be significant. For example, in 1985, the Arizona Supreme Court enjoined the operation of a soup kitchen in a Tucson neighborhood, and the facts of that case provide little comfort for neighbors worried about new shelters: "Transients frequently trespassed onto residents' yards, sometimes urinating, defecating, drinking and littering on the residents' property. A few broke into storage areas and unoccupied homes, and some asked residents for handouts. The number of arrests in the area increased dramatically. Many residents were frightened or annoyed by the transients and altered their lifestyles to avoid them." Homeless campuses, in other words, may be expensive, but they also are virtually lawsuit proof.[7]

Disorder Dispersal through Regulatory Enforcement: Housing Code "Sweeps"

Judicial deference to private-property regulation also makes a second disorder-relocation strategy—the targeted use of aggressive property inspections discussed in chapter 4—an attractive alternative to order-maintenance policing. While the previous discussion considered the use of housing codes to *suppress* disorder, regulatory sweeps have the effect of *relocating* it as well. To borrow the colorful language of economists John Accordino and Gary Johnson, "[c]rooks, killers, and losers tend to infest areas with dead buildings, like maggots on a carcass." Targeted aggressive inspections can address these problems by closing abandoned buildings and dispersing the criminals who use them for "hangouts." In an unguarded moment, a student of mine—a former police officer in a large midwestern city—admitted that officers sometimes would enlist building inspectors to close down buildings inhabited by drug dealers, gang members, and other troublemakers. The officers viewed the closures as a way to prevent further neighborhood decline by forcing these individuals to find somewhere else to hang out, hopefully outside of the neighborhood. He further remarked, however, that although his precinct commander had ordered the officers in his charge to adopt this practice, he and his fellow officers refused to do so. They reasoned that the situation in his precinct was so bad that the rest of the city was better off if the criminals just stayed put. At least one study confirms my student's instinct, finding that crime "displacement" is a significant benefit of housing inspections. Officers can enlist inspectors, in other words, to do what the Supreme Court suggests in *City of Chicago v. Morales* that they cannot do on their own—that is, ask perceived troublemakers to "move along."[8]

Moreover, the regulatory code book is, as James Delgado observed, "pretty thick." Academics tend to treat this "thickness" as a problem, for various reasons discussed in chapter 4. But for Delgado, the thickness "open[s] up miraculous possibilities." A recent case in the United States Court of Appeals for the Ninth Circuit illustrates why. Several years ago, San Bernardino, California, conducted housing code "sweeps" in a low-income area. As the Ninth Circuit observed, the "sweeps were massive undertakings, with city officials, police, firefighters, and housing code inspectors descending on the area to inspect dozens of pre-selected buildings." Over a six-month period, the city closed ninety-five buildings. The property owners alleged that the city trumped up a building-code emergency to force the eviction of tenants with criminal records and gang affiliations. A panel of the Ninth Circuit rejected the owners' claim that the sweeps were arbitrary and therefore unconstitutional. The majority reasoned that even if the city "faked" a housing-code emergency, "the reduction of crime by relocating criminals and reducing urban blight bears a rational relation to the public health safety and general welfare." The panel reached this conclusion over the vigorous dissent of Judge Stephen Trott, who argued, "[t]he action cannot be justified as a means to control crime. If criminals are living in the units, the police should arrest them. If crime . . . is rampant, the police should put a stop to it. The city cannot simply start throwing innocent people out of private property to reduce crime in a troubled neighborhood. A contrary rule is simply unimaginable." The lax oversight that worried Judge Trott undoubtedly is one reason many cities are incorporating sweeps into order-maintenance efforts.[9]

Disorder Dispersal through Public-Space Zoning: Neighborhood Exclusion Zones

Other local government entities have begun to use zoning techniques to exclude the "disorderly" from troubled communities. Several years ago, Robert Ellickson hypothetically suggested that zoning laws, which usually dictate the appropriate uses of private property, might be extended to govern the acceptable uses of public spaces as well. He proposed dividing a city's public spaces

into three zones, with "three codes, of varying stringency, governing street behavior" within each zone. Most city streets would fall into a "yellow zone,"
where episodic (but not chronic) disorder is permitted. The remainder would
be divided between "green zones," where aberrant behavior is strictly curtailed
in an effort to create "places of refuge for the unusually sensitive" and "red
zones," where significant social disorder is tolerated. Ellickson's zoning scheme
would manage disorder primarily by concentrating it in "red zones," which he
specifically analogized to skid rows.[10]

In contrast to Ellickson's hypothetical concentration strategy, most formal
public-space zoning policies employ a disorder-dispersal strategy. In Ellickson's terms, some local governments are seeking to use public-space zoning to
make their "red" zones "yellow." A number of public housing authorities exclude nonresident troublemakers from projects, much as a private landlord
might. Additionally, Portland, Oregon, and Cincinnati, Ohio, have adopted
"drug exclusion zone" laws that apply the anti-trespass principle to entire troubled neighborhoods. For example, Cincinnati's drug-exclusion law banned all
persons arrested for drug offenses within any designated "drug exclusion zone"
from the "public streets, sidewalks, and other public ways" in the zone for
ninety days; upon conviction, the exclusion was extended to one year. Persons
excluded under the ordinance were subject to prosecution for criminal trespass if they returned during that time.[11]

In its regulatory takings cases, the Supreme Court often has stated that
the "right to exclude" is "one of the most essential sticks in the bundle of
rights that are commonly characterized as property." With neighborhood
exclusion zones, local governments seek to borrow this treasured strand from
the property-rights bundle to augment order-maintenance efforts. Trespass-
zoning laws incorporate two different property-regulation devices—zoning
laws, which divide cities into various "use districts," and trespass laws, which
protect the right to exclude. Trespass-zoning laws differ from traditional zoning laws in important and constitutionally significant respects, of course. A
neighborhood-exclusion-zone scheme establishes the appropriate *users* of public streets and sidewalks, rather than the appropriate *uses* of private property.
Neighborhood exclusion zones are, in many respects, the mirror images of
homeless campuses. While campuses concentrate the disorderly in a central
location, exclusion zones disperse them. The two strategies also advance very
different policy goals. Homeless campuses seek to draw disorder away from
the central business district to aid redevelopment. In contrast, neighborhood
exclusion zones—like regulatory sweeps—seek to protect the most vulnerable

neighborhoods from the ravages of disorder. The underlying theory is that some communities are so overwhelmed by drugs and violence that the threat of additional disorder is simply untenable. In order to protect these communities, it becomes necessary to exclude individuals who previously helped create disorder. For this reason, exclusion zones target neighborhoods with unusually high levels of disorder and drug-related crime.[12]

In contrast to the two disorder-relocation policies discussed previously, city officials cannot expect courts automatically to extend carte blanche approval to exclusion-zone policies. Regulations governing the acceptable *users* of public spaces raise different constitutional concerns than regulations governing the acceptable *uses* of private property. While exclusion zones may avoid the "vagueness" concerns that plague new order-maintenance-policing efforts, these policies have been the subject of other constitutional challenges, including the following.

First Amendment Claims: The Supreme Court unanimously turned away a First Amendment "overbreadth" challenge to a public-housing exclusion-zone policy in *Virginia v. Hicks.* Kevin Hicks challenged his exclusion from a public housing project on the grounds that housing authority officials might, in the future, exclude individuals who wished to engage in expressive activities. The Court reasoned that Hicks's exclusion resulted from *nonexpressive* conduct (trespassing and vandalism) and that expressive activity presumably would be the kind of "legitimate business or social purpose" exempted from the trespass policy. *Hicks* is the second recent decision to grant the government qua landlord significant leeway to restore order. The other, *U.S. Department of Housing and Urban Development v. Rucker,* sanctioned a different kind of "exclusion" strategy. In *Rucker,* the Supreme Court ruled that public housing authorities could insert clauses in public housing leases authorizing "one-strike-and-you're-out" evictions for the illegal drug activity of a tenant, guest, or household member.[13]

Neither *Hicks* nor *Rucker* represents a constitutional green light for all neighborhood exclusion-zone policies, however. When applied in a public housing project, no-trespass rules arguably are a straightforward application of a landlord's right to exclude outsiders from a quasi-private development. In fact, the parties in the *Hicks* litigation briefed, but the Court did not address, whether public housing authorities were entitled to special solicitude not generally afforded government actors in their roles qua landlords. It is therefore unclear whether the Court's approval of the use of trespass laws in the public housing context would extend to the exclusion of individuals from public thoroughfares in a large section of a city. Tellingly, however, the Supreme Court has previously rejected "expressive association" challenges to content-neutral laws that limit *where* individuals may associate. The Court reasoned that "it is possible to find some kernel of expression in almost every activity a person undertakes—for example, walking down the street . . . but such a kernel is not sufficient to bring the activity within the protection of the First Amendment."[14]

Right to Travel Claims: In 2002, the U.S. Court of Appeals for the Sixth Circuit held that Cincinnati's drug exclusion law violated the Fourteenth Amendment "right to intrastate travel."* While the decision renders Cincinnati's ordinance unenforceable, it does not close the book on all exclusion-zone policies. As the Sixth Circuit acknowledged, the Supreme Court has consistently declined to recognize that right explicitly and has arguably rejected it *in dicta*. (Indeed, only a few months before invalidating the Cincinnati law, the Sixth Circuit rejected a right-to-travel challenge to a public housing authority's "no trespass" policy, reasoning "that right is essentially a right of interstate travel.") And the federal courts of appeals remain divided on the right-to-intrastate-travel issue, which frequently arises in the context of yet another exclusion strategy employed by local governments—curfews excluding young people from public streets late at night. Finally, even if the Supreme Court were to endorse a right to intrastate travel, exclusion policies might be upheld as analogous to travel restrictions routinely imposed as a condition for parole or probation.[15]

Right to "Intimate Association" Claims: The Sixth Circuit also ruled that the exclusion policy violated the Fourteenth Amendment right of "intimate association" as it applied to two individuals excluded from the Over-the-Rhine neighborhood. (Over-the-Rhine was designated the city's first drug exclusion zone in 1998.) The plaintiffs each claimed that their exclusions interfered with important personal relationships—one was prevented from helping to rear her grandchildren and another from visiting his attorney. In

---

*The Ohio Supreme Court also invalidated the Cincinnati ordinance on right-to-travel grounds, reasoning that "[e]very citizen of this state . . . enjoys the freedom of mobility . . . to roam about innocently in the wide-open spaces of our state parks or through the streets and sidewalks of our most populous cities." *State v. Burnett*, 755 N.E.2d 857, 862–63 (Ohio 2001).

contrast, the Ohio Supreme Court rejected a freedom-of-association challenge to the Cincinnati ordinance because the plaintiff failed to establish
that his exclusion actually interfered with his associational rights, suggesting that associational challenges could be avoided on an "as-applied" basis
with an appropriate variance provision.[16]

Double Jeopardy Claims: Exclusion-zone policies have also been challenged on
"double jeopardy" grounds, with excluded individuals asserting that they
are being punished twice (criminally, and through exclusion) for the same
drug offense. The Double Jeopardy Clause, however, is implicated only
when an individual is subjected to multiple criminal punishments for the
same offense, and courts have consistently found that exclusion-zone policies have a civil purpose—namely, to restore the quality of life for residents
in drug-plagued neighborhoods.[17]

Even considering the serious constitutional concerns raised by neighborhood
exclusion zones, disorder-relocation strategies entail less legal risk than their
order-maintenance-policing alternatives. Officials can usually presume that a
decision to establish a homeless campus or conduct a regulatory sweep will not
become embroiled in litigation. And a narrowly drawn exclusion-zone policy
may also survive review. It is hardly surprising, therefore, that local government
officials are turning to disorder-relocation strategies with increasing frequency.

Historical Disorder-Relocation Strategies

Local efforts to relocate urban disorder are nothing new. For many generations, police officers served as informal "urban disorder regulators," variously
employing both disorder-concentration and disorder-dispersal strategies. The
historical experience with these informal relocation strategies helps shed light
on the "cost of rights" problems raised by new, more formal ones.

Skid Rows

While homelessness is nothing new, the development of "skid rows" to serve
the needs of a subset of the homeless population has been called a uniquely
American phenomenon.* Skid rows developed in the years after the Civil War,

---

*The term *skid row* apparently originated with the "skid road" used to drag logs into
Seattle's Puget Sound. See Levinson, *Skid Row in Transition,* 80, n.1.

when widespread economic dislocation left many people homeless and poor. Skid rows served as lodging and employment centers for this large, transient, male population. In addition to inexpensive accommodations, skid row neighborhoods also featured employment agencies and other businesses serving itinerant workers. By the late nineteenth century, most large urban centers had one, with populations peaking between 1880 and 1920, a time when rapid industrialization, the railroads, and the opening of the West created demand for transient workers.[18]

Skid rows always were unquestionably disorderly places. High concentrations of bars and burlesque shows and the ubiquitous presence of prostitutes probably made them, in many cases, indistinguishable from red-light districts. Furthermore, while many workers on skid row remained "homeless" for a short time, a distinct subclass lived transient, unattached lives in "hobohemia" for many years. Most of these men were employed much of the time, but available work was never permanent and tended to be seasonal. As a result, many thousands of men had significant leisure time to frequent the skid row establishments that catered to the needs and desires of unattached, single men. Despite the tendency in some circles to idealize this lifestyle, most mainstream accounts depicted skid rows as dangerous and depressing places, and urban officials made efforts to prevent them from encroaching upon respectable parts of town.[19]

Still, skid row in its heyday was probably a vibrant—if disorderly—community. Contemporary accounts depicted busy sidewalks full of migratory workers who found employment and camaraderie there. These economic and social conditions stand in stark contrast to the later declining skid rows, which were "in the minds of both the public and the academic community . . . very different and more deviant place[s]." Skid rows began to decline around 1920, and their populations fell precipitously after World War II. The raw numbers, however, tell only part of the story. While skid row had always been associated with social deviancy and especially alcohol abuse, after World War II, these factors became the areas' defining characteristics. Several major studies of postwar skid rows all presented the same picture of dire conditions—extreme poverty, disability, alcoholism, mental illness, and social isolation.[20]

These studies also vividly illustrate how skid row came to be viewed as a land-use problem. For decades, city officials primarily had regulated skid row in the same way that urban disorder had been addressed throughout American history—through order-maintenance policing. In his classic study, Egon Bittner asserted, "the traditional attitude of civic-mindedness toward skid-row has been dominated by the desire to contain it and to salvage souls from its clutches. The specific task of containment has been left to the police." Police officers made every effort to maintain the boundaries of skid row, confining its residents so as to shield middle-class neighborhoods from the disorder that they were thought to generate. As skid row declined, however, police officers felt pressure to exercise a greater amount of control within skid row, as well. While police remained more tolerant of disorder on skid row than elsewhere, "sweeps" to clean up the areas became more frequent occurrences. By the mid-1960s, the skid row containment strategy had unraveled. Indeed, most post-war studies focused on how to address the dislocations resulting from skid row demolitions.[21]

While most skid rows have disappeared, homelessness has not. A number of commentators have asserted that the demise of skid rows fueled the home-lessness crisis by reducing the supply of affordable housing and dispersing the homeless. Moreover, skid row containment policies were abandoned at roughly the same time that public-order offenses were decriminalized. As a result, according to Peter Rossi, "the public could observe firsthand shabbily dressed persons acting in bizarre ways, muttering, shouting, and carrying bulky packages or pushing supermarket carts filled with junk and old clothes." As the homeless became more visible, city officials and nonprofit service providers struggled to find ways to address their needs. Politically progressive, middle-class religious congregations replaced skid row missions, with some congregations intentionally locating soup kitchens in more-affluent areas to draw attention to the homeless problem. Problems previously concentrated on skid row began to affect respectable communities.[22]

By the early 1990s, this kind of dispersed disorder began to generate a back-lash against the homeless. "Compassion fatigue," combined with a growing endorsement of the broken windows hypothesis, led many cities to pass ordi-nances cracking down on homelessness-related disorder, particularly panhan-dling and sleeping in public places. Through the creation of "campuses," homeless policy seemingly has come full circle, as local governments seek to formally reestablish skid row containment strategies.[23]

Red-Light Districts

Local governments' efforts to control sexually oriented businesses have fol-lowed a similar pattern of disorder concentration, followed by dispersal. Tradi-tionally, the "sex industry" was concentrated in special disorder zones known colloquially as red-light districts. As with skid rows, these containment policies were—with a few notable exceptions—informal in nature. Also, as with skid rows, the informal containment compromise unraveled when unruly red-light districts came to be viewed as a threat to the cities' greater welfare. In response to that concern, economic and legal forces combined to eliminate the red-light districts and disperse their concentrated disorder. This pattern played itself out in two related contexts: the municipal "vice districts" of the early twentieth century, and the late twentieth-century "adult-use" districts.

Municipal Vice Districts

Some Western European nations have designated official "vice zones" within which prostitution is tolerated. While this practice has been rare in U.S. history, several American cities created official municipal vice districts in the late nineteenth and early twentieth centuries. The best known example is "Storyville" in New Orleans, which was created by an 1897 ordinance confining brothels to a narrow area of the city. St. Louis, Missouri, and several Texas cities also established similar districts around the turn of the twentieth century. Technically, prostitution remained a crime within these districts, but lax enforcement approximated legalization.[24]

All of these districts were eliminated by World War I, for reasons related to the predictable consequences of concentrating disorder. In Texas, a state law encouraged cities to create vice districts by providing that a private nuisance lawsuit could not "interfere with the control and regulation of bawds and bawdy houses ... confined by ordinance ... within a designated district." When the aggrieved neighbors of brothels challenged this exemption, the courts ruled that the cities had effectively and illegally authorized prostitution. Moral outcry led to the demise of the St. Louis vice district only four years after its creation in 1870. Storyville lasted longer. In 1900, the Supreme Court rejected a quasi-regulatory-takings challenge claiming that the ordinance had resulted in an increase in disorderly and immoral behavior and diminished adjacent property values. Concerns about disorder did, however, lead the U.S. Navy to close Storyville in 1917 in order to preserve the health and good order of American servicemen.[25]

While the formal designation of vice districts was relatively rare, most large cities had large, quasi-official vice districts during this same time period. The police contained prostitution through selective arrests, turning a blind eye to solicitation within these districts, but arresting prostitutes elsewhere. Respectable society accepted this compromise because it shielded other neighborhoods from prostitution; however, prostitution-related disorder was amplified within these districts, where theft, physical abuse of prostitutes, and even violence spawned by inter-brothel rivalries was commonplace. Despite the disorder, and the concerted efforts of Progressive-era "social hygiene" reformers to eliminate prostitution, most vice districts remained intact until the second decade of the twentieth century. At that point, Progressives joined forces with Prohibitionists to pass "red light abatement acts" that authorized private citizens to file a complaint against any building used for prostitution. As the United States prepared to enter the First World War, Congress also authorized the military to arrest any prostitute operating within five miles of a military cantonment. These acts, combined with increased demand for police enforcement, meant the end of the vice districts.[26]

Eliminating vice districts did not, however, eliminate prostitution. Rather, prostitutes were dispersed, exposing more neighborhoods to the "oldest profession." Street walking—long viewed as the most disorderly and dangerous form of the trade—became commonplace. Tea rooms, massage parlors, and palm-reading establishments became fronts for prostitution rings. Prostitution became more difficult to regulate as control shifted from the madams and police to pimps and organized crime syndicates.[27]

"Adult-Use" Districts

Underground prostitution undoubtedly took root in the "adult-use" districts that developed during the last century. As with their vice-district predecessors, these areas featured high concentrations of sexually oriented businesses— adult book stores, pornographic movie theaters, peep shows, exotic dance clubs, massage parlors, and so on. The extent of the disorder present in these areas was epitomized by New York's Times Square. By the 1970s, visitors encountered "a smorgasbord of books, magazines, films, peep shows, . . . stripteases, and even live sex performances," many of which concealed prostitution as well. The area also became flooded with criminal activity—so much so that 42nd Street alone "recorded more than twice as many criminal complaints as any other street in the area, with drug offenses, grand larceny, robbery, and assault topping the list."

Most adult-use districts, including Times Square, resulted from an informal "containment" strategy similar to the vice-district model: Order-maintenance policing, rather than formal land-use policy, was used to regulate and contain the sex industry. A few cities, however, adopted formal land-use policies establishing adult-use districts. The best known example is Boston's "Combat Zone," which was designated the "adult use entertainment district" in 1974.

Unfortunately, after the containment strategy was formalized, the crime and disorder in the Combat Zone skyrocketed. Whereas prostitution, gambling, and hard-core obscenity were already present in the area, the "official" designation that these activities *belonged* there led to a rapid erosion of any discretion previously exercised by its purveyors. Norman Marcus, then counsel for the New York City Planning Commission, cautioned against emulating this model, warning that a sense of "criminal license" prevailed in the Combat Zone. Moreover, neighboring areas, especially Chinatown, suffered serious economic and social consequences from disorder spillovers and began to thrive as the Combat Zone contracted.[28]

Over the past few decades, adult-use districts have gradually disappeared, as a result of the same economic and legal forces that precipitated the elimination of skid rows and vice districts. Importantly, the districts' downtown locations have subjected them to the pressure of urban redevelopment efforts. Some, such as Albany's "Gut," were razed during the urban renewal period, as local officials came under increasing pressure to quell the disorder within them. More recently, after decades of failed efforts, private and public forces combined to transform the Combat Zone and Times Square. Urban-development expert Lynne Sagalyn recently described the "new" Times Square as an "internationally recognized symbol of urban redemption." In 2003, only two adult businesses remained in the Combat Zone.[29]

While zoning laws were rarely used to create red-light districts, they have contributed to their demise, thanks in part to the Supreme Court. The Court's decisions extending First Amendment protection to sexually explicit materials undoubtedly contributed to the growth of red-light districts in the 1960s and 1970s. But later decisions permit cities to use zoning laws to control the "secondary effects" of sexually oriented businesses, either by dispersing or concentrating them. The proliferation of "secondary effects" studies focusing on the negative consequences of concentrations of adult businesses provides strong anecdotal evidence that many cities have opted for dispersal. A predictable consequence of these policies has been, in the words of one commentator, "pornosprawl." Communities without dispersal zoning find themselves inundated with adult businesses pushed out of major cities.[30]

In each of the contexts discussed above, local authorities initially sought to control disorder by concentrating it into "disorder zones." Concentration efforts usually were an unofficial compromise that shielded respectable communities from urban disorder. Concentrating disorder, however, amplified it and caused spillovers that threatened neighborhoods outside of the containment zone. Eventually, the disorder-concentration compromise became socially and politically unacceptable, and government officials sought to disperse disorder in order to minimize its costs.

A "Cost of Rights" Problem?

Order-maintenance-policing proponents argue that judicial decisions preventing the police from addressing urban disorder create a "cost of rights" problem—that is, that legal protections designed to shield individuals from the *possibility* of police abuses result in a *certainty* of crime and disorder in our nation's most vulnerable communities. As the discussion above illustrates, disorder-relocation strategies dodge many of the legal pitfalls of order-maintenance policing by transferring the power to regulate disorder away from the police. The question remains, however, whether these strategies solve the cost of rights problem rather than creating a different one. The remainder of this chapter asks whether, in an effort to avoid legal challenges, local officials may be turning to disorder-relocation strategies that impose high costs of their own.

Disorder Relocation as Disorder Suppression

The historical experience described above casts a shadow of doubt upon current disorder-relocation efforts. Over the past century, urban policymakers discovered that efforts to contain or disperse urban disorder impose serious social costs. Unfortunately, there are reasons to worry that the costs of contemporary disorder-relocation efforts that shift power from police to land-use planners will exceed those of their historical counterparts. When police officers informally managed disorder, local officials could modulate the costs of relocation because of the flexibility enjoyed by officers on the beat. Today's disorder-relocation policies seriously limit that flexibility. Disorder-relocation strategies—like all land-use regulations—require *ex ante* determinations of who the disorderly are and where disorder is most harmful. A number of legal scholars have criticized American land-use policy precisely because it relies upon such predictive decision making. The codification of these predictions also deprives policymakers of the flexibility needed to rapidly respond to changing circumstances. While it is possible that policies adopted with the express intent of acting directly to suppress disorder by relocating the disorderly will overcome these difficulties, both the historical experience with disorder-relocation efforts and the social-norms arguments used to promote order-maintenance policing do not provide grounds for optimism.

Disorder Concentration: The New Skid Rows

At first glance, homeless campuses seem to be an excellent response to the criticisms of "policing" the homeless through the criminal law. Cities seek to use the promise of services and shelter, not the threat of arrest, to lure homeless individuals away from downtown streets. Ideally, this disorder-relocation strategy will reduce the amount of police intervention needed to suppress disorder—and therefore minimize the possibility that police officers may abuse their authority. Furthermore, if, as Professor Dan Kahan has observed, "[p]ublic drunkenness, . . . aggressive panhandling and similar behavior signal . . . that the community is unable or unwilling to enforce basic norms," then it seems self-evident that reducing such disorder will help send the opposite signals. This likelihood is particularly important for those who worry that an absence of street decorum drives law-abiding individuals away, thus impeding efforts to enliven moribund central business districts. In this sense, the homeless campuses can be seen as part of a broader movement to create local government institutions that will help reinvigorate decaying downtown neighborhoods. While new "sublocal" governments, like business improvement districts, enable downtown property owners to solve collective-action problems in order to tackle the physical (and to a lesser extent social) disorders that plague redevelopment efforts, homeless campuses seek to minimize downtown disorder by concentrating it away from city centers.[31]

If the only goal of order-maintenance policies was downtown redevelopment, or perhaps the gentrification of some urban residential neighborhoods, then disorder-concentration efforts might "work." After all, concentration strategies long served to shield respectable neighborhoods by drawing disorder into unrespectable ones. The story is not so simple, however. Social-norms scholars promise that disorder suppression is not a zero-sum game; that is, a reduction in disorder in one neighborhood need not mean an increase in disorder elsewhere. According to the social-influence theory, disorder suppression should have a multiplier effect. Government intervention to curb disorder will bolster private efforts to do the same. The result will be less disorder *everywhere*.

But history suggests that disorder concentration often is, in fact, *worse* than a zero-sum game. Relocating homeless services (and their patrons) may well make central business districts healthier, more vibrant places, but the cost of reducing disorder downtown may be increasing it elsewhere. Moreover, concentration strategies tend to amplify disorder. Policymakers who informally maintained disorder zones accepted the higher level of disorder within them to prevent the erosion of norms of order elsewhere. Yet, eventually, the amplified disorder that resulted led them to switch from a concentration to a dispersal strategy. This point is particularly important because proponents promise that order-restoration efforts will not just save downtown but will also save the poorest, most disorder-plagued urban communities.

These communities are the least likely to benefit from a concentration strategy. A homeless campus is a classic LULU ("locally undesirable land use"); a proposal to establish one frequently is greeted by screams of protest from neighbors. These objections undoubtedly reflect a healthy dose of "NIMBYism" ("Not In My Backyard"). A neighbor of Colorado Springs's proposed campus referred to the project as "Wino Wal-Mart." But they also may suggest that the campuses raise the economic- and racial-equity concerns flagged by opponents of order-maintenance policing. Unfortunately, the "environmental justice" literature illustrates why political decision makers may concentrate homeless services in poor minority neighborhoods, even absent discriminatory intent. Neighborhood opposition may be weaker, residents have less political clout, and planners view their communities as "hopeless" or "unsalvageable." And, importantly, land may be more readily available and less expensive than in more-affluent communities.[32]

For example, Phoenix chose to locate its campus in an area where existing service providers had concentrated informally. Residents in the neighborhood already suffer from so much disorder that existing zoning laws actually discourage new social services from moving into the area. Teachers at the local elementary school worry that homeless men in the soup-kitchen line may pose a threat to students' safety, keep students inside during recess to avoid contact with prostitutes, and encourage area parents to walk their children to school after welfare checks are distributed to avoid muggings. In other words, the campus will be located near a community that is unlikely to have the social capital necessary to withstand an onslaught of new disorder. Indeed, the vulnerability of such neighborhoods to disorder—and the weakness of social norms that might counter it—undergird arguments in favor of order-maintenance policies.[33]

The history of skid row vividly illustrates what such a community might expect from a new homeless campus. A new campus would operate under conditions at least as bad as skid rows in their darkest days. Indeed, sociological studies of the "new" homeless suggest that many suffer from more severe social pathologies—especially mental illness and severe drug addiction—than the classic "skid row drunk." Furthermore, a new campus will lack the private businesses that had economic incentives to enforce some social norms of decorum on the old skid rows. Importantly, the disappearance of the single-room-occupancy (SRO) hotels that traditionally provided the bulk of skid row housing would be likely to exacerbate the disorder of "campus" life. Today, emergency shelters serve as the primary means of addressing the homelessness problem. The very poor, however, have always viewed shelters as a last resort. While the physical conditions of SRO and cubicle hotels were likely to be deplorable, even the worst "cage hotel" unit offered privacy and autonomy that shelters cannot—and the resulting lack of privacy causes some homeless people to shun shelters. Moreover, containing skid row disorder will be much more difficult today than in the past, when municipal officials simply expected patrol officers to maintain the "line of respectability" within the city. Not only has the decriminalization of public-order offenses deprived police of the legal tools employed to back up their informal order-maintenance efforts, but neither the courts nor decent society would countenance some of the informal methods to control disorder in the past, which undoubtedly included the occasional "roughing up" of "bums" found in the wrong part of town.[34]

The City of Los Angeles's effort to formally combine land use and homelessness policy illustrates some of the challenges that a campus would face. During the 1970s, the city scrapped plans to demolish its downtown skid row area, partly in response to the suggestion by poverty advocates that dispersing the homeless would also disperse disorder, and instead adopted an official skid row containment policy. The local Community Redevelopment Agency spent millions of dollars to support service agencies and rehabilitate skid row housing. It also relocated missions and other homeless services away from downtown and into the skid row and has (until recently) resisted any efforts to provide homeless services outside of skid row. The containment policy was bolstered both by police efforts and by physical barriers, such as landscaping and building designs, which emphasized the separation of skid row from the rest of downtown.

During the homelessness "crisis" of the 1980s, this skid row containment policy unraveled. In 1984 and 1985, informal temporary accommodations, such as "tent cities" and cardboard shelters, appeared on skid row. Efforts to remove these structures were met with public protest and lawsuits by homeless advocates, and city policy vacillated between accommodation and crackdown. While the city struggled to come up with some permanent solution (experimenting, for example, with an "urban campground"), police occasionally cleared the homeless from public parks and skid row streets when prompted by complaints from skid row businesses. By the end of the decade, city officials and homeless advocates both clearly were disillusioned with the compromise. A skid row bursting at its seams threatened downtown renewal efforts, and homeless advocates worried that concentrating the homeless allowed others to turn a blind eye to their plight and impeded efforts to reintegrate them into society.

In November 2002, the Central City Association, which represented three hundred downtown businesses, issued a report characterizing skid row as a "downtown[ ] human tragedy" and blaming the "over concentration of 'homeless' service centers" for an "anything goes" mentality in the area. That same month, Los Angeles Police Chief William Bratton targeted skid row for street sweeps that aimed to search for parole and probation violators. (The ACLU challenged these sweeps in a lawsuit ending in an out-of-court settlement.) More recently, Bring LA Home!—a partnership of civic and city leaders formed in 2003—released a ten-year strategic plan to end homelessness, which calls for greater dispersal of homeless services throughout the entire metropolitan area. On September 24, 2006, city officials announced plans to launch the Safer Cities Initiative, a plan to put an additional fifty police officers on the ground in skid row to reduce crime. Bratton stressed that the condition of being homeless was not in and of itself a crime, but the police were going to focus on the behavior, not the condition, of being homeless. The initiative's efforts to target narcotic-related crimes as well as littering, defacement of property, and theft appear to have reduced the number of homeless as well as crime on skid row. While the police are continuing attempts to make strides in skid row, others insist the key battles taking place over the future of skid row involve real estate. More specifically, skid row has been experiencing high-end real estate development, to the delight of some but chagrin of others, including single-room-occupancy-hotel operators seeking to provide low-income housing to skid row residents.[35]

Disorder Dispersal: Neighborhood
Exclusion Zones and Regulatory Sweeps

But what of policies designed to shield such vulnerable communities from disorder by expelling the disorderly, either through the formal designation of an "exclusion zone" or as the not-so-unintended result of regulatory sweeps?

The case for relocating disorder away from drug-infested neighborhoods would appear to be at least as strong as the social-norms justifications for relocating it to a new skid row. While many city neighborhoods struggle, few have fallen to the depths of despair reached in Cincinnati's Over-the-Rhine neighborhood, which was designated the city's first (and only) "drug exclusion zone." If open-air drug markets have come to symbolize inner-city chaos, then Over-the-Rhine is an urban disaster poster child. Featured in the 2000 movie *Traffic* as the urban wasteland where the U.S. drug czar (played by Michael Douglas) searches for his wayward daughter, Over-the-Rhine is home to seventy-six hundred people and averages twenty-three hundred drug arrests per year.[36]

Obviously, to the extent that drug crime sends the negative social signals that encourage antisocial and disorderly behavior—and it is difficult to imagine otherwise—then removing drug dealers from such a neighborhood should have positive social-influence effects. The social-influence hypothesis would predict that exclusions could help create an atmosphere where norms favoring law-abiding, orderly behavior will reemerge. Not only will the exclusions reduce the most visible sign of disorder in the community—rampant drug criminality—but residents may feel less apprehensive venturing out of their homes, reasserting their right to use public spaces, and so forth. Similarly, drug exclusion policies may enable residents who otherwise would seek to "escape" to remain in the community and even encourage other law-abiding individuals to relocate there. Finally, both of the dispersal strategies discussed above minimize the exercise of police discretion: Sweeps transfer disorder-control authority to regulators, and exclusion-zone policies target particular offenders. Both therefore address opponents' concerns that the police will abuse their authority to control disorder.

Nevertheless, adding a spatial dimension to order-maintenance policy raises other serious concerns. As is the case with homeless campuses, land-use policies like neighborhood exclusion zones and regulatory sweeps single out poor, minority communities for enforcement—albeit to protect them from disorder, rather than to foist disorder upon them. Despite this, targeting the "worst" neighborhoods may send counterproductive signals. A number of property-law scholars have suggested that regulations "singling out" individual property owners for disparate regulatory treatment may heighten the perception of unfairness (and weigh in favor of compensation for regulatory takings). Similarly, "singling out" a poor minority neighborhood—either as a drug exclusion zone or for particularly vigorous regulatory enforcement—may generate resentment. For example, following recent racial riots in the Over-the-Rhine neighborhood, commentators rushed to provide a sociological explanation for the violence. Cincinnati's drug exclusion law was indicted, along with various other land-use policies, as contributing to a powder keg of racial tensions. One commentator observed, for example, that more than fifteen hundred people were "banished" from the area between 1996 and 2000, and that the exclusions had soured police/community relations. Similar issues have been raised about Chicago's response to the *Morales* decision. In addition to narrowing the definition of gang loitering, Chicago also limited the areas where the ordinance can be enforced to gang "hot spots" designated by the chief of police. A major controversy over the designation of these hot spots has ensued, with opponents arguing that they escalate the perception of arbitrary and discriminatory enforcement against minorities.[37]

The literature on "expressive theories" of law may help explain these controversies. There are two versions of "expressivism." One focuses on the moral claims made by the law (for example, "racial discrimination is wrong"); the other is concerned with the instrumental consequences of the values expressed by the law. For example, Richard McAdams has argued that the law, and especially local ordinances like exclusion-zone policies, can serve an "attitudinal" function. That is, the law "changes behavior by signaling the underlying attitudes of a community." Both theories shed light on the wisdom of disorder-dispersal strategies. Reactions to the drug exclusion policies in Cincinnati and the strategies employed in Chicago to target gang loitering suggest that some people interpret policies targeting minority neighborhoods for heightened enforcement as signaling official disfavor of minorities. While city officials hope that the norm-reinforcing function of these policies will outweigh these potential expressive harms, the consequential effects of neighborhood-specific dispersal strategies also are unclear. A policy designating a drug exclusion zone or targeting a neighborhood for a sweep might, in essence, become an official declaration that crime is out of control in the community. Thus, policies seeking to "save" poor neighborhoods by excluding individuals engaged in drug criminality can backfire, leading both to the appearance of racial bias and signaling that community renewal efforts are hopeless.

Ultimately, it is difficult to sort out the expressive effects of dispersal strategies. For example, conventional wisdom among criminologists questions the efficacy of criminal (and presumably regulatory) enforcement "sweeps." Kelling and Coles observe, for example, that "[s]weeps, inherently a short term and legally marginal placebo, often worsen the situation for residents and local police: they alienate innocent youths caught up in them (as well as their parents), and are meaningless to real troublemakers for whom an arrest is a minor irritant." On the other hand, some studies of order-maintenance policing suggest that residents prefer proactive tactics like sweeps to more-amorphous "community policing" efforts.[38]

Rebalancing the Cost of Rights?

The risks inherent in disorder-relocation strategies illustrate what might be called a constitutional irony. Beginning in the 1960s, the judicial imposition of strict constitutional limits on police discretion accelerated the radical deregulation of urban public spaces. In recent years, the order-maintenance revolution has reignited the debate about the appropriate scope of police authority to curb disorder. Yet as a result of judicial skepticism of police discretion—and, importantly, of opponents' determination to use that skepticism to their every advantage—the responsibility for curbing disorder is being transferred to *planners* with essentially limitless, unchecked discretion. This is the "unimaginable" regime that the dissent warned of in *Armendariz v. Penman*. Judge Trott was *incorrect* to observe that a "city cannot simply start throwing innocent people out of private property to reduce crime in a troubled neighborhood."[39]

The intuitive justification for treating property regulation and law enforcement differently is that more-significant civil-liberty interests are at stake in the criminal law context. Put simply, it is generally assumed that the police can throw you in jail but regulators cannot. Yet the transfer of authority to control disorder from the police to planners is more complex than conventional wisdom, or current constitutional law, recognizes. The consequences of the predictive decision making that pervades land-use policy are particularly troublesome when policymakers are designing disorder-relocation policies. The costs for a poor community of a rule prohibiting, for example, home businesses should not be underestimated. But the consequences of policies that codify the very stereotypes that motivate concern about order-maintenance policing arguably are more harmful. Moreover, it is not the case that regulators cannot throw you in jail. Property regulations frequently carry criminal penalties, including fines and imprisonment.

That said, so long as the courts impose relatively strict constitutional limits on the police and relatively lax ones on regulators, land-use policy will remain an attractive alternative to order-maintenance policing. More-searching scrutiny of land-use policies undoubtedly would curb enthusiasm for disorder-relocation strategies. But such scrutiny would also come at a cost. Local officials struggling to control urban disorder operate with one hand tied behind their backs by constitutional limits on order-maintenance policing. The wisdom of judicial intervention to tie the other hand by carefully review-ing disorder-relocation policies is questionable. The final chapter will return to this problem in the broader context outlined in this book, asking whether searching judicial review of land-use strategies, including disorder-relocation strategies, should be employed as a tool limiting local governments' zeal to stop disorder in all its forms.

6

The Order-Maintenance
Agenda as Land-Use Policy

We used to have a nice neighborhood. We don't have it anymore. . . . I am scared to go out in the daytime. . . . I don't go to the store because I am afraid.

I have never had the terror that I feel everyday when I walk down the streets of Chicago.

—*Testimony before the Chicago City Council in favor of the Chicago Gang Loitering Ordinance, 1992*

In his short history of urban life, *The City: A Global History,* Joel Kotkin argues that all successful cities have three core characteristics: They are sacred, they are safe, and they are busy. Few would argue with Kotkin's emphasis on city safety, or with his conviction that urban societies fail unless they keep their citizens safe. City life has long depended upon two kinds of security—the protection from invading outsiders and from deviant insiders. Until quite recently, urban civilizations' very existence depended upon the ability to repel invaders. Ancient cities—Assyrian, Greek, Indian, Roman, and American—developed and flourished when that security was established and foundered when it failed. As Kotkin observes, the rise of city walls once marked the beginnings of an urban society. When large walled towns first appeared in China (as early as 1110 B.C.), the characters for "wall" and for "city" were identical. Even during the Pax Romana, when unprecedented security enabled the free movement of people, goods, and ideas, many cities— especially on the frontier—depended upon the protection of walls and legionaries. The return of urban life to Europe in the centuries after the fall of Rome was similarly marked by the "erecting of a defensive perimeter."

While protecting inhabitants from invading outsiders is no longer a primary function of cities, local governments must continue to guarantee their residents' security by adopting and enforcing the rules necessary to protect them from deviant insiders. Many cities in the developing world are crippled by a lack of internal security. In these places, those citizens who can afford to do so retreat into guarded, walled suburban enclaves or emigrate abroad. As the discussion in chapter 1 highlights, by the time that the "Broken Windows" essay was published in 1982, many people expected American cities to suffer, in time, a similar fate. Any informed observer might have concluded that cities were falling apart at their seams and that any reasonable person would have cause to abandon them, at least in part because urban life had become too dangerous. Kotkin argues that order-maintenance efforts have done much to renew city prospects in recent years: "One critical element in the late-twentieth-century revival in some American cities . . . can be traced to . . . the adoption of new policing methods and a widespread determination to make public safety the number one priority of government." Kotkin's assertion received empirical support in the recent work of urban economists Edward Glaeser and Joshua Gottlieb. Glaeser and Gottlieb argue that city fortunes have revived thanks to an increased demand for the informal social interactions enabled by city densities and mixed-land-use patterns. Glaeser and Gottlieb purport to demonstrate that demand for these interactions—that is, for what chapter 3 refers to as "vibrancy"—has been fueled by increased security in urban communities. According to Glaeser and Gottlieb, "negative social interactions," including crime, had previously made it difficult to enjoy the amenities of urban life.[1]

These arguments are critically important. Debates about the wisdom and efficacy of order-maintenance policies tend to focus narrowly on whether the order-maintenance agenda represents wise criminal-law policy—specifically on whether, when, and to what extent order-maintenance-policing techniques reduce serious crime. This question certainly is worthy of serious reflection,

especially because the order-maintenance revolution has primarily revolutionized policing techniques. Over the last twenty years, the broken windows hypothesis has led police departments across the nation to alter their approach
to crime control. The widespread, if tacit, endorsement of the social-norms
premises of the order-maintenance agenda has led to a proliferation of policies
that aim to curb disorder, including an emphasis on police-community relations, arresting individuals for minor crimes and increasing police presence in
public places. As the most recent evaluation of Chicago's Alternative Policing
Strategy, discussed below, noted, "[t]he daily work of thousands of patrol officers [was] reshuffled so that newly formed beat teams could concentrate on
their assigned neighborhoods." If the policies leading to such a reshuffling are
in fact ineffective crime control techniques, critics are right to question whether
they misallocate limited law-enforcement resources.

But this debate about policing priorities and policies may miss what might
be called "land-use" benefits (and costs) of the order-maintenance agenda. As
the discussion in previous chapters highlights, land-use policies focus primarily (but not exclusively) on the regulation of private property. But their goal
has long been to maximize overall community health. Therefore, evaluating
order-maintenance policies through the lens of land-use policy lends itself to a
more holistic consideration of benefits other than crime reduction. Unfortunately, not enough is known about how the order-maintenance agenda fares
as land-use policy. This chapter seeks to fill in this important gap in the current understanding about order-maintenance policies. It considers benefits
other than crime reduction, including reducing the fear of crime (even when
the crime itself does not decrease), bolstering neighborhood stability, and improving police-citizen relations.

The "Broken Windows" essay urged that attention to disorder was important not just because disorder was a precursor to serious crime, but also because disorder undermined residents' sense of security. The later scholarly
explications of the broken windows hypothesis also emphasize the connection
between restoring the *perception* of security and its reality. One reason that
social-norms scholars link disorder and crime is that disorder has a predictable
effect on law-abiding citizens: Those with financial resources move away
from, or choose not to move into, disorderly neighborhoods; those without
resources remain inside and avoid public places. Even if these reactions (somewhat surprisingly) do not lead to more crime in a community, they certainly
disadvantage city neighborhoods vis-à-vis their suburban alternatives. Moreover, and importantly, the goals of reducing crime and of helping poor,

inner-city residents feel better about and more vested in their communities are not necessarily coterminous. Order-maintenance policies might achieve the latter without achieving the former. In other words, it might be the case that order-maintenance policies do not curb serious crime, *yet* they nevertheless make cities more attractive places to live, thereby improving the lives of current residents and helping them compete with suburban alternatives. Survey evidence suggesting both that residents' perceptions of security do not map neatly onto crime rates and that safety is regarded as one of the primary factors affecting housing choice tends to support this conclusion.[2]

Beyond Crime Reduction

To begin, it is important to emphasize once again that not all order-maintenance policies are policing strategies. Nor are they all crime-reduction strategies, solely predicated on the existence of a causal link between disorder and serious crime. Many order-maintenance policies are better understood as urban development strategies. They primarily aim to improve the quality of life in disorder-plagued urban neighborhoods, both for the sake of current residents and as a strategy for attracting newcomers. Certainly curbing crime, especially violent crime, is one of the most important ways to improve many urban neighborhoods. Violence is unfortunately the single most pressing quality-of-life issue facing many Americans today, especially the urban poor. But the broad array of policies falling under the order-maintenance umbrella—street sweeping and litter pickup, graffiti and junk removal, "weed and seed" programs targeting rubble-strewn abandoned lots, the demolition of abandoned buildings, and policies aimed at curbing the common "social disorders," such as public drinking, prostitution, and drug dealing—may generate a number of benefits, even if they do nothing to reduce serious crime. This chapter focuses primarily on one potential benefit—the reduction of the fear of crime—but there are many others, including, importantly, simply improving residents' quality of life in our poorest communities.

Fear of Crime

In "Broken Windows," Wilson and Kelling acknowledged—on the first page—that order-maintenance policing will not necessarily reduce crime. The essay was prompted by the Newark Foot Patrol Experiment, which increased the presence of police officers "walking the beats" instead of driving patrol cars. Kelling participated in an evaluation of the program, which found, in Wilson and Kelling's words, that "to the surprise of hardly anyone . . . foot patrols had not reduced crime rates." Despite this, however, Wilson and Kelling still concluded that the foot patrols had made the targeted neighborhoods *safer.* They reasoned that "residents of the foot-patrolled areas seemed to feel more secure . . . , tended to believe that crime had been reduced, and seemed to take fewer steps to protect themselves from crime (staying at home with the doors locked, for example)."[3]

Wilson and Kelling's admission that foot patrols had not caused crime rates to fall reflects their understanding, from its inception, that the order-maintenance enterprise is not just about reducing serious crime. It is also, perhaps primarily, about improving residents' sense of security. This distinction is an important one, especially because the available empirical evidence suggests that people tend to systematically *overestimate* the threat of crime. In other words, we tend to feel less safe than we actually are. Consider, for example, the most recent comprehensive evaluation of the Chicago Alternative Policing Strategy (CAPS) program, the city's comprehensive community policing effort that focuses on addressing crime and disorder at the neighborhood level. The program assigns officers to one of 279 beats in the city. In order to maximize their "turf orientation," police officers are given long-term assignments and made primarily responsible for responding to calls in their beat. CAPS officers also hold monthly community meetings in their beats, and District Advisory Committees, made up of residents, community leaders, business owners, and other stakeholders, meet regularly with police leaders to discuss community priorities.

Over the first ten years of the CAPS program, crime declined dramatically in Chicago (in keeping with national trends): Robbery declined by 68 percent, rape by 45 percent, murder by 30 percent, aggravated assault by 47 percent, burglary by 51 percent, and motor vehicle theft by 47 percent. Promisingly, crime declined most dramatically in the African American neighborhoods where violent crime was disproportionately concentrated during the early 1990s. Latino neighborhoods also experienced sharper declines than white neighborhoods did. Public perceptions of the city's crime also improved during this time period. Surveys found that African American and white residents both reported that crime fell sharply between 1993 and 2003. Importantly, African American perceptions of the crime problem, which were historically the most pessimistic, began to converge with the perceptions of white residents. Official crime statistics, however, suggest that crime actually declined much more sharply than Chicago residents thought that it did. While African

American and white residents both felt that their neighborhoods were much safer in 2003 than in 1993, the trends in officially recorded crime were even more positive. The divergence between survey data and recorded crime was most dramatic in predominantly Spanish-speaking Latino neighborhoods; Spanish-speaking Latinos reported a significant *increase* in crime, despite the fact that official statistics suggest it trended sharply downward.

The CAPS report also found that *fear* of crime in Chicago declined dramatically. Fear of crime is distinct from public perceptions of crime, as it incorporates individuals' predictions about the risk of future victimization. Importantly, because an individual's evaluation of his or her vulnerability also reflects a predictive judgment about the likelihood of public or private intervention to prevent or mitigate the effects of crime, fear of crime is an important variable for gauging police performance and the level of social capital in a community. Between 1993 and 2003, fear of crime fell across all demographic groups in Chicago. Fear was down by 10 percent among men and younger people—two traditionally low-fear groups; it fell 20 percentage points among the groups that traditionally expressed the greatest level of fear—women, African Americans, and the elderly.[4]

Fear versus Reality

For many years, conventional wisdom held that crime was the primary cause of fear of crime. Beginning in the 1960s, however, as fear of crime increased dramatically, it became clear that the association between fear and victimization is complicated and that other factors influence how fearful an individual feels. This is hardly surprising. To begin, not all crime is reported, so crime statistics systematically underestimate the extent of the actual crime problem. Surveys can partially remedy this problem by asking residents to report whether they were themselves victims of crime or know of friends and neighbors who have been victimized. Survey data may be particularly helpful in gauging the extent of underpoliced criminal activity, including classic "social disorder" crimes such as gangs, drug dealing, and prostitution. While official crime statistics generally measure the number of incidents and/or arrests, for these crimes, arrests reflect the level of police effort rather than the extent of the actual problem. Unfortunately, surveys are likely to overcompensate for the underreporting problem. Respondents may tend to overstate the prevalence of crime because informal and media reports of crime tend to have an amplification effect. For many Americans who have not been victimized, vicarious experiences become their primary contact with crime. Especially because these vicarious experiences often result from sensationalized media accounts of the least common—and most gruesome and bizarre—crimes, survey respondents may distort the extent and distribution of crime.[5]

Fear of crime is even more difficult to measure than the public perception of crime levels. There are no official "fear" statistics. Any effort to gauge the extent of fear necessarily depends upon self-reporting, usually in surveys, and survey results vary dramatically depending on the questions used to measure crime. Researchers are divided over whether to gauge fear levels by asking about personal concern about crime, about the perceived risk of victimization, or about precautions taken to avoid crime. By any measure, however, fear of crime is a significant urban problem. For example, a 2005 Gallup poll reported that 38 percent of Americans responded "yes" when asked whether "there is any area near where you live—that is, within a mile—where you would be afraid to walk alone at night?" Surveys soliciting information about specific crimes (assault, burglary, rape, murder) generally find lower levels of fear. Perhaps because a respondent's assessment of her level of fear reflects some combination of perceived risk and the perceived seriousness of the offense, people are not necessarily most fearful of serious, violent crimes.[6]

The relationship between personal experience with crime and fear is also unclear. The theory of "indirect victimization" suggests that fear is more widespread than victimization, because hearing about other people's experiences with crime causes nonvictims to become frightened. For this reason, there is some evidence that strong local social ties may amplify fear, apparently because neighborhood gossip is an efficient way to distribute information about recent crimes in an area. Most research suggests that prior direct experience with crime is weakly correlated with increased fear, although some authors have suggested that victimization actually may reduce fear under certain circumstances. (The theory being that some victims fear the worst and feel relief when they survive an incident relatively unscathed.) Somewhat paradoxically, the groups with the highest levels of fear—women and the elderly—have the lowest rates of victimization, and those with the highest rates of victimization, young men, have the lowest. These findings are consistent with the "indirect victimization" phenomenon, since older people and women are more physically vulnerable than younger men.[7]

The Costs of Fear

In his 1968 essay "The Urban Unease," James Q. Wilson argued that fear (or unease) brought about by the failure of informal community-level social norms was the root of the so-called urban crisis. At least since that time, fear of crime has been considered a serious impediment to urban health. Fear undermines urban community life in a number of related ways. First, when individuals are fearful, they tend to take steps to minimize the risk of victimization. (In fact, the level of precaution-taking in a community is a common measure of fearfulness.) These precautions are costly. Americans spend more on these private precautions—estimates range from $160 billion to $300 billion—than on the total U.S. law-enforcement budget. In other words, private individuals spend more to avoid being victimized than U.S. governments at all levels (federal, state, and local) spend on police, prosecutors, judges, and prisons. And these figures do not reflect the total cost of crime avoidance, such as the opportunity costs of remaining inside behind locked doors to avoid victimization. Many economists condemn private crime-prevention measures as socially wasteful, reasoning that private precautions do not reduce the total amount of crime but rather simply displace it. That is, precautions only deter criminals from victimizing protected individuals, not from committing crimes. Instead, criminals will choose to victimize those who have not taken steps to protect themselves.[8]

Private precautions ultimately may prove counterproductive for another reason. If social-influence theory is correct, steps taken to avoid crime may, perversely, increase its prevalence. Recall that social-influence theory predicts that people will be law abiding when they perceive that their neighbors are obeying the law. But private actions taken to avoid victimization cannot, by definition, support such a perception. Logically, would-be victims should not take steps to protect themselves from victimization if their neighbors are law abiding; they will take precautions only if they believe themselves to be surrounded by criminals. This is one reason why "depolicing" advocates may have erred. As discussed in more detail in chapter 4, depolicing proponents worried that a community can become too dependent upon official police protection, leading individuals to underinvest in private efforts to prevent and address crime. Yet the private deterrence measures that individuals fearful of crime are most likely to take—including neighborhood watch groups, alarm systems, extra locks, bars on windows, and so on—tend to signal that crime is prevalent in a community.[9]

Moreover, monetary estimates of prevention-related expenditures fail to capture the cost of reduced social capital resulting from fear. The concept of social capital is the subject of a voluminous and somewhat contentious literature. For the purpose of this discussion, however, Robert Putnam's "lean and mean" definition of social capital—"social networks and the associate norms of reciprocity and trustworthiness"—suffices. Fear undoubtedly impedes a community's ability to generate and capitalize upon social capital in a number of ways. The first is related to the social-influence effects of prevention. When a resident takes steps to prevent victimization, especially visible steps such as installing bars on her windows, she may signal to her neighbors that she does not trust them. Even if neighbors do not interpret precautionary measures as evincing a lack of trust—perhaps because the community is plagued by criminals from other neighborhoods—precautionary measures may have other deleterious effects. Consider, for example, the likely effects of one of the simplest and most common crime-avoidance strategies—remaining indoors. When law-abiding, but fearful, residents remain indoors to avoid victimization, they deprive their community of private surveillance opportunities— that is, of Jane Jacobs's classic "eyes upon the street." As a result, frightened residents may effectively become prisoners in their own homes, forced to turn the public spaces in a community over to their would-be victimizers.[10]

The "prisoner-in-my-own-home" phenomenon may also reduce the social capital generated by informal socialization among neighbors. In urban neighborhoods, an important predictor of both actual crime and fear of crime is what sociologists and social psychologists call "collective efficacy." Collective efficacy, according to the Project on Human Development Neighborhoods in Chicago, represents the "ability of neighborhoods to realize the common values of residents and maintain effective social controls." Collective efficacy is sometimes defined as a form of social capital, although it might be better understood as one way in which members of a community can successfully harness social capital. Collective efficacy and the social capital that enables it are critically important to neighborhood health. As James Q. Wilson explained in "The Urban Unease": "It is primarily at the neighborhood level that meaningful (i.e., potentially rewarding) opportunities for the exercise of urban citizenship exist. And it is the breakdown of neighborhood controls . . . that accounts for the principal concerns of urban citizens. When they can take for granted nor influence by their actions and those of their neighbors the standards of conduct within their own neighborhood community, they experience what to them are 'urban problems.' " Wilson's observations, made nearly four decades ago, proved prescient: Numerous empirical studies have demonstrated both that neighborhoods with low levels of collective efficacy are more dangerous than those with higher levels and that residents of such neighborhoods also are more fearful. Some studies suggest that low levels of perceived social control have a greater effect on fear of crime than actual crime rates and previous victimization. Not surprisingly, a resident who counts on her neighbors to address community problems has less cause to fear victimization.[11]

For this reason, policies that reduce the fear of crime arguably can succeed even if actual crime *increases.* As Guido Calabresi helpfully elucidated in *The Cost of Accidents,* the total cost of accidents includes the costs resulting from accidents and the costs of measures taken to deter or prevent them. "I take it as axiomatic," Calabresi argued, "that the principal function of accident law is to reduce the sum of the cost of accidents and the cost of avoiding accidents." Abstracting to the present context, one might similarly argue that the principal function of order-maintenance policies is to reduce the sum of the costs of crime and the costs of avoiding crime. Because the social-capital costs of crime avoidance are quite high, the benefits of policies that succeed in reducing them should not be discounted, especially given the critical role that social capital plays in undergirding neighborhood health. As discussed briefly in chapter 3, if either order-maintenance or land-use policies increase residents' perceptions of security, they may take fewer steps to avoid crime. If residents feel safer, they may, for example, spend more time in public space and/or get to know the neighbors who previously barred themselves inside behind locked doors. At least in the short run, the reduction in crime-prevention activities could lead to an increase in crime (either personal crime against the individuals in the now-populated public square or property crime against the now-empty residences). But if the decrease in prevention costs, especially the social-capital costs of prevention, outweigh the cost of the increased crime, it would be reasonable to consider the prevention-reducing policy a "success."[12]

Many cities' order-maintenance efforts seek to help neighbors overcome their fears by catalyzing new forms of collective efficacy. The CAPS program, for example, incorporates several forms of "assertive vigilance." Police work with local community leaders, including pastors, to organize marches in high-crime areas, prayer vigils at the site of gang- or drug-related shootings, "smoke-outs"—barbeque picnics—in drug-market areas, and "positive loitering" campaigns to harass prostitutes and their customers. In an interview, a police officer described the evolution of a successful positive loitering campaign to address a prostitution problem in her district:

> The [prostitution] problem was brought up at the beat meeting. [The officer] proposed positive-loitering, and they agreed to give it a try. . . . They started out with 30 people and were escorted by a police car. They began to alternate days and times so the prostitutes would never know when they'd be there. Soon the prostitutes ran

when they saw the group coming, while the police officers would stop them and check them for warrants, arresting them if there were any outstanding. . . . When a community member complained of seeing prostitutes from 9 P.M. to 11 P.M., positive loiterers came during those times. They got up to 60 volunteers.

There is a reason, of course, why Chicago uses the police to kick-start collective efficacy. Low levels of social capital deprive these communities of the ability to organize informally. Order-maintenance efforts like "positive loitering" take their cues from the broken windows hypotheses and flow from the belief that public intervention can reinvigorate collective efficacy when neighborhood self-governance disappears. Somewhat ironically, Wilson—who is now seen as the godfather of such efforts—questioned this assumption in "The Urban Unease," arguing that "there is relatively little government can do to maintain a neighborhood community. It can, of course, assign more police officers to it, but there are real limits to the value of this response." Although the apparent success of efforts like those featured in the CAPS program suggest that Wilson may have been correct to reconsider this assumption, it is clear that the healthiest, safest urban communities enjoy high levels of collective efficacy without public intervention. In these communities, neighbors know and trust one another well enough to organize informally to address community problems. By discouraging informal social interaction among neighbors, fear diminishes the likelihood that members of a community will organize without public intervention.[13]

Finally, and importantly, safety—reflected both in actual crime rates and the perceived risk of victimization—strongly influences residential location decisions. In his 1956 essay "A Pure Theory of Local Expenditures," Charles Tiebout influentially hypothesized that municipalities use public goods to compete for residents, or "consumer voters." According to the Tiebout model, which has been tested and refined extensively over the past half century, residents "sort" themselves within a metropolitan area according to their preferences for municipal services, which municipalities package and offer as an inducement to relocate. As Tiebout observed, "[e]very resident who moves to the suburbs to find better schools, more parks, and so forth, is reacting, in part, against the pattern that the city has to offer."[14]

If Tiebout is correct, then cities that succeed in convincing residents and would-be residents that they are, relatively speaking, safe—by actually reducing crime rates, by bolstering collective efficacy, and by undertaking policing practices that bolster residents' sense of security—are more likely to prosper than those that fail to do so. Why? Safety, which might be defined in public-goods terms as effective police protection, clearly influences residential sorting. It is fairly well accepted that crime and the fear of crime both work to undermine urban residential stability. The 1997 American Housing Survey, for example, found nearly half of all residents reporting that crime was a significant neighborhood problem also expressed a desire to move to a safer community. And in another well-known nationwide study, Julie Cullen and Steven Levitt found a strong correlation between crime and urban flight. Each reported that city crime was associated with a one-person decline in city residents; a 10-percent increase in crime corresponded to a 1-percent decline in city population. Cullen and Levitt also found that residents motivated to move by fear of crime were more likely to remain in the same metropolitan area than those moving for other reasons, which also supports the conclusion that fear of crime has encouraged *out-migration*, that is, moves from the city to suburbs. Cullen and Levitt's study focused on the connection between crime and out-migration. It is reasonable to assume that crime and fear of crime probably exert at least as robust an influence on residents' decisions about whether to move from one city neighborhood to another, with safer neighborhoods enjoying greater residential stability than more-dangerous ones. And, importantly, even studies that question the connection between fear and out-migration suggest that crime exerts a relatively strong and negative influence on in-migration, that is, on the decision to move from the suburbs to the city. This is not surprising, as survey data continue to indicate—despite declining crime rates—that a majority of Americans cite crime as the leading problem of living in a city.[15]

This connection between fear of crime and residential stability is important because residential stability is strongly correlated with collective efficacy. In a major study of 343 Chicago neighborhoods, Robert Sampson, Stephen Raudenbush, and Felton Earls found that residential stability, measured by average residential tenure and levels of homeownership, was one of three major factors explaining neighborhood variation in collective efficacy. They also found that collective efficacy, in turn, mediated the negative effects of the other two factors—economic disadvantage and immigration—enough to reduce violent victimization in a community. These findings, which are consistent with other social science research linking residential tenure and homeownership with high levels of collective efficacy, explain cities' nervousness about the ongoing foreclosure crisis. A resident's social integration into her neighborhood naturally increases over time, increasing the likelihood that she will build the kind of trust relationships with her neighbors that form the foundation of collective efficacy. Moreover, homeowners have obvious financial incentives to organize with one another to address neighborhood problems that more-temporary residents lack. This is one reason that fear of crime is a particularly salient land-use factor: Although home ownership raises the costs associated with moving and therefore may produce a kind of residential stickiness, highly educated wealthier households with children also are most responsive to crime—that is, most likely to relocate when they become fearful. These likely homeowners are also the very residents most needed to promote collective efficacy.[16]

That is not to say that security is the only, or even the primary, factor influencing most peoples' decisions about where to live. As chapter 2 documents, migration to the suburbs began long before public attention became intensely focused on the "urban crisis" in the postwar years. Most people move away from urban neighborhoods for reasons other than fear of crime, especially for so-called "life-cycle factors," such as a desire for more space and better public schools brought about by the birth of children. Recognizing this reality, many cities now seek to promote a "hip" image in order to compete for young, child-less professionals. For example, a 2003 *New York Times* article reported that cities like Memphis, Tennessee, and Cincinnati, Ohio, were "on a hunt for ways to put sex in the city": "In the same way that companies during the dot-com boom tried to present their offices as playgrounds, adding slides and masseurs, cities are now getting in on the act. In Michigan, Gov. Jennifer M. Granholm encouraged the mayors of 200 towns to form 'cool commissions' to attract and retain the state's young people. In Baltimore, a nonprofit group called Live Baltimore Home Center, partly financed by the city, has gone after young professionals as 'low hanging fruit.'" The logic of this strategy is obvious: Seek out the kind of would-be residents who can "risk moving to neighborhoods with subpar school systems, fixer-upper housing stock or a little street crime." The "young and hip" strategy also may draw in educated and creative young people—the very cohort that Richard Florida argued in his influential 2002 book, *The Rise of the Creative Class,* modern cities must attract in order to thrive. Cities, according to Florida, "have become the prime location for the creative lifestyle and the new amenities that go with it": They are benefiting from the energy provided by creative young professionals, who stay single longer than in previous generations, and who prefer to live in diverse, urban neighborhoods.[17]

Florida's work has been subjected to stinging criticism, but he does capture a sense of the changing aesthetics of urban and suburban life. As Robert

Bruegmann argues in his recent history of suburban sprawl, the very economic changes lamented by many scholars of urban life—including the decline in the urban industrial base—ultimately may save our cities. Freed from the congestion, pollution, and disease that once characterized urban life, cities will become more attractive to the "creative class" and other wealthy individuals who might previously have chosen to live in the suburbs. Bruegmann hypothesizes, "[i]t is quite possible that sprawl could recede everywhere as more citizens become affluent enough to live like the residents of the Upper East Side," because "as individuals pass from affluent to extraordinarily affluent they are better able to enjoy the benefits of density without the negative side effects." As a result, cities may thrive by abandoning their traditional roles as centers of social, cultural, and economic activity and becoming temporary way stations for the unattached, gentrified playgrounds for the wealthy, or, "essentially resort areas filled with second homes." Glaeser and Gottlieb's study, discussed above, suggests that this prediction may be coming to pass. As Glaeser and Gottlieb observe, "one plausible hypothesis is that urban resurgence can be understood as reflecting the rising demand for urban amenities caused by rising income and education levels nationwide."[18]

It remains unclear, however, whether targeting the young—and those wealthy enough to afford a comfortable, fear-and-disorder-free urban life—is a long-term strategy for urban success. Even assuming that the "creative class" is indeed attracted to urban life (despite the fact that most of its members, as discussed in chapter 4, are native suburbanites), there are reasons to worry that H. G. Wells's prediction of a century ago may be coming to pass: "Cities may now be morphing . . . from commanding centers of economic life toward a more ephemeral role as a 'bazaar, a great gallery of shops and places of concourse and rendezvous.'" The fact remains that most young professionals, even hip ones, do not remain unattached and childless forever. When their life circumstances change, they face the same pressures and demands that all parents face. And the research connecting social integration and residential tenure with collective efficacy suggests that the most successful, safest city neighborhoods ultimately will be the kinds of places where people choose to make their lives long-term—to live, work, and raise families. Unfortunately, fewer and fewer families—especially middle-class families—build their lives in city neighborhoods. Although the extent of concentrated poverty declined dramatically during the 1990s, major cities continue to contain a disproportionate number of poor families. And while a handful of cities are gaining wealthy residents, even growing cities continue to lose families in general and middle-class families in particular. A recent Brookings Institution study of twelve large metropolitan areas found that only 23 percent of central-city neighborhoods had middle-income profiles (compared to 45 percent in 1970).[19]

Disorder, Fear, and the Order-Maintenance Agenda

Convincing middle-income families with children to forego the amenities of suburbia and make their lives in cities—or, perhaps at least as importantly, to remain in any given urban neighborhood long enough to build the social capital needed to support a healthy urban life—obviously is no small task. But order-maintenance policies may prove critical to achieving it for three related and underappreciated reasons.

First, recall that wealthier families with children are most sensitive to fear of crime—that is, they are most likely to move if they become fearful. And while the causal connection between disorder and *crime* is hotly contested, the connection between disorder and the *fear of crime* is not. Nearly all efforts to measure the connection between disorder and fear find a strong positive correlation. People intuitively associate disorder and crime. Apparently, the average observer buys the broken windows hypothesis: When she sees physical disorder or experiences social incivilities in a neighborhood, she assumes that serious crimes are prevalent there as well. Indeed, disorder may generate more fear of crime than actual personal experience with crime itself, perhaps because residents who live in disorder-plagued neighborhoods encounter disorder on a daily basis, even if they are rarely, if ever, victimized.

Disorder generates fear at both the neighborhood and individual levels. At the neighborhood level, disorder is not only positively correlated with fear of crime, but higher levels of disorder correspond to higher levels of fear. At the individual level, residents within the same neighborhoods experience different levels of fear depending upon their individual perceptions of the amount of disorder in their communities. That is, the more disorder a person sees, the more fearful she is. For example, Jeanette Covington and Ralph Taylor interviewed more than fifteen hundred residents about the levels of disorder in sixty-six Baltimore neighborhoods and then compared the responses to physical assessments of neighborhood conditions conducted by trained observers. They found that fear was most strongly influenced by the disorder levels within a respondent's neighborhood. Residents of neighborhoods with higher levels of observed physical and social disorder had higher fear levels. They also found, moreover, that individual perceptions of disorder were strongly linked to individualized, within-neighborhood differences in fear. Residents who saw more disorder than their neighbors, or expressed greater concern about disorder, were more fearful.[20]

Second, disorder is negatively correlated with collective efficacy, which, as discussed above, is an important predictor of both fear of crime and residential stability. In their important study of Chicago neighborhoods (discussed in chapter 1), Robert Sampson and Stephen Raudenbush found no significant correlation between disorder and serious crimes other than robbery. But they also found that collective efficacy was significantly and negatively correlated with disorder. Sampson and Raudenbush posit that perceptions of disorder may color residents' judgments about the level of cohesion and control in their community, a hypothesis that is consistent with previous research suggesting that perceptions of disorder strongly influence individual perceptions of collective efficacy. Alternatively, it is reasonable to expect that communities with high levels of collective efficacy will be less disorderly; after all, members of cohesive communities with high levels of social capital are most likely to organize informally to keep disorder in check. Sampson and Raudenbush's findings led them to reject the strong version of the broken windows hypothesis, which posits a causal link between disorder and serious crime. But they took care not to dismiss disorder as irrelevant. Disorder, they suggest, might "turn out to be important for understanding migration patterns, investment by businesses, and overall neighborhood viability," especially if it "operates in a cascading fashion—encouraging people to move (decreasing residential stability) or discouraging efforts at building collective responses."[21]

Furthermore, order-maintenance policies may help generate much-needed social capital in struggling communities both by helping residents overcome fear and social isolation and by bringing together community leaders who might not otherwise collaborate. The first of these benefits flows from the fact that, as discussed above, efforts to organize community responses to neighborhood problems are a centerpiece of many order-maintenance policies. Endeavors like Chicago's "positive loitering" campaigns, "smoke-outs," and prayer vigils are not perfect substitutes for the collective efficacy organically present in healthier neighborhoods, but they do hold out the promise of promoting social capital. Consider, for example, the effects of police-sponsored prayer vigils in troubled Chicago neighborhoods. About ten years ago, an innovative police commander named Claudell Ervin took it upon himself to organize a massive anticrime prayer vigil on Chicago's impoverished West Side. Ervin invited hundreds of church leaders to attend a meeting at the police district headquarters. At this meeting, the group planned the vigil, which proceeded as follows: Participants stood and prayed in groups of ten on street corners that were usually occupied by drug dealers; following the vigil, the participants were joined by thousands of other residents in a large park for a "praise celebration" featuring food, speeches, and a four-hundred-member gospel choir. Variations of this prayer vigil have occurred dozens of times since. A study conducted over the two years following the first vigil found that the prayer vigils generated a number of important benefits. Religious leaders' opinions of the police improved, and they became more interested in, and likely to participate in, crime-prevention efforts. Since the initial vigil, churches and faith-based institutions also have come to play a prominent role in Chicago's community policing efforts. While this result might not please strict separationists, the improved relations allow police to enlist leaders of what are, in many inner-city neighborhoods, the most important community institutions. The prayer vigils also built social capital by fostering interdenominational relationships among clergy. Similarly, the initial public intervention enabled subsequent informal collective efforts to address community problems. For example, following the initial vigil, an interdenominational Ministers' Alliance was formed to promote subsequent vigils, and Ministers' Alliance meetings quickly became a popular way for secular service providers to disseminate information.[22]

Third, and perhaps more importantly, many order-maintenance policies apparently make people feel safer, even if they do not actually reduce serious crime. There is a sizable empirical literature suggesting that many central elements of order-maintenance policing—especially preventative patrols and increased police-citizen interactions—reduce the fear of crime. Over the past several decades, a number of urban police forces have created controlled experiments to test the effects of different policing techniques. The pioneering experiment, the Kansas City Preventative Patrol Experiment, sought to measure the impact of routine motorized police patrols. The goal of the experiment was to test what the researchers, who were led (somewhat ironically) by George Kelling, characterized as the long-standing and widely held belief that "the presence or potential presence of police officers on patrol severely inhibits criminal activity." To test this hypothesis, the Kansas City Police Department agreed to vary the level of police presence in fifteen of the city's beats: In five "reactive" beats, routine patrols were eliminated and officers instructed to respond only to calls for service; in five "control" beats, routine preventative patrols were maintained at the usual level of one car per beat; in five "proactive" beats, routine patrols were intensified to two or three times the usual level. The researchers found that increasing police presence had virtually no effect on crime levels, citizen satisfaction with police service, or citizens' fear of crime.

The Kansas City Preventative Patrol Experiment was interpreted at the time as supporting reform-era, reactive policing strategies. In the preface to the final report on the experiment, for example, the Kansas City chief of police asserted that the findings "repudiated a tradition prevailing in police work for almost 150 years" and "suggest[] that deployment strategies should be based upon specific crime prevention as service goals as opposed to routine preventative patrols." It is important to note, however, that the Kansas City study focused on *motorized* patrols, one of the reform-era innovations that Wilson and Kelling criticized in "Broken Windows." Two subsequent field studies found that routine *foot patrols* do in fact reduce the fear of crime, although they do not necessarily reduce crime itself. For example, in 1979, Flint, Michigan, established a neighborhood foot patrol program with the hope that foot patrols would prevent crime, increase police-citizen interaction, and catalyze neighborhood organization. Over several years, researchers from Michigan State University studied the effects of the foot patrols and found that, in most of the experimental beats, crime decreased, and, importantly, that residents *believed* that foot patrols had decreased crime, regardless of whether they actually had. Residents' perception of personal safety also dramatically improved in the experimental areas, especially when a foot patrol officer was present. Residents living in the foot patrol areas also reported increased levels of communication with one another, a finding supporting the conclusion that order-maintenance-policing efforts can increase neighborhood-level social capital. Similarly, the Newark Foot Patrol Experiment—the catalyst for the "Broken Windows" essay—found that foot patrols reduced the fear of crime, even as actual crime levels remained stable (or, in some cases, increased).[23]

Evidence from controlled experiments in other cities also supports the conclusion that certain elements of community policing can reduce the fear of crime and improve citizen perceptions of police performance. For example, controlled policing experiments conducted in Houston, Texas, and Newark, New Jersey, conducted during the late 1990s measured the effect of several community-policing techniques—including a police-community newsletter, neighborhood-level police multiservice centers, and frequent police contacts with residents to solicit input about local problems. Researchers found that, in both cities, programs that fostered more-frequent citizen-police interactions reduced fear of crime and improved residents' perceptions of crime and disorder levels as well as their evaluation of police service. Similarly, in the Citizen Oriented Police Enforcement (COPE) project, Baltimore, Maryland, varied the intensity and organization of police presence over three years: The first involved intensive mobile patrols in targeted areas; in the second, officers increased their contacts with citizens, and some mobile patrols were shifted to foot patrol; in the third, officers engaged in intensive problem solving and community mobilization. The COPE program's aim was specifically to reduce the *fear* of crime. The evidence showed that fear was reduced in the transition from phase one to phase two, but that phase three—intensive contact and problem solving with community members—had the most significant effect on fear reduction. Other experiments yield similar results: A comprehensive review of studies of the relationship between policing strategies and fear reduction, conducted in 2002, found that order-maintenance-policing strategies reduced fear in thirty-one of fifty studies; eighteen found no change; and one reported an increase in fear. The authors noted that merely increasing police presence appears to do less to reduce fear than proactive, targeted policing efforts and community policing. Interestingly, however, some studies suggest that police-citizen collaborations that involve citizens directly in crime-prevention activities, such as the prayer vigils discussed above, may actually increase fear of crime, at least among participants.[24]

The Costs of Order

The costs of implementing the policies most likely to achieve these benefits—including efforts to increase the frequency and quality of citizen-police interactions (such as intensive community policing efforts and foot patrols)—are not insubstantial. This is undoubtedly one reason why order-maintenance proponents promise that their policies will reduce serious crime, rather than simply make people feel safer and more vested in their neighborhoods: Crime rates are tangible and measurable, reflected in official statistics. In contrast, the benefits of reducing the fear of crime and increasing collective efficacy are difficult to quantify, their very definitions contestable. The remainder of this chapter reflects upon two frequently cited possible costs of order-maintenance policies: First, they are too resource-intensive; second, they threaten to undermine civil liberties. A third potential cost—that an order-maintenance mindset may lead urban leaders to stifle the kinds of social and economic activities necessary for a healthy urban life—is set to one side, as it is discussed in detail elsewhere in this book. The purpose of this closing reflection is not to weigh empirically the costs and benefits of the order-maintenance enterprise, but rather to suggest that it is overly simplistic to conclude that, absent proof that reducing disorder *in fact* reduces serious crime, the order-maintenance agenda should be abandoned.

Economic Costs

Order-maintenance-policing tactics are resource intensive. Some, like Mayor Giuliani's "quality of life" policing regime, devote significant resources to the arrest and processing of individuals for relatively minor offenses. Others, such as foot patrols, require more police officers, if only for the simple reason that an officer can cover far more ground in a car than on foot. The most predominant order-maintenance technique, community policing, requires officers to devote significant time to building community relations, attending community meetings, and so on, and tends to expand the range of problems on officers' plates. Some critics, therefore, have used data questioning the crime-disorder nexus to argue order-maintenance policing does not make economic sense. As Bernard Harcourt and Jens Ludwig recently argued, "Our analysis provides no empirical evidence to support the view that shifting policing toward minor disorder offenses would improve the efficiency of police spending and reduce violent crime." While Harcourt and Ludwig agree with order-maintenance proponents that "police matter," they urge that other practices, for example intensive policing in criminal "hot spots," represent a better allocation of policing resources.[25]

Civil-Liberties Costs

Perhaps the most troubling concern raised by critics is that order-maintenance-policing techniques may threaten civil liberties, especially of poor minorities who live in struggling urban neighborhoods. This prediction (which is discussed in greater detail in chapter 1) reflects a deep skepticism of police discretion. Critics worry that order-maintenance policies present opportunities for police abuse of power, by increasing the frequency and intensity of police-citizen interactions and failing to channel the discretion that officers necessarily exercise during them. Critics also express concern that the emphasis on police-citizen interactions will politicize the police, inviting the kind of corruption that reform-era innovations sought to eliminate and causing officers to side with citizens that they know well or believe to be politically influential. According to this view, if officers become too close to the citizens that they are assigned to protect, they might begin to enforce "vigilante values" rather than the criminal laws.

Order-maintenance proponents counter that increasing police-citizen interaction and collaboration diminishes, rather than exacerbates, the risk of abuse and corruption. As Tracey Meares and Kelsi Brown Corkran assert: "Critics of community policing fear that encouraging the alignment of law enforcement and community interests will result in the compromise of individual rights—usually criminal-procedure rights. Yet . . . aligning the interests of those in high-crime urban neighborhoods with the goals of law enforcement might well enable residents . . . to hold law enforcers accountable in order to better guide their exercise of discretion." The highly militarist reform-era policing model, according to Meares and Corkran, encourages officers to consider themselves crime-fighting warriors who are pitted against lawless citizens, enemies who are unworthy of their respect and protection. Stephen Mastrofski and Jack Greene express this sentiment slightly differently, asserting that community policing will give greater weight to "men" in the balance between "laws and men," reasoning that "the bonds of formal laws and bureaucratic rules must be loosened to allow police policies and practices to be guided by community norms and sentiments."[26]

It is also possible that vesting police officers with more discretion ultimately will improve police officers' attitude about the legal rights of citizens. As Jerome Skolnick and James Fyfe argue, the "crime fighting" model of policing "has the effect of putting the police on the front lines of crime wars they cannot win." Some lose heart and become frustrated and demoralized; others become convinced that "they are losing the war only because *others* . . . have handcuffed them. They hear fundamental Constitutional principles and due process rights . . . described as technicalities and unreasonable limits on their ability to fight the enemy among us." The turn toward problem-oriented or community policing, prompted by the order-maintenance agenda, might, as Mark Moore has suggested, encourage officers to view themselves as "street corner judges," rather than "street corner politicians," and to begin to perceive legal rights as valuable tools for resolving disputes, rather than constraints that limit their ability to perform their jobs effectively.[27]

Unfortunately, not enough is known about the connection between policing techniques and police behavior. Some commentators have sought to connect order-maintenance-policing techniques, especially the aggressive misdemeanor arrest practices that characterize New York City's quality-of-life policing efforts, with an increase in excessive-force incidents. A comprehensive review of national and local data on the use of force, conducted for the National Institute of Justice in 1999, however, concluded that virtually no data exists on how different policing techniques affect the use of force. A more-recent nationwide survey of police officers from 113 departments, conducted by the Police Foundation in 2001, found that officers overwhelmingly rejected the idea that community-oriented policing increases abuse of authority (including corruption and excessive force). Most officers, however, also rejected the proposition that community policing *decreases* the risk of corruption, although a slight majority believed that community policing reduces the risk of excessive-force incidents. These findings are generally consistent with other studies seeking to gauge police attitudes about community policing: Officers report that community policing improves their morale and their relationships with citizens.[28]

Positive police attitudes toward community policing are certainly a hopeful sign. Ultimately, however, as Debra Livingston has observed, whether order-maintenance policies, especially problem-solving and community policing, act to curb police abuses may be inextricably linked with whether they enable police to successfully address real community problems. Skolnick and Fyfe may be right that asking police to engage in an unwinnable "war" on crime leads to cynicism, alienation, and even brutality among the ranks. If so, officers are least likely to feel frustrated and cynical if they are asked to identify and accomplish achievable goals. The sizable literature investigating the factors that influence public satisfaction with the police tends to support Livingston's hypothesis. One of the most important predictors of public satisfaction with the police is public perception that the police are doing their jobs effectively. For example, fear of crime is inversely related to public satisfaction with police performance; that is, the safer people feel, the happier they are with police performance. There is undoubtedly a risk that expanding the universe of policing priorities to include order-maintenance and other community problems will overwhelm officers with tasks with which they are ill-equipped to deal. (Interestingly, citizens who *fear the police*—that is, who are afraid that police will abuse their authority—also express high levels of fear of crime, suggesting a different kind of connection between police performance and public satisfaction.)[29]

It is less clear under what circumstances *order-maintenance-policing* practices improve public satisfaction with the police. The early foot patrol experiments, discussed above, found that increasing police presence in a neighborhood led both citizens and police officers to report that police performance improved. In Boston, foot patrols became so popular that local politicians quickly seized upon the opportunity to take credit for their deployment; some began to issue press releases when additional officers were assigned to a neighborhood. Other studies, however, indicate that increased police presence does not itself improve public satisfaction, although policing techniques that successfully reduce fear of crime do. For example, a 2003 evaluation of data from twelve cities, collected by the U.S. Justice Department's Bureau of Justice Statistics and Office of Community Oriented Policing Services, found a strong correlation between increased community policing efforts and citizen satisfaction with the police. The connection between community policing efforts and citizen satisfaction apparently holds true across all racial groups. In Chicago, the researchers conducting the ten-year review of the CAPS program found that while perceptions of police performance had improved among all racial groups, the gap between the perceptions of whites and other racial groups did not close. While the continued gap is cause for concern, the overall increase in policing satisfaction remains hopeful, especially because minorities tend to simultaneously demand increased levels of police protection and to express high levels of distrust for police officers. It is also promising that minority police officers often express higher levels of support for community policing than their white counterparts.[30]

Worth the Costs?

This chapter sought to expand the discussion of the order-maintenance agenda beyond the narrow question of whether order-maintenance-policing techniques reduce crime. By highlighting the important distinction between crime reduction and fear reduction, I hoped to illustrate that order-maintenance policies might "work" even if they do not reduce serious crime. Importantly, order-maintenance policies may mitigate the negative effects of the fear of crime, including reduced levels of collective efficacy and residential instability. These things matter because crime rates tell only part of a city's story. Nothing in this chapter should be interpreted as suggesting that the potential benefits of fear reduction necessarily justify all of the myriad policies falling under the order-maintenance umbrella. I am ill equipped to weigh the not-insignificant costs of any of these policies, or some combination of them, against any set of potential benefits. For example, the order-maintenance-policing techniques that appear to be most successful at reducing the fear of crime—foot patrols and community policing—also are perhaps the most resource-intensive. Some have suggested that other, less-resource-intensive policing techniques (for example, "hot spots" policing) do more to reduce actual crime. If so, policies that simply make people feel safer might not represent the best allocation of scarce law-enforcement resources.[31]

Moreover, generalizations about "the order-maintenance agenda" or "order-maintenance policing" are problematic because of the dramatic differences characterizing different policies. For example, the apparent link between order-maintenance-policing efforts, including community policing, and improved satisfaction with the police may also mitigate some concern that order-maintenance policies may lead to discriminatory enforcement. But general expressions of satisfaction with community policing efforts should not be interpreted as an endorsement of all order-maintenance tactics. Chicago's community policing efforts stand in sharp contrast to the aggressive policies of misdemeanor arrests that characterized New York's order-maintenance efforts during Rudolph Giuliani's mayoralty. The latter have drawn the most ire of order-maintenance opponents.

7

Reordering the City

Although most local government officials acting as regulators behave as if they continue to endorse the order constructed by zoning rules, many local officials acting as developers seem to have abandoned it. Indeed, imbedded in many cities' redevelopment policies is an implicit admission that past order-construction efforts failed. Less than a half of a century ago, cities spent billions of dollars in federal funds to demolish urban neighborhoods and reorder them to reflect the order-construction ideal: Traditional urban communities were leveled and replaced with modern, single-use developments, high-rise residential and commercial towers, and massive elevated freeways. Today, the same cities use the same wrecking ball and the same federal funds to undo these projects—demolishing urban renewal developments, high-rise public housing projects, and elevated freeways—in order to reconstruct neighborhoods designed to look much like the ones that were eliminated to modernize the order of our cities. This chapter examines reordering efforts in three cities that aim to undo each of the three kinds of order-construction endeavors undertaken in the postwar years. It begins by considering the ambitious plan of the

Chicago Housing Authority (CHA) to demolish all of the city's notorious high-rise public housing projects and replace them with low-rise, mixed-income private developments. The discussion then turns to Washington, D.C., where the city is replacing parts of one of the largest and most historically significant urban renewal projects. Finally, it considers Milwaukee's effort to re-create a neighborhood by demolishing a never-completed urban renewal–era freeway. The chapter closes with a reflection on whether these reordering efforts suggest that city officials may be coming to gradually abandon the order-construction ideal.

From High Rises to HOPE in Chicago

Chapter 2 briefly examined how public housing policies combined with urban renewal and highway construction to fundamentally alter the urban landscape in the postwar years. It goes without saying that the centerpiece of postwar public housing policy—massive, multibuilding high developments— is now considered an abysmal failure. And it is a failure that many cities are now seeking to undo. This section focuses on the construction, demolition, and redevelopment of public housing projects in the city of Chicago. There are a number of related reasons why Chicago provides a fascinating opportunity to consider how public housing policy has been used, and is being used, to reorder cities. Chicago has always been, and remains, one of the nation's most segregated cities. And as Arnold Hirsch notes in his excellent history of postwar housing policy in Chicago, *Making the Second Ghetto,* by the mid-1950s, public housing policy had become a powerful tool in the hands of those intent on maintaining segregated housing patterns. As a result, Chicago felt the negative consequences of the myriad failures of America's experiment with high-rise public housing projects in a particularly acute way. Until recently, the city was home to the densest concentration of public housing units in the country. At its peak, the CHA managed almost forty thousand public housing units, the vast majority of them in the high-rise developments most associated with disorder and crime. Moreover, in 1976, the CHA entered into a novel consent decree that obligated it to remedy its racially discriminatory tenant-assignment and site-selection practices by using housing vouchers to place black public housing tenants in low-poverty areas in the city and suburbs. The resulting program, named for the original plaintiff in the litigation against the CHA, Dorothy Gautreaux, has been widely studied. In 1994, the U.S. Department of Housing and Urban Development replicated the Gautreaux program in four additional cities—New York City, Los Angeles, Baltimore, and Boston. As discussed in chapter 1, Bernard Harcourt and Jens Ludwig have used data from this broader Moving to Opportunity program to test and challenge the social-influence foundation of the broken windows hypothesis. Finally, and most importantly for purposes of this discussion about the *re*ordering of the city, a decade ago, the CHA committed to demolishing *all* of the disorder-plagued high-rise family-housing projects and replacing them with new-urbanist-inspired, low-rise, mixed-income—and in some cases, mixed-use—developments. The extent of the transformation is both breathtaking and, in light of the history of these projects, breathtakingly ironic.[1]

A Short History of U.S. Public Housing Policy

High-rise public housing projects were not constructed or maintained for the sole purpose of concentrating urban disorder. However, high concentrations of poverty, and the crime and disorder related to it, were their foreordained result for a number of reasons. First, Congress acted to assuage private developers' worries about competition from government-owned housing with various policies that led to the projects' economic and social isolation and rapid obsolescence. For example, the "equivalent elimination" requirement, which required housing authorities to demolish one unit of substandard housing for each unit constructed, effectively guaranteed that most public housing units would be built in urban areas; suburbs simply had little substandard housing to eliminate. Local housing authorities, motivated by a desire to conserve land costs as well as by, in many cases, blatant racism, exacerbated the problem by choosing to locate projects in close proximity to one another in the least desirable and poorest city neighborhoods. Congress also mandated "economy" in the construction of public housing units in order to make them less attractive vis-à-vis market-rate units. The costs of frugality became apparent as early as the late 1950s, as buildings began to deteriorate almost as soon as they were occupied. When public housing authorities failed to make timely repairs, vacancy rates rose. In Chicago, almost half of the city's forty thousand public housing units had become uninhabitable by the turn of the twenty-first century. Not only did high vacancy rates increase crime, as vacant units served as staging grounds for criminal activity, but squatters began to inhabit vacant units, causing housing authorities to lose track of who was actually residing in their projects.[2]

Second, the multi-building "towers in the park," reflecting Le Corbusier's ideal of the "radiant city," proved singularly ill-equipped to house poor families. Not only did the architectural design of the high rises create the impression that the projects were nothing more than a "filing cabinet for the poor," but as Oscar Newman devastatingly demonstrated in his classic study *Defensible Space,* the building design also prevented residents from developing the feelings of "ownership" necessary for effective private controls over communal spaces. For example, the high-rise designs made it virtually impossible for parents to supervise their children outside of their apartments. Other design flaws—including limited-access stairwells and external hallways—proved dangerous as well. The elimination of the old street grids to create "superblocks" further isolated residents from what remained of the surrounding community after the demolition necessary to construct the projects.

Third, while public housing was initially conceived as a transitional way station for the working poor, over time, federal policy evolved toward reserving public housing units for the neediest families. The result was high concentrations of destitute families in rapidly deteriorating buildings. By the early 1970s, Congress began to take steps to reduce the concentrations of very poor tenants in public housing projects. Gradually, federal policy came to prioritize income integration and shifted to favor demand-oriented subsidies, like vouchers, that enabled poor tenants to rent private apartments. Despite two decades of such efforts, however, crime and disorder had come to define high-rise projects by the late 1980s.[3]

In 1989, the National Commission on Severely Distressed Public Housing issued a report finding that, while much of the nation's public housing stock was in fairly good repair, the most troubled projects were the very places in which poor families were most likely to live: More than half of all the units were located in "family" projects of more than two hundred dwellings owned by the largest urban public housing authorities. These projects, the commission found, were most likely to exhibit the characteristics of severe distress: "[r]esidents living in despair and generally needing high levels of social and support services, . . . physically deteriorating buildings," and "[e]conomically and socially distressed surrounding communities." Moreover, the commission found that *all* public housing residents were "very poor and getting poorer," a reality that translated into "an aggregation of particularly vulnerable households in many family developments" as well as "tremendous isolation" and "[i]nstitutional abandonment" of the most distressed projects.[4]

In its final report, the commission recommended that Congress appropriate $7.5 billion to renovate distressed public housing, even when renovation costs exceeded the cost of reconstruction. Congress, perhaps suffering from sticker shock, resisted. Instead, Congress took additional steps toward eliminating the concentrated poverty and disorder plaguing housing projects and their neighbors, including appropriating $300 million for a demonstration project that became the precursor to the HOPE VI program discussed below. In 1998, Congress solidified the preference for de-concentrating the disorders associated with public housing by enacting the Quality Housing and Work Responsibility Act of 1998. The law included a number of provisions designed to encourage public housing tenants to gain self-sufficiency, including work- and job-training requirements, and to empower public housing authorities to exercise more authority over their tenants, including the "one-strike-and-you're-out" eviction policies upheld by the Supreme Court in *Department of Housing and Urban Development v. Rucker*. Perhaps most significantly, the 1998 reforms sought to promote market-oriented public housing practices. The law formally authorized HOPE VI, which finances the redevelopment of public housing projects, including their demolition and replacement with privately developed, low-rise, mixed-income communities.[5]

HOPE VI projects are privately developed with a mix of public and private funds. As a condition of receiving the public subsidies, private developers must agree to make some of the replacement units available at below-market prices and to reserve some units for public housing tenants. HOPE VI, however, is not exclusively, or even primarily, an affordable-housing program. It is, at heart, a neighborhood-redevelopment strategy that aims to reorder and renew poor urban neighborhoods by saving them from the ravages of disorder-plagued public housing. HOPE VI has both order-construction and disorder-suppression goals. It seeks to reorder city neighborhoods physically by replacing modernist high-rise structures with new low-rise development reflecting a new-urbanist aesthetic and by reconstructing and reconnecting the old street grids that were eliminated to make public housing "superblocks." Some HOPE VI projects also incorporate commercial enterprises into the new residential developments, thus moving from single-use to mixed-use environments. HOPE VI also aims to suppress disorder by breaking up the concentrations of social and criminal disorder present in the old high-rise projects. Hope VI's income-mixing elements seek to build social capital in disorder-ravaged neighborhoods by attracting middle- and working-class residents.[6]

While HOPE VI is generally viewed favorably in the popular press, many affordable-housing advocates argue that the program further exacerbates serious inequities imbedded in U.S. public housing policy by infusing billions of dollars in federal subsidies into the private housing market with the express intention of *reducing* the supply of public housing. As Michael Schill has observed, U.S. public housing policy lacks both horizontal and vertical equity. That is, not all individuals who qualify for assistance by virtue of economic circumstance receive it, and the neediest individuals are not necessarily entitled to receive a subsidy before wealthier ones. Critics argue that HOPE VI aggravates these problems because projects usually contain only a fraction of the number of preexisting pubic housing units: A central goal of the program is, after all, to demolish high-rise public housing projects and replace them with new developments that are both low-rise (and therefore contain far fewer units) and mixed-income (and therefore further reduce the pool of units available for the very poor). For example, Chicago's Robert Taylor Homes once housed twenty-seven thousand people, although high vacancy rates meant that *only* eleven thousand residents were dislocated by their demolition. Yet the replacement projects anticipated in the Plan for Transformation will contain fewer than one thousand public housing units. In other words, critics assert, the federal government has committed to a policy of allocating scarce housing resources to subsidize private housing for families who are not eligible for public housing *at all*—that is, those wealthy enough to purchase market rate or "affordable" units beyond the financial reach of the poor. And, because private developers exercise significant control over tenant selection, the public housing units in HOPE VI projects tend to go to less-needy individuals (for example, those with good credit and without criminal records). The inequities imbedded in public housing policy were further exacerbated by the 1998 act's mandate that public housing authorities take steps to promote economic diversity in traditional public housing, including financial incentives for working-class families to move to very poor projects.[7]

HOPE VI proponents counter that the realities of life in the projects render untenable any proposal to preserve the high rises in the name of maximizing public housing units. Proponents argue that HOPE VI promises to break the cycle of fear and hopelessness that has trapped far too many public housing tenants for decades. Moreover, high-rise demolition removes a major source of concentrated disorder and crime from struggling neighborhoods. Pre–HOPE VI studies universally found that large public housing projects had dramatic and negative effects on their surrounding neighborhoods. One study of Chicago, published soon after the commission's final report, estimated that the presence of a public housing development increased a census tract's poverty rate by 11 percent.[8]

While acknowledging that HOPE VI entails an increased reliance on demand-oriented housing vouchers to make up for units that are demolished and not replaced, proponents strenuously resist the assertion that the program "succeeds" by depriving the neediest tenants of the resources that they need in order to secure housing. If the program works as intended, displaced tenants are given either a replacement unit or a housing voucher to secure private housing. And while opponents argue that voucher recipients are forced to re-settle in equally dangerous and segregated communities, empirical studies paint a more hopeful picture: Displaced tenants tended to relocate to slightly more wealthy, more-diverse neighborhoods—albeit to ones that remained rel-atively poor and segregated. Residents also report that their new neighbor-hoods are safer than their old neighborhoods, although, again, many still worry about crime. It remains to be seen, however, how well these communi-ties, many of them undoubtedly already disorder-weary, will cope with an in-flux of desperately poor residents.[9]

High Rises in Chicago

In order to contextualize the extent of the reordering undertaken by the Plan for Transformation, a few words about Chicago's sordid public housing his-tory are in order. During most of the twentieth century, the white residents of Chicago, like those of most northern cities, sought to "contain" African Americans by preventing them, economically, legally, and even violently, from moving into white neighborhoods. In Chicago, most African Americans lived in a narrow strip of neighborhoods on the city's South Side. Housing short-ages were a perennial problem, as continued migration north increased the number of residents vying for the limited supply of residential units within the "Black Belt" and pervasive discrimination prevented exit from it. The housing situation reached a crisis point in the postwar years, when returning soldiers and a new wave of migrants arrived in the already overcrowded neigh-borhoods.

By the end of the Second World War, however, Chicago was changing. Im-portantly, the economic situation for African Americans began to improve at a time that increasing numbers of whites suburbanized, creating housing va-cancies in neighborhoods surrounding the Black Belt. African Americans, un-derstandably, began to seek housing in areas previously closed off to them. White residents responded to the threatened "invasion" in various ways. Some organized "neighborhood preservation" committees, which sought to use le-gal means—such as the enforcement of racially restrictive covenants and housing codes—to drive away new black neighbors; others turned to violence—including arson and physical assault. Real estate speculators played a major role in the racial succession process, using "block breaking" tactics that took advantage of white fears about integration to enable the quick and below-market acquisition of homes in transition areas, which were subsequently transferred to desperate African American families at dramatically marked-up prices.[10]

In Chicago, as in most major urban centers, public housing and redevelopment policies shaped in significant ways how the city evolved in the face of integration pressures. That public housing played such a role was, for many obvious reasons, predictable. Most of the city's African American residents were poor and in dire need of quality housing. In an era of optimism about the government's ability to respond to social problems, it is only natural that the CHA stepped in to fill the void. But the CHA's motivations were hardly pure. From its inception, the CHA adhered stringently to the so-called "neighborhood composition rule," making every effort to ensure through tenant-assignment and site-selection policies that a project would not alter the racial composition of a neighborhood. The CHA also unapologetically operated "white" and "black" projects. One of the first CHA projects, in fact, the Ida B. Wells Homes, was built with federal Public Works Administration funds during the late 1930s explicitly to house poor African American residents.* In the postwar years, however, the need to secure housing for returning veterans strained the CHA's rigid racial quota system. Since the need for housing was most acute among African American veterans and the available temporary housing units were located primarily in white neighborhoods, the CHA began to place African Americans in projects built in white neighborhoods, leading, on more than one occasion, to a violent protest by white residents.[11]

During these years, however, the CHA had the indomitable Elizabeth Wood at its helm. Wood favored "nondiscriminatory" tenant-selection policies, although it is fair to say that the concessions Wood was willing to make—including, for example, strict racial quotas and promises not to place African American *Catholics* in projects in white neighborhoods in order to assuage those concerned that these tenants might send their children to nearby

---

*The bunker-style buildings of the Ida B. Wells Homes have largely been demolished to make way for a "traditional neighborhood" HOPE VI project, although one of the original buildings will be restored for historical preservation purposes.

parochial schools—shock the modern conscience. Over time, however, Wood began to lose her battles over integration for two related reasons. First, as the urban renewal process began to gain steam, the CHA's focus shifted toward providing transitional housing for families dislocated by redevelopment efforts. For example, when completed in 1950, the Dearborn Homes—Chicago's first high-rise project—served primarily as temporary housing for residents dislocated by redevelopment.* Initially, the relocation process also strained the neighborhood composition rule—because many dislocated families were black and available units were located in white neighborhoods—but the shift in priorities marked the gradual erosion of Wood's authority. Second, Wood's support in the city government evaporated. In 1947, Mayor "Boss" Edward J. Kelly—a powerful "machine" man who protected Wood—was replaced by the "clean" Martin Kennelly. When integration-sparked violence again broke out at a veterans' project, Kennelly declined to back Wood. He also capitulated to calls for an investigation of the CHA. While the ostensible charges were fraud and mismanagement, the alderman leading the charge made clear that his concern was that the CHA "persisted in theories of housing which are shared by no other representative local government agencies . . . and are not in accord with those of a great majority of citizens." Ultimately, Wood and the CHA were cleared of all wrongdoing, but not before the Illinois state legislature gave Chicago veto authority over the CHA's selection of sites for new housing projects.[12]

As a result, the Chicago City Council effectively dictated the locations of all of the federally funded projects in the city. The council delegated the decision about whether to accept or veto a CHA-proposed site to the alderman representing the affected area; white aldermen simply vetoed all proposed sites. The council also favored sites with existing public housing projects and insisted that no project be placed in "virgin" territory. The city ultimately proposed eight sites, for a total of 10,500 units, all in existing ghetto areas. Construction of these cites would uproot 12,465 black families. When the federal government demanded one additional "white" site, the city proposed a location in a racially transitioning neighborhood, which necessitated the demoli-

---

* Today, the Dearborn Homes, one of the few remaining high-rise projects, again serves that purpose. The CHA's Web site indicates, without a hint of irony, that "Dearborn Homes is currently operating as one of the CHA's 'relocation resources,' providing capacity for residents who have moved from other developments undergoing redevelopment or rehabilitation. Plans for the property's future are currently under consideration."

tion of a large swath of solid housing stock. All told, the final plans for feder-ally funded public housing in Chicago created a net addition of 47 housing units and required densities that exceeded the CHA's own standards. Eliza-beth Wood railed against the proposal—publicly proclaiming that the CHA had become a "captured" agency, but her cries fell on deaf ears. She was un-ceremoniously dismissed in 1954.[13]

The upshot was that public housing policy became a powerful tool for maintaining the existing racial balance on the South Side of Chicago. Of the thirty-three projects built by the CHA between 1950 and the mid-1960s, twenty-five were sited in census tracts containing at least 75 percent African American residents; six more were in areas undergoing racial transition. By the time that construction was completed, only one of the projects was in an area less than 84 percent black, and all but seven of them were in areas greater than 95 percent black. All told, 98 percent of the public housing units con-structed after 1950 were in all-black neighborhoods. The result was a dense forest of poorly constructed high rises in the former Black Belt, inhabited al-most exclusively by the poorest Chicago residents—those for whom poverty and housing discrimination provided few options. Given what we now know about the ills associated with concentrated poverty, postwar Chicago public housing policy could not have been more antithetical to neighborhood stabil-ity (a reality that planners, one might reasonably assume, anticipated at the time). As one critic observed in 1958, the CHA's policies led to the "pyramid-ing of existing ghettos" and the further concentration of the urban ills they contained. And when a federal court ultimately found in 1969 that the CHA's site-selection and tenant-assignment procedures violated the Fourteenth Amendment's Equal Protection Clause, "public housing construction in Chicago simply ceased."[14]

HOPE in Chicago?

But that was then. In 1995, after finding gross financial mismanagement, the U.S. Department of Housing and Urban Development assumed control of the CHA. Four years later, in 1999, HUD transferred authority to the City of Chicago. One year later, the new CHA announced the Plan for Transforma-tion. It is, at this point, impossible to avoid the irony: Today, a housing au-thority under the control of Mayor Richard M. Daley is leading the charge to revitalize, through public housing reform, the disorder-plagued projects that a different CHA, helpless at the whims of another Mayor Daley and his politi-cal machine, created and neglected for decades. But irony aside, the new CHA is in fact transforming public housing in Chicago. Nearly *all* of the high-rise projects are gone now, and the empty rubble-strewn lots where they once stood are slowly being filled with low-density HOPE VI developments so up-scale and attractive that no outsider would guess they were "public housing projects." In one sense, it is too easy to take potshots at the failures endemic to Chicago public housing policy. After all, both the fact and extent of the deba-cle were predictable: The buildings were poorly constructed and mismanaged, placed in the poorest communities, and crammed full of desperately poor people. Still, both the past calamity and current efforts to reverse it shed light on city officials' thinking about what kinds of land-use policies failed and on their hopes for what kinds might succeed. To understand these factors in con-text, and to fully grasp the extent of the *mea culpa,* consider the details of two of Chicago's HOPE VI projects—Lake Park Crescent/Jazz on the Boulevard and Legends South.

The Lakefront Properties (Now Lake Park Crescent and Jazz on the Boulevard)

When completed in 1963, the Lakefront Properties contained nine hundred pub-lic housing units. Their piecemeal construction over the course of nearly a de-cade resulted from a textbook application of the racially motivated policies outlined above. The high rises were located in the heart of the Black Belt. Con-struction required the demolition of the densely populated Douglas neighbor-hood and the dislocation of nearly fifteen thousand people. Over the following decades, neglect and concentrated poverty left the towers crumbling and plagued by crime and disorder (figure 7.1). In 1985, the CHA announced plans to reno-vate many thousands of public housing units, including the Lakefront Homes. The renovation plan was never carried out, however, thanks to a mix of local and federal impediments—the federal court supervision of the *Gautreaux* consent decree, neighborhood opposition, objections from residents who would have to be relocated during the course of the renovations, and, importantly, mismanage-ment by the CHA. Instead, in 1998, the Lakefront Properties were demolished after a decade-long debate over the fate of the towers and their residents (thou-sands of whom had been displaced for renovations that never occurred)—a de-bate dominated by the same forces opposing renovation, as well as by federal officials who had come to favor demolition and redevelopment over renovation, and by an entrepreneurial real estate developer named Ferdinand Kramer.

Today, the vacant lots where the Lakefront Properties once stood are slowly being filled with two mixed-income projects. Lake Park Crescent (figure 7.2),

Figure 7.1. Lakefront Properties, Chicago, immediately prior to demolition.
Photo © by Lee Bey.

Figure 7.2. Lake Park Crescent development, Chicago, rendering. Courtesy of Draper and Kramer.

developed by Draper and Kramer, will "offer a mosaic of distinctive housing types, featuring masonry, setbacks and other design features similar to the surrounding North Kenwood-Oakland area." When completed, the development will include 120 public housing units, 122 affordable-housing units, and 248 market-rate units. As of this writing, single-family row homes are offered at the "incentive" price of nearly $700,000. Construction began in 2003, although the first row houses are only now rising from the rubble and the CHA has yet to dispose of the property needed for the second phase of the project. A few blocks east of the original Lakefront Properties, the off-site Jazz on the Boulevard development is substantially completed. This smaller development (137 units), also a mixed-income project, incorporates both owner and rental units, most of which—in contrast to Lake Park Crescent—are located in multifamily buildings. Jazz on the Boulevard's relative success has been attributed to a general renaissance of the historic Drexel Boulevard corridor.[15]

The Robert Taylor Homes
(Now Legends South)

It is hard to imagine a more powerful monument to a failed order-construction strategy than the Robert Taylor Homes, which for decades lined a two-mile stretch of Chicago's Dan Ryan Expressway across from the White Sox's Comiskey Park. Featured in the 1970s hit sitcom *Good Times,* the Taylor Homes were considered the largest public housing project in the world upon their completion in 1962. By the time the CHA began to demolish them more than a decade ago, the Taylor Homes had become a national symbol of urban chaos and disorder (figure 7.3). In the early 1990s, the CHA instituted a policy of warrantless law-enforcement "sweeps" of units. The immediate impetus for the policy was a series of shootings. The CHA had hired contractors to install window guards on the units because several children had fallen out of them. When the contractors arrived, unknown individuals began to shoot at them from vacant apartments. Although a federal court subsequently invalidated the sweep policy as inconsistent with the Fourth Amendment's warrant requirement, the policy—and the events precipitating it—sparked a major debate about the appropriate bounds of government authority to suppress disorder.[16]

The inside story of how Chicago politics shaped the design and location of the Robert Taylor Homes is as telling and as troubling as any tale of public housing in Chicago. The Taylor Homes was the first project that was Mayor

Figure 7.3. Robert Taylor Homes, Chicago, 2002. Photo by Eli Reed. Reprinted from *Metropolis Magazine*, January 2002.

Richard J. Daley's own; he obtained city council approval for it a year after his election. The project was destined from the beginning to house an almost unprecedented concentration of poor people; when completed, the twenty-eight towers were home to twenty-seven thousand tenants. Although he later professed ignorance of the risks and consequences of concentrating large numbers of poor people in high-rise projects, housing experts had talked for years about the dangers of concentrated poverty. Elizabeth Wood, a onetime devotee of Le Corbusier, issued a warning in her last address before being pushed out of the CHA. Even Ferdinand Kramer, the same developer (five decades later!) instrumental in the redevelopment of the Lakefront Properties, asked Daley during the 1950s to consider scattering public housing throughout the city to avoid "great colonies of racially, socially, and politically segregated housing."* Daley's motivations are hardly a mystery. He was a Chicago Irish Catholic, born and raised in a neighborhood that was facing integration pressures by the mid-1950s. Daley sought to use all the anti-integration tools at his disposal. For example, it is widely believed that Daley gerrymandered the path of the Dan Ryan Expressway to protect South Side Catholic neighborhoods from the city's expanding "Black Belt." The initial plans called for a more direct route cutting deeper into the heart of Chicago's ethnic Catholic neighborhoods. As Daley biographers Adam Cohen and Elizabeth Taylor recount, however, when the "final plans were announced, the Dan Ryan had been 're-aligned' several blocks eastward . . . along Wentworth Avenue"—the city's traditional, and increasingly porous, racial dividing line. "It was a less direct route, and it required the road to make two sharp curves in a short space, but the new route turned the Dan Ryan into a classic racial barrier between the black and white South Sides." The construction of the Taylor Homes along the freeway further extended the massive cement buffer between "black" and "white" Chicago.[17]

Again, that was then. Over the past several years, millions of motorists along the Dan Ryan have watched the towers of the Taylor Homes gradually disappear, one by one. At times, skeletal buildings appeared to be literally devoured by giant cranes sitting atop their roofs. At others, piles of rubble cluttered the parking lots of buildings where lights from occupied units punctuated facades dominated by boarded-up windows. The Taylor Homes

---

* Ferdinand Kramer, a fixture of Chicago real estate and redevelopment for more than five decades, died in 2002 at the age of 100. Trice, "Developer's Vision Thrives in Lakefront Model."

are a wasteland again—an unnervingly massive fenced-off vacant lot. And the CHA is determined to remake them, and save the neighborhood in the process. The master plan for the Taylor site, known as "Legends South," anticipates the construction of 2,550 mixed-income rental and home-ownership units, including 851 public housing units, in a diverse array of housing types (figure 7.4). Unlike many of the other CHA HOPE VI projects, the Legends South plan also incorporates retail and commercial space. Thus far, redevelopment efforts have concentrated on off-site relocation housing, but the on-site development of "Hansberry Square"—named for the African American author Lorraine Hansberry—is now under way in the northern portion of the cleared property. Ultimately, Legends South will be linked with another HOPE VI project, Park Boulevard, located on the site of the demolished Stateway Gardens, the Taylor Homes' neighbor to the south.

The New, New Southwest

Today, insiders associate Southwest Washington, D.C., with austere federal office buildings and charmless modern apartment buildings and townhouses. The area, however, once contained some of the city's oldest buildings, most of which were destroyed during the 1950s as part of a massive urban-renewal-era redevelopment effort. This effort is best known as the factual backdrop of the Supreme Court's landmark 1954 *Berman v. Parker* decision, which paved the constitutional way for urban renewal throughout the United States. In *Berman,* the Court was asked to resolve whether the Takings Clause of the Fifth Amendment, which provides that private property shall not be taken for "public use" without "just compensation," prevented the federal government from using eminent domain to acquire hundreds of acres of private property with the express intention of transferring it to a private developer for redevelopment. The Court had little difficulty disposing of the issue, known to lawyers as the "public use" question. Justice William O. Douglas's unanimous opinion highlighted the perceived connection between physical order and social disorder:

> We do not sit to determine whether a particular housing project is or is not desirable. The concept of public welfare is broad and inclusive. The values it represents are spiritual, as well as physical, aesthetic as well as monetary. It is within the power of the legislature to determine that the community should be beautiful as well as healthy, spacious as well as clean, well-balanced as well as carefully patrolled. In the present case, the Congress and its authorized agencies have made determinations that take into account a wide variety of values. It is not for us to reappraise them. If those who

Figure 7.4. Advertisement for Legends South, Chicago. Courtesy of Brinshore Development.

govern the District of Columbia decide that the Nation's Capital should be beautiful as well as sanitary, there is nothing in the Fifth Amendment that stands in its way.

As Justice Douglas's words suggest, the constitutional issue in *Berman* was primarily about the separation of powers: Legislatures, not courts, the Supreme Court ruled, are vested with the power to decide land-use patterns. Just as *Euclid* stood for the proposition that local governments could establish such patterns *ex ante* through zoning, *Berman* authorizes them to alter them *ex post,* with bulldozers if necessary.[18]

Douglas's description of the choices facing the District of Columbia also hints at the ideological forces shaping the city's plans to redevelop the old Southwest. As discussed in chapter 2, *Berman* was decided at a time when elite opinion held both that our cities were obsolete and that government could overcome their obsolescence by demolishing and reshaping them. That this was an era of hopeful optimism about the ability of the government to wisely reorder cities is reflected not just in Justice Douglas's glowing praise of the district's grandiose plans for the troubled Southwest, but also in the public reaction to the decision. In 2005, when the Supreme Court ruled in *Kelo v. New London* that the Fifth Amendment's Takings Clause did not preclude a city from using eminent domain to acquire property for a private redevelopment project, the outcry was deafening. Editorial cartoons variously featured a Supreme Court justice with a meat cleaver ripping the heart out of the Constitution and another astride a crane with a giant wrecking ball aiming for the sacred "home as castle." My colleague, John Nagle, reports seeing a sign in a remote Alaskan outpost that declared "rape, robbery, and eminent domain . . . all the same!" I personally saw a giant billboard, erected (apparently at some expense) on top of an auto-repair shop in Shawnee, Kansas, that warned "The Supreme Court has declared war on private property. Your home could be next." These protests grew so heated that a number of state legislatures placed new restrictions on the use of eminent domain. In contrast, the public reaction to *Berman* was positive, praising the city's "bold" plans to remake the old Southwest. Ideological disputes over the fate of the Southwest played itself out not in the pages of the *Washington Post* or the pages of the *United States Reports,* but rather in the pages of obscure planning reports commissioned by competing federal agencies.[19]

The End of the Old Southwest

Southwest was one of the first areas settled in the District of Columbia. James Greenleaf, a real estate speculator and important Revolutionary War financier, developed some of the earliest row houses in the city there, and the area was home to a number of notable officials during the early republic. Although relatively close to the Capitol, development was hampered both by the physical isolation from the rest of the city, imposed first by the James Creek Canal and later by a major railroad, and by the dangerous health conditions generated by the fact that Southwest was bordered on three sides by bodies of water—the canal, the Washington Channel, and the Anacostia River. Residential development of the area virtually ceased by the end of the nineteenth century, and the Southwest began a steady decline. By the time it was selected as the district's first major urban renewal area, it had earned a reputation as one of the worst housing areas in the United States. In 1950, 43 percent of the area's fifty-six hundred dwelling units had outdoor toilets; 70 percent lacked central heating; 21 percent lacked electricity; and 44 percent were without indoor baths. The overwhelming majority of the area's twenty-three thousand residents were African American and very poor.[20]

The old Southwest was notorious for its "alley dwelling" problem. As early as the 1850s, property owners began to build slave, servant, and rental quarters along the alleys at the back of their properties. After the Civil War, the number of alley dwellings multiplied, as the influx of African Americans and poor whites led owners to divide their lots to permit construction of buildings only accessible through rear alleys. The living conditions along the alleys were a significant concern as early as the late nineteenth century: Congress forbade further construction along them in 1892. In his 1904 message to Congress, President Teddy Roosevelt called for a commission to study the problem. The commission's report—condemning the alley dwellings as both unhealthy and dangerous dens of criminality—was basically ignored, as many such reports were. Although the population living in the alley hovels did decline over the first decades of the twentieth century, many poor people—the overwhelming majority of whom were African American laborers—remained crowded together in them. Subsequent efforts to tackle the problem were undertaken just prior to the First World War and again during the Great Depression. Both led to ineffective federal legislation. In 1934, for example, Congress created the Alley Dwelling Authority and charged it with the task of clearing the alleys by 1944. Litigation and the Second World War, however, pressed the deadline back to 1955, by which time bulldozers had cleared the old Southwest of far more than alley hovels.

Serious attention turned to the question of redeveloping the old Southwest in its entirety during the Second World War. In 1942, Arthur Goodwillie, who directed the Conservation Service of the Home Owners' Loan Corporation, proposed a rehabilitation plan for the area. In making this proposal, Goodwillie had as a model the "unslumming" of Georgetown, which was accomplished privately beginning during the First World War by wives of war workers in search of convenient and affordable housing. There ensued a decade-long debate about the wisdom of this conservative approach as opposed to a radical facelift of the entire area. Although the National Capital Park and Planning Commission (NCPPC) supported rehabilitation, postwar planning ideology did not favor a surgical approach to the problem of blight. As early as 1946, General Ulysses S. Grant III, the Chairman of the Redevelopment Land Agency (RLA), which, importantly, held the power of the purse, drew up a master plan calling for the radical reconstruction of the old Southwest. To support his effort, Grant enlisted planning guru Alfred Bettman, who had written the *amicus* brief thought to have turned the tide in favor of zoning in the *Euclid* litigation. Bettman's bold suggestion that postwar redevelopment "should include the replanning and rebuilding of the built up and subdivided areas of cities and metropolitan regions," formed the blueprint for postwar redevelopment policy, including, importantly, the District of Columbia Redevelopment Act of 1945 and the Housing Act of 1949. With the enactment of the latter, Daniel Burnham's admonition to "make no small plans" became official federal redevelopment policy. American cities would never be the same.[21]

After the enactment of the Housing Act, the battle over the old Southwest continued. In 1951, the NCPPC, which hoped that the Southwest could remain an enclave for low- and middle-income workers, asked landscape architect Elbert Peets to prepare a renewal plan for the Southwest. In the spirit of the earlier Goodwillie plan, Peets sought to preserve the historical elements of the old Southwest, especially the older row houses and tree-lined streets. Peets argued that the basic soundness of the old housing stock signaled that the area might be ripe for rehabilitation. A survey of the Homebuilder's Association of Metropolitan Washington had described the houses in the old Southwest "as sound and in many cases as large and fashionable as homes in Georgetown" and with an unusually high level of residential stability for a poor community. The following year, the RLA commissioned a competing report from Louis Justement and Chloethiel Woodard Smith, asking them to explore possibilities for a more-ambitious redevelopment of the entire area. Smith's writings had previously made clear her view that such possibilities were endless, which is precisely why the RLA selected her. Not surprisingly, the Justement-Smith plan asked the RLA to consider the "whole process of rebuilding the city in a purposeful and accelerated fashion." The Southwest could be re-created, they argued, to attract suburbanites back to the city—a goal that pervaded the discussions of D.C.'s postwar redevelopment efforts. Justement and Smith proposed demolishing most of the existing structures in the area and replacing them with high-rise apartments and low-rise townhouses, carefully grouped "to take the greatest advantage of the various sites, orientations to the sun, prevailing winds and views, provision of maximum privacy . . . , best use of open space, etc." They also suggested a strip of high rises along the waterfront, with "corner stores" interspersed in the development to maintain the feel of a traditional urban neighborhood. The plan necessitated the closing and reconfiguration of many streets, including a new entrance or "front door esplanade" to the community. Public housing would be limited in scope and contained at the outskirts of the area. Shortly thereafter, the NCPPC, apparently sensing defeat, submitted a "compromise plan" that embraced a more radical approach but called for the preservation of historically significant sites and emphasized the need for low-income housing.[22]

In 1953, the RLA began the process of assembling land, demolishing buildings, and selling the land to developers (figure 7.5). *Berman* set aside any constitutional roadblocks to the new Southwest a year later. The end result seems almost inevitable in retrospect: 99 percent of the buildings in the Southwest were torn down to make way for a more modern city. In their place stood what Daniel Thursz described (positively) as the "futuristic Southwest complex," and another commentator described it as "an architect's paradise of high rise apartments balanced on concrete fingertips, colonial town houses in verdant culs-de-sac, Olympic-size swimming pools . . . and a renovated waterfront [that] has been regrettably scaled down to a narrow sterile promenade and a row of warehouse-elegant restaurants." With the old buildings went the former residents of the old Southwest, overwhelmingly poor and African American. Throughout the redevelopment process, the all-black Southwest Civic Association had decried the lack of plans for low-income housing and described the effort as a "shameful un-American displacement program." In 1949, the *Pittsburgh-Washington Courier* complained that the desire to "make Washington the most beautiful city in the world" was causing city leaders to ignore the "plea that thousands of Negroes will lose their life savings and become renters or objects of charity; hundreds of Negro business enterprises will be wiped out; hundreds of Negro churches will be destroyed and their members scattered. . . ." And scattered they were. Thursz's

important study of five hundred relocated families found that they had settled throughout the city. The largest concentration landed in public housing
in the Southwest, including two small projects built at the edge of the redevelopment area; many others wound up in new public housing elsewhere in
the city. While most of those displaced enjoyed improved housing conditions,
many were left psychologically devastated. Thursz concluded: "The New
Southwest may yet develop into the 'Good City,' but its birth has been at a
cost. It has risen over the ashes of what was a community of well-established,
though poor, inhabitants."[23]

Figure 7.5. The destruction of the old Southwest. Photo courtesy of St. Dominic's
Catholic Church, Washington, D.C.

A Newer New Southwest

The "New Southwest" never did develop into the "Good City" envisioned by the planners who destroyed the old one. Although the wrecking ball eliminated the squalor, it also erased the pockets of charm that have elsewhere proven crucial to neighborhood regeneration. Planners eventually dropped even the planned "urban" touches—corner stores and restaurants—from residential sections, a decision that drained the area of any sense of urban vitality. The inhabitants of the new Southwest tended to be wealthier than those displaced by the renewal effort, but hopes that the new community might compete successfully with the burgeoning suburbs never materialized. The new residents were overwhelmingly short-termers, especially young professionals and paraprofessionals drawn to the area by its proximity to federal office buildings, who were unlikely to invest the time and energy needed to build the social capital that characterizes healthy community life.

By the late 1990s, local leaders had become convinced that many of the central elements of the urban renewal effort prevented them from capitalizing on the area's potential, especially its location along the Anacostia River. In 2002, the EPA's decision to move its offices out of the area that the *Washington Post* described as "the drab concrete office buildings of the Waterside Mall" provided a catalyst for a new wave of redevelopment in Southwest. The Waterside Mall was demolished in late 2007 (figure 7.6) to make way for a new development, known simply as "Waterfront." If all goes as planned (and it has not to date), the modernist concrete-buildings conceived by Justement and Smith will be replaced with a new-urbanist-inspired community that will, according to the developers' promotional materials, "create 18-hour activity and vibrancy through a strong live/work/play mix that provides more residential, more neighborhood retail establishments, and more open and public spaces." Somewhat ironically, the predicted success of the new Waterfront development hinges in part on the city's decision to reconnect the area to the rest of the city by reopening Fourth Street, which was closed when planners reconfigured the old grid pattern during the urban renewal era. Now, more than four decades later, the city promised that reopening Fourth Street will create "a new Main Street" that will energize the area by creating a "walkable community."[24]

Just south of the Waterside Mall site, another substantial redevelopment project is planned for the northern banks of the Anacostia River. The riverfront

Figure 7.6. Demolition of the Waterfront Mall, Southwest D.C. Photo by Angela R. Schoonover.

has long been underutilized, both because much of the property is owned by the government and, as elsewhere in the Southwest, because the creation of urban renewal "superblocks" and the erection of major freeways cut the area off from the rest of the city. In 2002, the National Capital Revitalization Corporation, the quasi-public agency that acquired title to the land during the urban renewal effort, drafted a redevelopment plan for the waterfront. The plans call for demolishing parking lots and other concrete barriers in the area and replacing the existing retail establishments with a mixed-use development featuring hundreds of units of mixed-income housing, hotels, neighborhood-friendly retail establishments, and public open space.

The city's plans for the new, new Southwest are closely tied to other redevelopment efforts along the Anacostia River, including a new Washington National's baseball stadium and the massive mixed-use development accompanying it. A little farther east still, the District of Columbia Housing Authority has demolished two of the public housing projects—the Arthur Capper Homes and Carrollsburg Dwellings—which absorbed some of the displaced residents of the old Southwest. A private developer has committed to redeveloping, with the assistance of a federal $35 million HOPE VI grant, the reclaimed land into a mixed-use development known as "Capital Quarter." Capital Quarter will replace all of the 707 demolished pubic housing units and will incorporate an additional 700 market- and affordable-rate housing units, 730,000 square feet of office space, and 50,000 square feet of retail space. The one-for-one replacement of the public housing units—rare for HOPE VI redevelopments—is made possible by the fact that the Capper-Carrollsburg projects were bunker-style, rather than high-rise, projects and by regulatory changes permitting denser development, enabling the developer to double the number of housing units on the site. Prices for the market-rate townhomes begin in the mid-$600 thousands.[25]

If successful, all of these waterfront projects will substantially reorder the city, in part by undoing what urban renewal planners accomplished in the years following *Berman*. While the redevelopment of Southeast, D.C., including the development around the stadium and Capital Quarter, is well under way, the efforts in the Southwest have been plagued with delays. Indeed, frustration over delays and inadequate collaboration, especially on the two Southwest projects, led the city to abolish both of the agencies charged with redevelopment earlier this year and to assume direct responsibility for promoting and supervising the projects.[26]

Milwaukee's Road to Nowhere

In the early 1950s, Milwaukee, Wisconsin—like other major cities—began construction of a comprehensive expressway system. In 1958, Milwaukee's Expressway Commission announced plans to add the Park East Freeway, one of several major arteries that were never completed, to the system. The plans called for the Park East to dissect much of central Milwaukee, connecting to another never-completed expressway that would have run along the shore of Lake Michigan. Property acquisition for the Park East began in 1965, and hundreds of houses and dozens of businesses were demolished to clear the right-of-way. In 1971, the first stretch of the Park East—a one-mile elevated segment extending off of Interstate 43—was opened to traffic, and a block-wide strip of land had been acquired and cleared to continue construction to the lakefront.

By this time, however, neighborhood and environmental activists combined forces to oppose further construction of the Park East and other Milwaukee expressways. In 1971, opponents succeeded in obtaining an injunction barring construction of the freeway through Juneau Park. While a subsequent Wisconsin Supreme Court opinion modified the injunction to permit construction to recommence, political opposition rendered that option unacceptable. In 1972, Mayor Henry Maier refused to appropriate the funds necessary to relocate utilities in the Park East corridor. "America is the only nation in the world to let her cities ride to bankruptcy on a freeway," he remarked at the time. "My city has discovered that the freeway is not free."[27]

For the next two decades, the Park East cast its shadow over central Milwaukee (figure 7.7). The corridor cleared for the never-completed portions also remained undeveloped, thanks to its continued state-law designation as a "transportation corridor." Outside of Milwaukee, the Park East Freeway was best known for its cameo appearance in the 1980 comedy *The Blues Brothers.* In the movie, which was set in Chicago, John Belushi and Dan Aykroyd, on "a mission from God" and seeking to evade the authorities, cause an Illinois state highway patrol car to drive off the end of the uncompleted road.

In 1972, when Mayor Maier finally halted construction of the Park East Freeway, John Norquist was a young lathe-operator-turned-community-organizer working under the tutelage of Ted Seaver, the activist who led the battle against the Park East and other Milwaukee freeway projects. Norquist's anti-freeway activity landed him a seat in the state assembly, the beginning of a political career that ended with a fifteen-year stint as mayor of Milwaukee.

Figure 7.7. Park East Freeway, Milwaukee, prior to demolition. Photo courtesy of the City of Milwaukee.

As a result, the man partially responsible for halting the Park East Freeway construction happened to be in charge of the city when the state lifted the "transportation corridor" designation in the mid-1990s, clearing the way for redevelopment in the never-completed path of the freeway. In the following years, the vacant corridor, known as the "East Pointe neighborhood" stood out as a redevelopment success story, quickly filling with $50 million worth of new apartments, condos, and retail stores (figure 7.8). The contrast between the vibrancy of the redeveloped area and the squalor surrounding the Park East infuriated Norquist. "Look at this!" he exclaimed in a 1999 interview. "They build this right through downtown and you can't see anything from here." Tellingly, Norquist reportedly asked his staff to read Robert Caro's epic biography of New York highway baron Robert Moses, *The Power Broker*. In it, Caro poignantly describes the decline of Brooklyn's Finn Town following construction of the Gowanus Parkway: "[T]he avenue was cast forever into darkness and gloom, and its bustle and life were forever gone. . . . Moses' steel and concrete, 'lifted into the air' above a neighborhood for the convenience of motorists driving through the neighborhood to get somewhere else, had destroyed the neighborhood."[28]

Norquist was a strong proponent of removing underutilized urban expressways, which he argued divided and drained vitality from the communities they dissected. Milwaukee was not the first city to consider this step. In 1989, the Loma Prieta earthquake severely damaged the elevated Embarcadero Freeway in San Francisco. Faced with the choice of either repairing or demolishing the never-completed expressway, San Francisco chose demolition. The mere announcement that the Embarcadero would be demolished caused nearby property values to skyrocket 300 percent. The city used the federal emergency funds to remove the structure and reconstruct the street beneath it as a seven-mile waterfront promenade. Hundreds of redevelopment projects have been attributed to the Embarcadero's demolition, including the reconstruction of the historic Ferry Building, a major hotel, and a redeveloped warehouse district of apartments, shops, and restaurants. Other cities have also tackled their freeways with a wrecking ball. While Boston's scandal- and problem-plagued "Big Dig" project is the best known and most ambitious demolition effort, smaller projects are under way in Portland, Oregon, Toronto, Ontario, New York City, and Niagara Falls, New York (which is, fittingly, tearing up a waterfront parkway named for Robert Moses).

In Milwaukee, the need to invest significant resources to rebuild several elevated freeways in the central city presented Norquist with his opportunity.

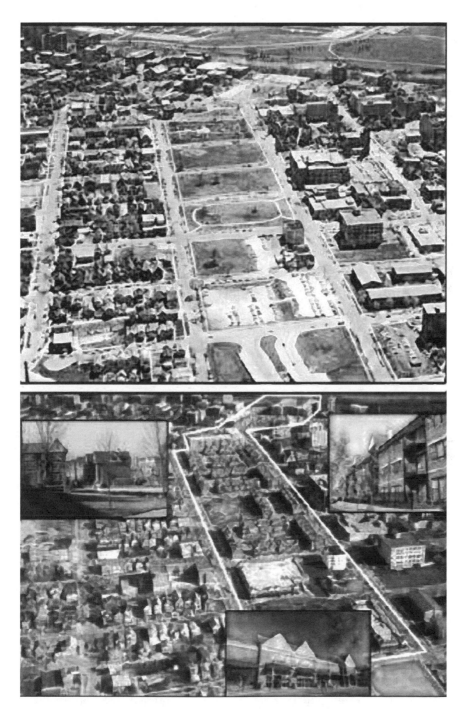

Figure 7.8. East Pointe neighborhood, Milwaukee, during and after "transportation corri-dor" designation. Photo courtesy of the City of Milwaukee.

When the Wisconsin Department of Transportation estimated in the mid-1990s that it would cost $80 million to make needed repairs to the Park East Freeway, Norquist announced that the road had "become so inefficient that it didn't make sense to re-build." His administration also enlisted a private firm to prepare a comprehensive plan for downtown Milwaukee. The firm's final report suggested that removing the highway "opened enormous potential for a waterfront plaza, new park, housing, commercial space, and extension of the existing grid system." The potential development benefits of freeway removal quickly captured the public imagination, and an overwhelming majority of downtown businesses and civic organizations rallied to support it. In May 1999, Norquist announced that he had reached an agreement with the governor that would allow him to spend some of the federal transportation funds earmarked for highway renovation on the removal of the Park East Freeway. Within a month, Norquist's proposal to remove the freeway cleared both the county board and the Milwaukee Common Council. Demolition began in 2002.[29]

By 2004, the elevated structure had been replaced by a six-lane grid-level boulevard, which connects to a reconstituted street grid. The result was the "creation" of twenty-eight traditional city blocks, opening twenty-four acres of downtown property for redevelopment. At the time the project was announced, Milwaukee officials boasted that it would spur at least $250 million in new investment. They had reason to be optimistic. The project announcement alone had immediate results, with a number of major developments— including a new Harley-Davidson Museum and the conversion of a nearby power plant by Time Warner—commencing just outside of the redevelopment area in anticipation of the freeway demolition. But development inside the Park East project area has lagged. Most of the cleared property remains vacant, with the first new construction commencing in late 2007. One recent study, commissioned for the Milwaukee Common Council, estimated that it might take as long as eighteen years for the vacant lots cleared by the highway demolition to fill with new buildings.[30]

Reordering Reconsidered

By the early 1970s, after two decades of aggressive reordering efforts, citizens and government officials alike began to exhibit what might be called "redevelopment fatigue." Large-scale redevelopment efforts screeched to a halt, and federal efforts became intensely focused on neighborhood-level improvement through programs such as Community Development Block Grants. High-rise public housing construction ceased at approximately the same time, and the first high-rise demolition, of St. Louis's notorious Pruitt-Igoe housing project, occurred in 1972. A quick survey of the urban landscape, however, suggests that local governments are taking steps—some more tentative than others—to reenter the redevelopment business. In addition to the three discussed above, the controversy over the redevelopment effort at issue in *Kelo v. City of New London* also brought to light a number of cases where local governments exercised, or threatened to exercise, the power of eminent domain to acquire private property for redevelopment purposes. And certainly HOPE VI projects represent efforts to redevelop publicly held property.

Modern-day redevelopment projects tend to pale in comparison to the grand ambitions of those of the urban renewal era. They also *look* radically different from their urban-renewal-era predecessors. Urban-renewal-era planners replaced dense mixed-use environments distributed along grid street patterns with single-use developments set at a distance from the surrounding communities. In each of the projects described above, a local government is seeking to fix past mistakes by re-creating neighborhoods that look like a nicer version of what their predecessors destroyed in the name of order construction. At the very least, the three projects described above, and others like them, suggest that many local officials now believe that past efforts to re-order the city were ill conceived. The fact that these reordering efforts reject the single-use model imposed in the urban renewal era in favor of "traditional" neighborhood design, however, does not necessarily suggest that local officials are abandoning the quest to construct the order of American cities. On the contrary, these projects illustrate that local government officials continue to view government-sponsored and -controlled development as a solution for cities. Indeed the control over project detail that the role of developer provides may well be what makes local officials comfortable with promoting mixed-use developments. If so, then the design of redevelopment projects does not necessarily signal that city officials acting as regulators, rather than developers, are coming to question the long-standing assumption that ordered land uses suppress disorder. On the contrary, experience, especially in Milwaukee, suggests that a desire to control the details of a mixed-use community may lead regulators to replace single-use zoning with an alternative—the "form-based" codes promoted by new urbanists—that poses different impediments to urban regeneration. Drawing in particular upon the Milwaukee experience, where officials have wholeheartedly embraced the new-urbanist model, the remaining pages of this chapter offer a few brief closing thoughts on the potential consequences of local officials' continued desire to maintain control over the order of urban neighborhoods.

As discussed above, the pace of the redevelopment in the Park East area has lagged. Even before the current recession, some estimates suggested that it may take nearly two decades to fill the empty lots. While explanations for the delay vary, a primary culprit appears to be government micromanagement of the development process. The city has partially underwritten the Park East project with tax-increment financing. "TIF," as it is commonly called, is a popular local government innovation that permits designated areas of a city to "recapture" the revenue increases associated with a redevelopment project. After the local government designates a redevelopment area as a "TIF district," any revenue associated with increases in property values is spent on improvements within the district's boundaries. Theoretically, the revenue increases are the "increment" resulting from the redevelopment effort. In Milwaukee, TIF was used initially for the public works improvements necessary for the project. Later, under pressure from developers, the city opted to use TIF funds to partially underwrite some private projects. Cost overruns for infrastructure improvements, which proved about five times more expensive than initial expectations, led the city to be very cautious in selecting projects eligible for TIF financing. Many private developers chafed at the delays associated with the financing approval process. And when a city-sponsored study cautioned against financing projects that would compete with unsubsidized redevelopment just outside the Park East area, one developer withdrew its request for TIF financing and announced that it was dropping much of the eighty-one thousand square feet of retail space that was to accompany a proposed Hyatt Place boutique hotel.[31]

Other developers complain that they devote inordinate time and resources to complying with the land-use regulations adopted for the Park East area. Under Norquist, who is currently serving as president of the Congress for the New Urbanism, the city adopted a mixed-use zoning designation for the Park East area, supplemented by a detailed new-urbanist design code. Park East thus provides a unique test case for the new urbanists' project, which, at its core, proposes to impose a very different kind of order—aesthetic rather than use-based—upon an urban environment. During his tenure as mayor, Norquist frequently was labeled a libertarian—and sometimes criticized for abandoning his liberal-progressive political roots. Certainly some of Norquist's positions reflected a distrust of government institutions; his determined support for Milwaukee's controversial school-voucher program, for example, rankled many of his traditional political allies. But neither the new urbanism nor the code adopted for the Park East area is a libertarian project. While new urbanists echo Jane Jacobs in their embrace of the urban aesthetic, their preferred method of achieving it represents a significant departure from her belief that cities best thrive when the government leaves them alone.[32]

The new urbanism, of course, arises as a response to, and a rejection of, the world created by order-construction regulations. Proponents of the new urbanism therefore understand that government-created order is the norm and that officials charged with land-use regulations generally assume that order-construction suppresses disorder. In this context, new urbanists do not advocate deregulation, as did Jacobs. Rather, they propose substituting traditional use-based zoning with a radically different form of land-use regulation, which they promise promotes careful planning *and* balances the need for city busyness with the concern about urban disorder. Specifically, new urbanists argue that cities should regulate property based upon *building form* not *building use*. For example, architect Andrés Duany's "SmartCode" proceeds upon the assumption that development naturally progresses from urban (most intense) to rural (least intense). The new urbanists call this progression the "transect" and urge cities to replace use-based zoning with the regulation of building forms appropriate to the various "transect zones" along the progression. Theoretically, the concept is relatively simple: Buildings appropriate for the city center should go in the city center (regardless of what they are used for); suburban buildings should look suburban, and so on.[33]

As the saying goes, however, the devil is in the details. And the new urbanists' alternative to zoning is detailed indeed. As a practical matter, the new urbanists favor replacing use-based zoning with a very meticulous and exhaustive aesthetic code. They have specific ideas about how buildings should look: Ugly, unwelcoming buildings, in their view, can be just as detrimental to community as sterile, single-use planning. The movement is dominated by architects, and new-urbanist coding consequently relies heavily on detailed architectural design standards. (Political resistance to scrapping traditional zoning usually guarantees that these standards tend to supplement, rather than supplant, traditional zoning tools when they are adopted.) The regulatory code for the Park East redevelopment district includes hundreds of pages of architectural renderings and photographs of "appropriate" building types. The area "master plan" observes that "the quality of experience in a downtown" is "critical" and dependent upon ground-level land uses that are open to the public. "To effectively contribute to the quality of experience," the document continues, "these uses need to be visible, accessible, and memorable. This involves careful consideration of windows, entries, signage, and many other design details. The full public realm involves both the inside and outside of buildings—effective connection of these two types of areas makes downtowns more valuable."[34]

In order to "help achieve this necessary relationship" and promote "visible, accessible, and memorable" design, Milwaukee also promulgated a "Development Code" for the Park East area. This code provides the following guidance for those wishing to develop in the area:

- Street level facades shall include visual features and design details that enrich the pedestrian experience. While visual interaction with all stories of the building is encouraged, visual interaction by means of clear, non-tinted windows (glazing) is required along the street frontage of a building.
- [T]he area behind the glazing must be Street Activating Uses. . . . Street Activating Uses are those open to the public, including shops, restaurants, lobbies, and other service activities that move goods and people in and out of the building. Street Activating Uses can also include areas that are not open to the public, yet still activate the street.
- Detailing of the base of the buildings should be used to enhance the human scale qualities of the building.
- When horizontal changes in materials are desired, different materials should generally meet only at a change of plane, particularly at an inside corner. This gives the material a sense of thickness and a perception of permanence and quality. Different materials should never meet at an outside corner as this reveals the thinness of the material.

These kinds of aesthetic guidelines promise to make some city projects—perhaps including infill efforts like Park East—look very nice. And many new urbanists believe that building aesthetics can help build social capital. For example, new urbanists favor relatively shallow setbacks, front porches on residences, and "Street Activating Uses" on the ground floors of commercial buildings not simply because these features look nice. New urbanists also argue that these architectural features generate the informal social mixing that Jacobs argued is critical to building healthy communities.[35]

Intuitively, I agree with the new urbanists' argument. Anecdotally, my husband and I added a front porch to our early twentieth-century home about five years ago. After we built the porch, we both noticed that we spent more time outside interacting with neighbors and other passersby on the sidewalk

in front of our home. Mandating "community friendly" architecture, however, is not cost free. On the contrary, adding compliance with complex architectural standards to the list of impediments to urban reinvestment is a risky
proposition. By seeking to dictate the details of what a busy neighborhood
should look like, new urbanists' proposals may backfire, further depressing
urban development hopes. In Milwaukee, there is evidence that the new-
urbanist-inspired "order" imposed by the Park East Development Code has
slowed the redevelopment process. In July 2007, for example, an anchor tenant for one of the area's largest projects backed away, citing delays in development and the need for the city to show greater flexibility in the regulatory
approval process.[36]

The risk of replacing or augmenting zoning rules with detailed aesthetic
regulations is particularly high in those neighborhoods that are most in need
of economic activity. Consider, for example, how a code like Milwaukee's
might affect development prospects in the communities where the bulk of
Chicago's HOPE VI projects are located. I visited the vacant Taylor Homes
site, and it is obvious why the Legends South plan incorporates retail establishments. Site clearance for the Taylor Homes created, in the words of the
Chicago Urban League at the time, a "wilderness" bereft of "virtually every
existing institution, every line of familiar and personal stability, and every
semblance of formal and informal organization." As a result, there is virtually
no retail in the community. I saw one business: It was a tombstone company
with a giant billboard advertising "Elmo's Tombstones, made while you wait.
Before you go, call Elmo."[37]

Some of Chicago's HOPE VI efforts, notably North Town Village on the
site of the partially demolished Cabrini-Green Homes, appear to be succeeding in the appointed task of stemming the disorder associated with notorious
"projects." But North Town Village is located at the edge of the prestigious
Lincoln Park neighborhood. It remains to be seen whether the HOPE VI
ingredients—intentional mixing of income groups, "neighborhood-scale" and
"community-friendly" design, and, in some projects, the mixing of residential
and commercial uses—can "save" a neighborhood lacking such geographic
advantages. New urbanists might argue that in communities that lack these
advantages—like the South Side neighborhoods in the shadows of the former
Robert Taylor Homes—attention to design is particularly appropriate because
designs that are "anticommunity" will undermine efforts to rebuild the social
capital of the community. But design standards undoubtedly also drive up the
price of the replacement units and may make them marginally less attractive

to individuals who might otherwise take a chance on a risky redevelopment succeeding.

Convincing these urban pioneers to invest in HOPE VI developments is critical, not just for the success of the individual developments but also for the overall stability of the neighborhoods where they are located. The Robert Taylor Homes undoubtedly contributed to the decline of the adjacent neighborhood, but their removal also has led to an influx of new, desperately poor residents into the surrounding neighborhoods. There is some evidence, mostly anecdotal, that public housing demolition acts as a disorder-dispersal device. A recent *Atlantic Monthly* article, for example, linked HOPE VI with an uptick in violent crime in previously secure neighborhoods. And Sudhir Venkatesh's ethnography of a South Side Chicago neighborhood that abutted the Taylor Homes chronicled how the demolition led to an influx of gang members in search of new turf. More generally, social scientists are debating the extent to which the dramatic decline in concentrated poverty (discussed in chapter 8) has dispersed violent crime as well. Social scientists agree, however, on the ills of poverty concentration, so it is difficult to argue that poverty dispersal is an unfortunate development. These potential costs will be mitigated, of course, if the CHA and developers succeed in attracting wealthier residents to risk investing and living in new developments like Legends South. The jury is still out on whether they will. In 2008, even before the extent of the subprime mortgage foreclosures became evident, the *Chicago Tribune* reported that only 30 percent of the city's HOPE VI replacement housing has been completed, nearly nine years into a ten-year program. The article reported that, in many developments, "the market-rate homes have proven to be an albatross" because developers are "struggling to sell high-priced homes amid a glut of new construction across the city."[38]

In 2003, Chicago substantially rewrote its zoning code for the first time since 1957. Perhaps concerned about the costs associated with moving toward a more detailed aesthetic code, or perhaps simply uncomfortable abandoning use segregation, the city declined to embrace new-urbanist regulatory principles comprehensively, although it did authorize more mixed-use zones than the previous code and also incorporated some relatively minor "character standards" for building facades. Tellingly, many HOPE VI sites were given a "planned development" designation, which essentially provides an opportunity for the city to control, through negotiations with developers, land-use patterns and building design. These designations also permit city officials to consider and control the individual elements of a mixed-use development—

including, in the HOPE VI context—the socioeconomic makeup of the would-be residents. In other words, they permit diversity but manage it.

It may be the case, as Susan Fainstein observed recently, that "diversity represents the new guiding principle for city planners." But the diversity is not, as Jacobs and early enterprise-zone proponents urged, an organic one. Just as a careful management style has overtaken the initial laissez-faire approach to the original enterprise-zone concept, controlled diversity is coming to dominate redevelopment efforts. Certainly, a case for land-use-diversity management can, and has, been made. A growing urban aesthetic may, for example, be one factor leading some to relocate to cities. As discussed in more detail in chapter 4, even suburbs are assuming a more "urban" flavor, at least when it comes to the design of commercial and retail projects. Even if the economic costs imposed by regulations like those in place in Milwaukee hinder development efforts in poor communities, perhaps the careful control of aesthetics of urban life is needed to attract suburbanites, who are used to more "orderly," less-organic development patterns. Furthermore, some kinds of land uses appear to be correlated with higher levels of disorder and crime, both of which undermine residential stability and limit cities' abilities to compete for residents with suburbs.[39]

Urban officials might also seek to use the planning law as a tool to maximize the likelihood that a diverse neighborhood will succeed. For example, Robert Putnam's recent troubling finding that diversity apparently undermines social capital by limiting both in-group and between-group interactions might lead urban officials to seek to use planning tools to maximize the likelihood that a diverse neighborhood will succeed by seeking to maintain greater class and race diversity than could be achieved organically. However, even within intentionally diverse communities, like HOPE VI projects, barriers to the interactions that build the social capital needed to overcome the economic and social isolation that plague many inner-city communities remain. And, as Bob Ellickson has argued, regulatory tools such as inclusionary zoning, which planners use to achieve and maintain class diversity, also tend to drive up development costs across the board. Thus, the experience in many communities that have undertaken diversity management in the past demonstrates that the fiscal costs of managing membership in a community fall most heavily on those who are excluded in the name of community preservation.[40]

It remains to be seen, in other words, whether the costs of "diversity management" strategies outweigh their benefits: Perhaps city officials will choose the wrong neighborhoods, or the wrong land uses, to manage—with poor neighborhoods deprived, through the vigorous enforcement of zoning rules, of the microenterprise endeavors that might foster a healthy, organic renewal. Moreover, the perverse fiscal incentives that drove past redevelopment mistakes remain largely unchecked. Importantly, when local officials act as developers, they frequently are not spending local funds. When the funding for a project comes from a higher level of government—for example, the federal government in the HOPE VI context, or a mix of state and federal funds in Milwaukee—local officials' incentives are skewed. They might, for example, be less reticent about imposing costly planning mandates than if they were on the hook for the entire bill associated with a failed redevelopment strategy. In an excellent case study of the notorious Poletown redevelopment project, which required Detroit to seize several thousand homes to make way for a new General Motors plant, William Fischel notes that "the voters and elected officials in Detroit had little financial interest in determining whether the Poletown project made economic sense." This was because the project was financed almost entirely by "nonfungible gifts"—in other words, the city was given a large amount of money to finance the GM Poletown plant, but nothing else—from the state and federal governments. The need to deter inefficient projects and to establish the right incentives for city officials to adopt efficient regulatory strategies, therefore, may weigh in favor of reform proposals that limit the ability of local officials to spend state and federal funds on redevelopment. Local government officials spending *local* money are constrained politically by the need to keep taxes low. Local officials also operate under a number of legal constraints that disfavor an aggressive redevelopment policy: Many state constitutions restrain local taxation; most limit local government's ability to borrow money—by capping total indebtedness, by requiring voter approval of new debt, or both. Were local governments forced to internalize the costs of their redevelopment projects, it is reasonable to assume that they would engage in careful consideration of the regulatory strategies most likely to lead to success.[41]

8

Letting Go?

A Case for Land-Use Incrementalism

When I began this book, I did not plan to end by making a case for incremental land-use reform. I embraced Jane Jacobs's ideas wholeheartedly and without reservation—the soundness of her judgment about land-use policies being as self-evident to me as the sharpness of her observations about city life. I did not like zoning, and I still do not like it. Rules that impose a regulatory straightjacket and that, in many cases, require cities to behave as suburbs strike me as wrongheaded and silly. But to think hard about cities is to confront their complexity and the complexity of proposals to change them. If a term like *disorder*, which drives so much of urban policy these days, proves contested and contextual, then surely the relationship between commercial land uses, disorder, and social capital cannot be the same in every city neighborhood. Moreover, the forms of our "cities" themselves vary dramatically: Chicago, Illinois, the nation's third-largest city, has as little in common with Houston, Texas (fourth), as San Jose, California (eleventh) has in common with Baltimore, Maryland (twelfth). What's more, many of the "urban" communities that have been the focus of this book were once "suburban" ones, absorbed into the central city by annexation, and there is no particular reason to believe that this evolutionary process is over.

The proposals made in the remaining pages of this book flow from a conviction that there are two significant reasons to shy away from Daniel Burnham's famous admonition to "make no small plans" for our cities. The first is a humility wrought of past land-use mistakes. Small plans, to borrow from Burnham again, may not "stir men's souls," but grand ones often fail, a reality captured beautifully in a 2006 *Washington Post* headline: "Southwest Waterfront Will Finally Get Over the '60s: Development Plans Would Shun Tall Towers, Dead-End Streets." This is a hard lesson for city officials, who now admit the error of past efforts to impose order on traditional neighborhoods but exhibit a willingness to abandon the order-construction enterprise only when it is replaced by an equally restrictive (or more so) system of development controls. Places like Legends South and the Park East redevelopment areas *look* much different than the Robert Taylor Homes and the "new Southwest" that followed *Berman v. Parker,* but they too represent "grand plans" of city officials eager to impose a different, better, model of urban development. I happen to agree that the model is both different and better—and enjoy the irony of the fact that the difference reflects an effort to reimpose the look and feel of the older, more-organic urban form that previous generations of planners destroyed. The question remains, however, whether these "grand plans" can reverse the negative consequences of other, grander, ones that failed.[1]

Second, planning policy is, and in most cases will remain, a local political matter. There are, of course, examples of and proposals for removing or limiting the discretion of local governments over land-use policies. Many of these proposals flow from the belief that the costs of our fragmented system of local government authority—suburban sprawl, urban disinvestment, a lack of coordinated planning of infrastructure investments, exclusionary zoning, and so on—outweigh the benefits of the competition generated by metropolitan fragmentation predicted by Charles Tiebout. These proposals, by and large, focus on changing the identity of the regulator; generally speaking, they seek to vest land-use regulatory authority in a regional- or metropolitan-level entity rather than to change the order constructed by the existing land-use regulations, although some regional government proposals seek to achieve denser, more "urban" patterns of development by channeling new development into built-up areas. Elsewhere, I have expressed concerns about the distributional- and transitional-fairness consequences of these regional-growth-control proposals, but the debate over them is far too complex to restate briefly in these pages.[2]

In the order-maintenance context, civil libertarians seek to limit local authority in another way—namely, through relatively strict constitutional limits on police discretion. Earlier in this book, I made the case that local officials resort to land-use strategies to control disorder because of a judicial skepticism of order-maintenance policing. If I am correct about their motives, then searching judicial scrutiny of land-use policies undoubtedly would curb enthusiasm for using the tools of property regulation to curb disorder. For example, the Sixth Circuit's decision invalidating Cincinnati's exclusion zone makes such policies less attractive to city officials. Despite my skepticism of the animating assumption behind most American land-use policies—that government intervention to order urban land uses is necessary—I am hesitant to advocate substantive judicial review of local land-use policies. Since the Supreme Court upheld zoning in the *Euclid* decision, courts (especially federal courts) generally have refused to second-guess local governments' predictive judgments about the proper ordering of land uses. A searching review of local land-use policies would alter our constitutional order far more than relaxing constitutional restrictions on police discretion. Moreover, and importantly, judicial scrutiny of land-use policies would further limit the options available to local officials struggling to control urban disorder. These officials operate with one hand tied behind the back by constitutional limits on order-maintenance policing. It is arguably unwise to encourage judges to tie the other hand by carefully reviewing land-use policies as well. Robert Ellickson made this argument with respect to disorder-relocation strategies. Despite his view that police are likely to be better disorder managers than land-use planners, Ellickson suggests that "[h]aving pushed cities in the direction of formal public-space zoning, judges should not strictly scrutinize the policies of municipalities that have accepted this invitation."[3]

Since the power to regulate land uses will, in most instances, remain vested in local political hands, suggestions for reform must take account of the political economy of land-use regulations. Thus, it is important to make explicit an impediment to reform that previous discussions of redevelopment policies tacitly acknowledged—namely, local government resistance to relinquishing or diminishing their authority over land-use regulation. This resistance stands as a primary obstacle to regional-government and growth-management proposals. As regional-government proponents have observed, in our system of fragmented local authority, each locality jealously guards its authority to regulate land uses.

And for good reasons: Given the fact that local governments are the ugly stepchildren of the American political system, with no inherent power and subject to usurpation at the will of their state legislatures, it is understandable that local officials would fight to preserve the arguably most significant power entrusted to them by state law. Furthermore, as Tiebout influentially predicted, decentralized local governments compete for residents by providing an attractive package of services at the lowest possible cost. Some economists have noted that this dynamic tends to produce suburban sprawl, as suburban regulations exhibit a pattern of invitation and exclusion, pushing new residential development farther away from the city center. And while urban governments have not historically fared well in the competition for "consumer voters," city officials continue to see land-use policy as a tool for attracting and retaining residents and businesses. They therefore will be predictably wary of proposals that radically change or diminish their regulatory authority over land uses.[4]

Not only does local officials' significant interest in maintaining their broad authority over land-use regulation make them resistant to reform, but the interest groups exerting influence on the shaping and reshaping of urban land-use policies have little incentive to pressure city governments to abandon or dramatically alter order-construction regulations. As Neil Komesar has helpfully elucidated, the land-use planning literature generally assumes a "two-force" political model, in which local democratic actors are prone to both minoritarian and majoritarian biases, giving cause for both a "fear of the few" and a "fear of the many." Minoritarian theories of land-use planning generally focus on the influence of private developers. These "developer influence models" posit that private developers of both residential and commercial projects—including the developers of the reordering efforts described in the previous chapter—are a dominant force shaping the outcome of the planning process, rather than passive followers of the rules that emerge from it. The dominant majoritarian theory—captured in William Fischel's "homevoter hypothesis"—asserts that homeowners frequently exert more influence than developers in local planning processes. Conventional wisdom holds, however, that the "influence model best fits central cities, and the majoritarian model, elite suburbs," as Ellickson points out.[5]

Developers' incentives to support dramatic changes to existing land-use regulations are limited by their ability to work within, and influence, the local regulatory process. Contemporary regulatory tools, including planned-unit-development regulations and, in many states, development agreements, offer the opportunity for developers to negotiate on a case-by-case basis the regulatory concessions necessary for a given project. And, although certainly not a universal phenomenon, urban governments' willingness to go so far as to condemn private property and *give it away* to a private developer promising a redevelopment miracle suggests that regulatory officials' eagerness for "economic development" generates an openness to accede to many developer demands. Consider, for example, HOPE VI in Chicago. Not only does the program give developers great latitude in selecting new tenants, but most of the city's projects are zoned "planned development," specifically to enable negotiations over the governing land-use regulations. To the extent that the existing regulatory regime works *for* developers, they have little incentive to change it. This is especially true if, as the experience with Milwaukee's Park East project suggests, the regulatory alternative might prove more burdensome and less flexible than the existing regulations.

Residents (and, especially, homeowners) also exert influence over urban land-use policies, of course, even if not the degree of influence they enjoy in the suburbs. While "exclusionary zoning" is usually considered a suburban phenomenon, city residents do not necessarily favor more city development generally or dense, mixed-land-use environments in particular. On the contrary, city residents regularly support policies that have the effect of *minimizing* the mixing of urban land uses and *decreasing* city densities. In his recent history of sprawl, Robert Bruegmann offers as examples of urban exclusionary zoning the restrictions on residential "teardowns" in older, inner-ring suburbs (in the name of community preservation) and the "downzoning" of city neighborhoods to reduce their population. But other examples abound. City residents oppose urban infill development, citing concerns about "randomly filling up the vacant lots around the city," "vertical sprawl," and the loss of urban "green space." The attorney general of New York went so far as to file a lawsuit seeking to freeze construction of nearly three thousand new apartments that threatened community gardens. Elsewhere, environmentalists express health concerns about new infill developments featuring affordable, multifamily housing units and complain that subsidies for urban "brownfield" redevelopment are "corporate welfare." As Michael Schill succinctly explains, "many inner-city residents would be happy not to have new neighbors, new barriers to their views, and new competitors for parking spaces. . . . [Their] opposition to new development manifests itself every day in opposition to rezoning, drawn-out land use and environmental approval procedures, and endless lawsuits, meritorious and frivolous." In poorer communities, concerns about gentrification and attendant displacement also contribute to residents' suspicion of land-use reforms. And, at least with respect to proposals for significant *deregulation,* residents weary of disorder may greet with significant suspicion the claim that the familiar order constructed by zoning laws is unrelated, or even harmful, to disorder-suppression efforts.[6]

Against this backdrop, it is predictable that many efforts to reform land-use policies (like the zoning reforms in Spanish Harlem discussed in chapter 4) will be incremental in nature. Indeed, these public-choice factors go a long way toward explaining why the deregulatory aspects of the enterprise-zone idea have disappeared despite the widespread adoption of other elements of the proposal. Just as local governments appear willing to embrace mixed-use developments that can be carefully controlled during the development process, they are similarly willing to embrace a system of development incentives that can be carefully managed by city planners.

Incremental Policies That Matter

Reforming Home-Occupation Restrictions

Although a primary aim of zoning laws is to purge residential zones of incompatible commercial activities, local officials have long had to contend with the fact that many people work from home. Since the first zoning laws were enacted at a time when home occupations remained quite prevalent, most early codes did not prohibit working from home altogether, but rather permitted either "accessory uses" of residential property, "customary" home occupations, or both. Many modern codes still contain these types of provisions. Perhaps in an effort to reduce the uncertainty caused by these vague restrictions, other municipalities have enacted zoning restrictions that more specifically address home-based businesses. Some cities simply prohibit all home occupations, either in all residential zones or at least in areas zoned for single-family residences. Zoning codes in jurisdictions that do not prohibit all home occupations often list permitted occupations, prohibited occupations, or both. Many allow "professionals" to ply their trades in residential areas, at least if the home office is not the primary one, but, in keeping with the idea that "commerce" does not belong in the home, prohibit nonprofessionals from doing so.

Virtually all cities that permit some home-based enterprises, however, restrict their size and scope. For example, zoning codes commonly restrict the physical configuration of a home business by placing limitations on the space that a resident may devote to a home business—usually to 25 percent of the floor space or less; requiring that the home business be conducted solely within the confines of the home and not in any exterior structure, including attached garages; and prohibiting a resident from physically altering her home to accommodate the business. Almost all codes also strictly limit who can work in a home business. Most require the proprietor of the business to reside in the dwelling and limit her ability to hire employees that do not also reside there. Zoning codes further regulate the internal practices of home businesses by precluding client or customer visits and/or by prohibiting all commercial transactions in the home. Many codes also make it illegal for a home business to manufacture a product, to maintain any inventory on the premises, or to use any "equipment" that is not customarily used for household purposes. Finally, proprietors are often precluded from advertising their business through product displays and/or signs visible from the street.

While many of these restrictions are on a collision course with the technological revolution, they are particularly problematic for individuals lacking formal education and job skills. Despite the promising decline in concentrated poverty, and the apparently qualitative improvement of many of our poorest urban communities, underemployment remains a persistent problem of our urban poor. In 1996, Congress eliminated the sixty-year-old federal welfare entitlement and replaced it with a new program, Temporary Assistance for Needy Families, which requires all recipients to begin working within two years and bars recipients from receiving benefits for more than a total of five years, although certain recipients qualify for either exceptions and exemptions from the limit and/or for state welfare programs. While early results of the welfare reform effort have exceeded expectations, many individuals struggle to make the transition from welfare to work. It remains unclear how the current economic downturn will affect individuals who only recently exited welfare rolls and may be barred forever from returning. The low-skilled individuals who face welfare time limits and work requirements are among the most vulnerable in the modern economy. Not only are they likely to lose under the "last-hired/first-fired" principle, but over the past forty years, the "blue collar" jobs that traditionally provided high wages for workers lacking formal education and training increasingly have been supplanted by jobs in service-oriented industries, where employers tend to require specialized skills and higher levels of education. Indeed, the federal economic-stimulus package enacted in early 2009 sought to blunt the effects of the welfare measures enacted in 1996, leading critics to complain that Congress was "secretly ending welfare reform."[7]

Home businesses might offer a partial buffer against these stark economic realities, leading some state legislatures to consider the option of increasing opportunities to work at home as an economic development tool. The fact that welfare recipients lack the skills demanded by large, service-oriented employers does not necessarily mean that they lack marketable skills altogether. The success of "microenterprise" programs, which provide small loans that enable low-income individuals to become entrepreneurs, demonstrates that many welfare recipients have skills that could help them achieve self-sufficiency without depending upon an employer. Consider two examples—first, the dire need of the single mothers, who make up the bulk of welfare recipients, for quality, loving childcare. Obviously, many thousands of welfare recipients have the skills to provide this important service; women have long earned extra money by caring for a few children in their homes. Second, the "Muffin Lady": Linda Fisher, a single mother from Westminster, Maryland, drew national attention a few years ago when she was fined for selling fresh-baked muffins door-to-door in an effort to support herself and her son. Fisher learned to her surprise that her business was illegal, but she was ultimately able to return to baking after the local volunteer fire department made its oven available to her.[8]

The success of women like Linda Fisher hinges on their having a place to work. Unfortunately for many of the low-skilled individuals struggling to exit welfare rolls, that place is home or nowhere. The Muffin Lady was lucky, but the local fire department can hardly rescue all low-income mothers in need. For many, the inability to work at home dashes all hopes of becoming an entrepreneur. Leasing commercial space costs money—a significant sum of money—and most recent welfare recipients lack resources or credit. In contrast, however, the vast majority of home-based businesses require less than five thousand dollars in startup capital, and most entrepreneurs, especially women and minorities, do not rely upon bank loans to get these businesses off the ground. Furthermore, working from home enables former welfare recipients to balance work and family responsibilities, a prospect that, if daunting to any parent, can be overwhelming for a young mother struggling to achieve economic self-sufficiency.

It is not surprising, therefore, that a majority of the loans funded by microenterprise programs are small home-based businesses. Nor is it surprising that many of these businesses operate in the underground economy. Zoning codes are skewed in favor of high-end white-collar occupations, limiting the privilege of working at home to "professionals" such as doctors, lawyers, and accountants. This is despite the fact that a majority of women- and minority-owned home-based businesses produce goods and services in industries that are likely to be considered "commercial" rather than "professional." Consider, for example, how home-occupation restrictions might effect the typical resident of Englewood, the poor Chicago community discussed in chapter 4. Most of Englewood is zoned "RS-3" or "RT-4," both general residential districts allowing a mix of single- and multifamily dwellings; churches, convents, libraries, day-care centers, and community homes are also permitted. Home occupations are permitted in residential zones, but several occupations that low-skilled individuals might find attractive, such as automobile repair, cosmetology, catering, contracting, landscaping work, and light "piecemeal" manufacturing work, are expressly prohibited. And further restrictions prohibit residents from hiring employees, altering their homes in any way to accommodate their businesses, "display[ing] or creat[ing] any external evidence of the operation of the home occupation," or serving more than ten patrons per day.[9]

Disorder-weary residents might be wary of welcoming too many of these activities—especially those that might be noisy and dirty (for example, auto repair). Yet, there is a case to be made that home-based businesses also promise to bolster efforts to improve poor urban neighborhoods, for at least two related reasons. First, regulatory reforms that release the entrepreneurial energies of residents in poor neighborhoods are, as previously discussed, one way to mitigate the negative social-influence effects of chronic underemployment. Reforming home-based-business restrictions promises to provide economic opportunities for individuals who are unable to afford commercial space. And, because child-care services are among the most popular home-based businesses, they also should enable more women to work outside of the home. Second, recall the concern (discussed in chapter 3) that commercial land uses may reduce collective efficacy by making it more difficult for residents to discern who "belongs" in a community. While home-based businesses may increase the number of "strangers" in a residential community, their proprietors have a distinct advantage over many other business owners: Home-based-business owners *live* and *work* in the communities that they serve. Not only does this insider status lend itself to effective informal monitoring, but home-based entrepreneurs have dual incentives (as residents and as business owners) to ensure neighborhood health. Furthermore, it is important to remember that some evidence suggests that commercial enterprises are *beneficial* (in terms of disorder- and crime-reduction) in poor neighborhoods, even if they are harmful (in these terms) in wealthier ones. Finally, it is likely that many aspiring entrepreneurs in inner-city communities view working from home as a substitute for, or supplement to, working in public spaces. If so, their neighbors might well prefer home-based entrepreneurship to street-based entrepreneurship, since commercial activities compete with other uses of public spaces.

Nonconforming-Use Regulations

Many city neighborhoods predate zoning regulation. The first zoning codes were crafted to map onto preexisting land-use patterns—which by the early twentieth century had assumed use-segregated patterns. Still, early zoners were forced to account for land uses that did not "fit" within the pattern desired; they believed that such uses could not be outlawed outright without running afoul of constitutional protection of property rights. The solution was to "grandfather" in these "nonconforming uses." The first generations of zoning regulators assumed that nonconforming uses would disappear over time, and they encouraged them to do so by forcing them to operate under regulatory restrictions designed to make life difficult. For example, in many cities, nonconforming uses may be repaired but not altered or enlarged, and a temporary abandonment of the use results in the loss of the right to operate. Furthermore, many zoning codes have since been amended to incorporate "amortization" provisions to gradually eliminate nonconforming uses altogether.

While the goal of these regulations is to impose uniformity (and thus to restore order), these restrictions may prove counterproductive. Since they tend to discourage upkeep and lead to the physical decline of buildings, the result of these regulations may be particularly perverse in the poorest neighborhoods. Not only are these communities perhaps most in need of commercial vitality, but they are also plagued by the myriad negative effects of vacant and abandoned buildings—the single biggest predictor of disorder, according to the evidence discussed in chapter 3. And, as one commentator has noted, while "it was thought that the existence of nonconformities would lead to lowered property values, affect the area's desirability, and result in physical deterioration. . . . what has more often been the case is that traditional regulation has fostered vacancy, with buildings falling into disrepair due to their loss of marketability." Making life easier for nonconforming uses—by permitting reasonable alterations and expansions and changes of ownership and use, and by resisting the temptation to amortize them out of business—would remove one regulatory obstacle to urban neighborhood health.[10]

Cities should also consider how other property regulations may contribute to the physical decline of urban neighborhoods. For example, building codes may make the rehabilitation of older buildings prohibitively expensive, a reality that has led some states to adopt rehabilitation-specific codes. Similarly, as the discussion of land-use reforms in East Harlem highlights, zoning laws frequently require commercial enterprises to provide large amounts of off-street parking as a condition for rehabilitating a building or changing its use. These requirements drive up the cost of operating a business in the very communities that most need economic energy; they also prevent the development of an attractive urban streetscape and require deep setbacks that impede informal monitoring of streets and sidewalks. And they frequently impose these costs unnecessarily. After all, in many of our poorest neighborhoods, open space, for parking or otherwise, is quite abundant.[11]

Beyond Incrementalism, Beyond Land Use

The discussion thus far in this chapter has proceeded from the public-choice realities of local land-use regulation. Reforms to home-occupation restrictions, nonconforming-use regulations, off-street parking requirements, and so on are promising for a number of related reasons: First, these reforms would reduce the cost of operating a business in many communities where access to capital is limited, at best. Second, they offer the opportunity to experiment with a greater mixing of uses than zoning regulations currently allow in many urban neighborhoods. And because the commercial incursions into residential neighborhoods would be minimal—and largely driven by those who have a preexisting stake in neighborhood life—they minimize the threat of increased disorder. Third, the incremental nature of the reforms reduces the public-choice impediments to their implementation. Although experience suggests that even incremental proposals for reform can be significantly complicated by neighborhood political forces, they have at least a shot at making it through the local political process. On the other hand, because these reforms are by design incremental, they are unlikely to change significantly either the economic life or land-use patterns of many city neighborhoods. For example, many individuals who would welcome the opportunity to work from their homes *legally* are probably already doing so *illegally*. While legality promises many benefits for both the entrepreneurs and the communities where they work, it is difficult to predict the extent to which it will encourage *new* entrepreneurs to enter the marketplace, or existing entrepreneurs to expand. Second, the time that has elapsed since zoning laws were enacted has dramatically decreased the number of nonconforming uses, a reality that is likely to minimize the impact of reforming nonconforming-use regulations as well.

The remainder of this chapter outlines a few nonincremental policies that also offer city officials and community leaders the opportunity to overcome or minimize some of the public-choice impediments to land-use reform.

Mixed-Use Zoning without the Strings

The new urbanists' influence is reflected not simply in the design of contemporary redevelopment projects but also in the growing number of cities that have designated "mixed-use" zones, where certain commercial uses are permitted to mingle, as of right, with residential ones. It is possible that a new regulatory equilibrium may develop favoring mixed-use zoning, especially in urban centers. Mixed-use zoning would, at least theoretically, reduce the kinds of regulatory barriers to economic activity discussed previously. Mixed-use zoning also eliminates the need for cumbersome and expensive case-by-case consideration of variances, special exceptions, and requests to "spot zone" small parcels to authorize commercial uses—all regulatory burdens significant enough to prompt some cities to establish "one-stop permit shops," and regulatory ombudsmen to assist frustrated applicants. Mixed-use zoning would also enable property owners to respond more seamlessly to the evolutionary changes in neighborhood character that are a natural part of the economic life cycle of all urbanized areas. And, importantly, mixed-use zoning would enable cities to be cities and to thereby capitalize on what is likely to be their comparative advantage over their suburban competitors.

As the previous chapter's discussion highlights, however, city officials are most comfortable moving away from the order-construction ideal when they are able to carefully control the mixed-use environment that will replace it. Milwaukee's Park East project, in particular, illustrates city officials' impulse to replace one version of legislated order, based upon land use, with another arguably more-complicated one, based upon aesthetics. The control offered by the new urbanists' alternative to use-based zoning may give regulators worried about the effects of abandoning order-construction regulations comfort. Even cities eschewing comprehensive new-urbanist-inspired codes may prefer to make exceptions to order-construction regulations in the planned-unit development process, which also enables negotiations between the government and regulator and consideration of individual elements of a development on a case-by-case basis. Yet case-by-case consideration of individual elements of a development project takes time and requires the repeated intervention of paid experts—lawyers, architects, and so on—which can drive up development costs dramatically. Perhaps for this reason, the enterprise-zone proposals in Great Britain, which generally requires individualized consideration of all land-use changes, evolved toward a zoning model that permits at least some kinds of development as-of-right.

The new urbanists promote mixed-use communities on aesthetic and communitarian grounds, and these factors—especially, in my view, the aesthetics—may prove critical to attracting and retaining middle-class residents. The aesthetics of new urbanism can offer a distinctly urban "product" for would-be residents deciding between urban and suburban life (although some of the most successful new-urbanist developments are suburban ones, and continued suburban successes ultimately may threaten to deprive cities of this comparative advantage). Still, while mixed-use neighborhoods may enable middle-class city neighborhoods to compete with suburban ones, the primary benefits of mixing land uses in poor neighborhoods and struggling urban centers are likely to flow from increased levels of economic activity. If so, the fiscal burdens imposed by new-urbanist-inspired regulatory codes—and even the negotiated development model characterizing many large-scale projects—may undermine the benefits of mixed-use zoning in struggling communities.[12]

Land-Use Devolution

Questions of "subsidiarity"—that is, "the principle that a central authority should have a subsidiary function, performing only those tasks which cannot be performed effectively at a more immediate or local level"—have come to dominate contemporary debates about land use and local government law. Most of these debates focus intensely on whether some or all authority to regulate land use should be removed to a higher-level governmental entity—a regional-, metropolitan-, or state-level institution. Proponents of these proposals argue, in short, that local governments in fact cannot effectively regulate land uses because they act parochially, demonstrating an inability or unwillingness to take into account the extra-jurisdictional effects of their actions. The thinking about the allocation of local government power *within* cities, however, increasingly runs in the opposite direction. As Richard Briffault has observed, recent decades have seen a rise in "sublocal" government innovations—business improvement districts, tax-increment financing districts, enterprise zones, special zoning districts—all of which are predicated on the assumption that some local government functions are best performed at the neighborhood level. This trend in local government law toward the devolution of authority to "sublocal" institutions presents interesting opportunities to accomplish the important goal, identified in this book, of rethinking the order-construction/disorder-suppression equation.[13]

Sublocal decisions about land-use policies may be particularly appropriate in light of the fact that large cities tend to be made up of numerous distinctive urban enclaves. It is reasonable to assume that the residents' regulatory "tastes" vary from neighborhood to neighborhood and that this diversity offers neighborhoods, like cities, an opportunity to compete with one another for residents. In fact, several scholars have used neighborhood distinctiveness to advocate for devolving certain decisions about land-use regulation to neighborhood institutions similar to the now-popular "business improvement districts." While some scholars have applauded (and others lamented) the extent of neighborhood-level influence on existing land-use regulations, others, including Robert Ellickson, George Liebmann, and Robert Nelson, have made the case for formalizing this influence by permitting neighborhood-level or block-level community institutions to either regulate or deregulate land uses. As Ellickson argues, these reforms would effectively retrofit poor urban neighborhoods to enable land-use controls to be exercised by the equivalent of the residential community associations prevalent in many wealthy, planned suburban communities.[14]

These proposals are not uncontroversial—many scholars lament the rise of residential community associations and have no enthusiasm for expanding their reach to urban communities. Critics argue that sublocal institutions like business improvement districts represent, in Robert Reich's words, the "secession of the successful." That is, they enable wealthier communities to improve in ways that may negatively affect their poorer neighbors. Generally speaking, I believe that the proponents of devolution have the better of the argument. Skeptics are correct to urge vigilance that poor communities are not systematically neglected in the distribution of city services and infrastructure improvements as wealthier ones begin to provide their own. It is important to remember, however, that business improvement districts arose as a mechanism to revive moribund urban centers—and flowed from a conviction that city governments were failing to provide satisfactory services *anywhere* in the city. Moreover, Ellickson's proposal for "Block Level Improvement Districts" is informed by a desire to improve poor residential communities, not wealthy ones. At the very least, the interest of equity would seem to be served by empowering these communities to take the same steps to improve themselves that business improvement districts offer commercial districts.

Leaving to one side this important debate, it remains the case that the devolution of land-use authority presents complicated institutional design problems. In planned residential communities, including suburban subdivisions and urban condominiums, residents voluntarily submit to covenants establishing the ground rules of community life. Any proposal to retrofit older neighborhoods ultimately necessitates a mandatory, rather than voluntary, governance structure. Moreover, most sublocal government structures privilege property ownership. That is, property owners receive the lion's share of political authority; residents who do not own property are substantially disenfranchised. These voting procedures have survived Equal Protection "one-person-one-vote" challenges primarily because most sublocal structures are quasi-private entities that lack formal regulatory authority. Any proposal to vest them with regulatory authority would most certainly raise serious constitutional concerns.[15]

Finally, and perhaps most importantly for purposes of this discussion, the devolution of regulatory authority to the block or neighborhood level would not necessarily lead to any systematic rethinking of the order-construction ideal. Critics and fans of sublocal governments, especially business improvement districts, both observe that they tend to act more like business entities and less like governments—although the critics and fans differ on whether this is cause for celebration or concern. As previous discussion has demonstrated, however, city officials themselves demonstrate a willingness to abandon the order-construction ideal when acting as developers rather than regulators. It is possible, if not probable, that a *neighborhood-as-business* model would generate the same demands for controlled diversity as the *city-as-business* model apparently does. The resulting regulatory regime might still be preferable to the current one. After all, neighbors may well know better than city regulators what kinds of land-use patterns will foster social capital and healthy community life. But the reforms might result in a regulatory model that replicates the negotiations characterizing the city-as-developer model. If so, the economic costs of the sublocal regulations would probably exceed the no-strings mixed-use zoning proposal outlined above.

Land-Use Reform as a
Community-Policing Subject

Short of creating new neighborhood institutions with legislative authority over land use, another possibility is to broaden the agenda of the community-policing discussions that are central to formulating order-maintenance policies in most cities. These discussions could provide a forum within which community members consider how land-use regulations shape the order of urban neighborhoods. Even if neighbors sought regulatory reforms, implementing the results of such discussions would require local legislative action. But, hopefully, if community discussions generated a formal land-use-reform proposal, city officials would endeavor to overcome the significant public-choice impediments to changing the order-construction regime, as they did in response to the East Harlem proposal. Furthermore, the results of neighborhood-by-neighborhood examinations of the order-construction/disorder-suppression equation might serve to educate legislators about the need for urban land-use reforms in diverse urban neighborhoods.

Community-policing programs encourage local residents to work with police to identify and target disorders that impede community renewal. Community policing is not perfect—indeed, even its strongest proponents admit that in some cases it "has come to mean all things to all people." Ideally, however, community policing efforts begin with discussions asking community members to identify problems that traditional law-enforcement strategies may overlook or discount. And one benefit of this model is that, theoretically, everything is on the table, including priorities that traditionally were not classified as "law-enforcement" problems. Community policing practices also may generate social capital independent of strategies that it produces by bringing together diverse, and sometimes antagonistic, elements of a community and asking them to take a collaborative role in addressing the neighborhood's problems.[16]

Not surprisingly, in light of the evidence linking property disorder and crime (discussed above), community policing efforts sometimes have led to the increased use of disorder-suppression regulations. For example, when Baltimore, Maryland, instituted a formal community-policing program a decade ago, residents of the struggling Boyd Booth neighborhood immediately identified property decay and abandonment as a priority. As a result of discussions with Boyd Booth residents, state and local officials provided funds for boarding up vacant housing, erecting fences, improving lighting, and making cosmetic improvements in the neighborhood. A local public-interest group helped residents pursue public-nuisance actions against drug houses and take legal actions against negligent landlords. And the neighborhood association established a summer jobs program that focused on cleaning public spaces. After these reforms, crime decreased dramatically in the community and residents testified that they no longer feared leaving their homes.

Thanks to the ascendancy of community-policing practices, these citizen-government discussions now are being carried out in hundreds of poor neighborhoods throughout the country. And there is no reason why disorder suppression should be the only property-regulation subject on the table. Just as Boyd Booth residents prioritized property abandonment, residents should be encouraged— as part of broader discussions about order-maintenance priorities—to consider the ways in which order-construction regulations shape their neighborhoods, for good and ill. This is precisely what happened in East Harlem. While the effort there was not formally part of a "community-policing" program, the land-use reforms there grew out of broader discussions about various priorities, and residents' own beliefs that some zoning regulations drained the area of needed vitality. As a result, community leaders identified order-construction regulations that stood in the way of renewal and proposed reforms to city regulators who embraced them.[17]

Including the subject of land-use reform in community-policing discussions could empower residents to critically examine how order-construction and disorder-suppression regulations shape the order of their neighborhoods. What types of reforms might this process produce? Neighborhood distinctiveness would probably yield results that vary dramatically from neighborhood to neighborhood. For example, by virtue of the community's location on Manhattan Island, the densest urban center in the United States, the preexisting regulatory scheme in East Harlem probably allowed more mixing of commercial and residential uses than most zoning codes permit. (For example, virtually all of the north–south streets, and a handful of east–west streets, are designated commercial "overlay" zones.) East Harlem's land-use needs are therefore quite different from less-dense urban communities, such as Englewood, where commercial activities tend to be limited to major thoroughfares set several blocks apart. And Englewood's land-use patterns—a prezoning community in a major midwestern city—stand in almost as sharp contrast to neighborhoods in a sprawling western metropolis like Phoenix. Still, the East Harlem experience suggests the types of regulations that inner-city residents might view as problematic. As noted above, residents there did not opt for radical deregulation; rather, they advocated a relatively narrow set of reforms—a new commercial overlay zone, the reduction of off-street-parking requirements for businesses in commercial overlays generally, and shallower setbacks in residential zones. The supporting documents submitted to the city indict these regulations for standing in the way of healthier, more orderly, community life.

Other communities might identify similarly counterproductive regulations. In a community like Chicago's Englewood neighborhood, residents might worry that the very types of commercial establishments—restaurants, bars, food stores, and so on—that Jacobs and others argue serve as "informal meeting places" and foster healthy community life are prohibited, except along major thoroughfares, spaced approximately eight blocks apart. To the extent that such establishments once existed in Englewood's residential districts as nonconforming uses, many have since been eliminated by amortization rules. Englewood residents might also take exception with the home-occupation regulations described above. Elsewhere, perhaps in a neighborhood with large numbers of immigrants, residents might seek regulatory reforms permitting more street vending.

As discussed above, there are no guarantees that devolving the regulatory authority over land uses, either through new sublocal government institutions or through community-policing discussions, would lead to meaningful regulatory reforms. For example, some of the home occupations attractive to residents with limited skills can disrupt neighborhood life. Venkatesh, for example, describes how "hustlers" who fix cars in alleys pose a safety hazard for small children because they frequently fail to dispose of oil and sharp metal parts. Many neighbors, especially in poor, disorder-ravaged communities, might resist the suggestion that more economic activity would generate social as well as economic capital. And while these neighbors might be wrong, of course, their strong sentiment on the matter—as residents of the communities that struggle with low levels of both—is entitled to some measure of deference. In fact, the dire need for economic activity in many urban neighborhoods, coupled with residents' understandable wariness about sanctioning activities that might generate disorder, may weigh in favor of allowing neighbors to monitor economic activities following approval. Such monitoring might be achieved either by a system of revocable permits, such as the "special-exception" and "conditional-use" permits already utilized for many land uses under current zoning rules, or (more radically) by nuisance-like fines, as suggested by Robert Ellickson in his classic 1973 article, "Alternatives to Zoning: Covenants, Nuisance Rules, and Fines as Land Use Controls." Residents' ability to monitor their neighbors who are engaged in commerce might overcome their natural apprehension about authorizing potentially "noisy" economic activities.[18]

Deregulating Vacant and
Abandoned Buildings

In a recent article, Stephen Clowney set forth another proposal to reverse the troubling economic decline of many inner-city communities, which he calls the Vacant and Abandoned Land Transfer program, or VALT. Clowney suggests that local governments might eliminate land-use restrictions on vacant and abandoned buildings and then transfer titles to these businesses to inner-city entrepreneurs. As Clowney notes, many cities already have voluminous *in rem* portfolios of buildings seized as a result of tax delinquencies; some have been quite aggressive in acquiring titles to abandoned buildings through public-nuisance actions and tax foreclosures. As discussed previously, vacant buildings—whether held by a local government or an absentee private owner—are always detrimental to neighborhood life. Clowney intuits that neighbors would prefer to have these buildings utilized for commercial activity than to remain vacant, and, moreover, that this desire might overcome public-choice impediments to implementing his proposal. The VALT proposal is, in my view, both ingenious and promising. If successful, it would advance several of the land-use-policy goals outlined in the introduction—improving the quality of life of poor urban communities, promoting vitality by filling vacant buildings with viable businesses, and generating new social capital by eliminating major contributors to its decline (namely, abandoned buildings and the physical and social disorder associated with them). Put differently, even if commercial enterprises sometimes disrupt neighborhood life, filling vacant buildings with viable commercial enterprises would, by definition, produce a net increase in social capital. Common sense strongly suggests that a legal barbershop in an occupied building is always better than an illegal brothel in an abandoned one.

The VALT proposal, however, also surfaces two other impediments to the regeneration of poor urban communities that I have not discussed in detail thus far. First, some economists argue that the tax delinquencies that enable cities to acquire titles to abandoned buildings are a significant contributing factor to urban decline. Property tax rates are, according to this view, excessive—they lead owners of rental housing and commercial properties to abandon their buildings. Second, the new owners of abandoned buildings in poor neighborhoods would face high renovation costs—deferred maintenance being an inevitable result of abandonment. But regulations other than zoning restrictions drastically drive up the cost of renovations. For example, building codes may require rewiring and replumbing, and the accommodation requirements of the Americans with Disabilities Act (ADA) may require significant structural changes. Anecdotally, I know of a beautiful beaux-arts building in South Bend, Indiana, that sits vacant because the owners cannot afford the cost of installing a second elevator—a renovation requirement imposed by the ADA, which would cost more than the total value of the building itself. More-systematic evidence of renovation costs comes from studies of the relocation expenses incurred by businesses seized by eminent domain. These studies universally find that the renovation costs imposed by regulatory compliance, especially the ADA, pose the most substantial impediments to the successful relocation of displaced businesses. These fiscal and regulatory impediments have also probably contributed to the relative lack of success in "urban homesteading" programs.[19]

Beyond Root Problems

The broken windows hypothesis, and the order-maintenance policies that flow from it, are concerned primarily with addressing the symptoms rather than the causes of urban decline. In contrast to policymakers' long-standing focus on solving the "root problems" underlying these symptoms—including poverty and unemployment, drug use, illegitimacy, and sub-par education— Wilson and Kelling offered an innovative insight: They opined that life in urban communities will improve if policymakers simply focus on addressing, primarily through policing practices, a significant consequence of those root problems, namely, disorder. They challenged the prevailing wisdom, which suggested that the consequences of pathologies of urban life could be separated into causes and their inevitable symptoms—symptoms that could only be cured by treating the causes. Instead, Wilson and Kelling urged that the symptoms are, in a sense, part of the problem. That is, the symptoms have feedback effects; they are important inputs into the root causes. If this intuition is correct, policies that address the symptoms may obviate the need to address root problems. (Of course, to the extent that order-maintenance policies are predicated on the assumption that disorder *causes* crime, they also flow from the assumption that disorder is itself a "root problem.")

Over the past few decades, just as order-maintenance strategies began to capture the imaginations of urban leaders, urban neighborhoods—even those written off as "hopeless"—began an apparent rebound. The fact that this rebound coincided with the institutionalization of the order-maintenance agenda and the dramatic decline in serious crime suggests that Wilson and Kelling were right to connect city fortunes with residents' perceptions of security. Order-maintenance-policing efforts, of course, do not work in a vacuum. Other policies adopted during roughly the same time period, which also focus on addressing the symptoms of urban decline, undoubtedly contributed to city successes: For example, many cities have focused on improving both public infrastructure (sidewalks, curbs, roads, parks, and so on) and the delivery of governmental services. Fixing these "broken windows" undoubtedly improves the quality of life in urban neighborhoods. An important catalyst for increased investment in these basic urban building blocks has been the rise of, and the spending decisions made by, the sublocal governmental institutions discussed above—business improvement districts, tax-increment financing districts, and enterprise zones. The very fact that these sublocal entities prioritize infrastructure improvements suggests that many residents consider them important neighborhood priorities. Improving the physical plant of city neighborhoods also makes them more attractive to individuals whose economic circumstances afford mobility.[20]

The "urban rebound" also has coincided with efforts to restructure and reform another important local government institution—public education. Over the past few decades, as the influence of federal judges enforcing desegregation decrees has waned, state legislatures have prompted, prodded, and pushed urban school reforms. While many of these reforms have met with great resistance, they have gradually changed the face—the order, if you will—of public education. The long-dominant model of the geographic-based neighborhood school, which began to unravel during the busing era, has given way to a complicated mosaic of elementary and secondary educational options—magnet schools, charter schools, schools-within-schools, and, in a handful of cities, publicly funded school-voucher programs. These options are augmented by private philanthropic efforts, including private scholarship programs (some of which are encouraged by state tax-credit legislation). Most of these reforms are root-causes efforts; they aim to improve the educational options and outcomes for those of the least means, thereby breaking the cycle of poverty that plagues so many urban communities. Most charter schools, for example, are located in center cities and cater to low-income, low-achieving students.[21]

It is a mistake, however, to view the need to improve the quality of educational options available to city residents solely in root-causes terms. If, as many critics have argued, cities need more than the "creative class" to thrive, then education reform may ultimately prove as critical to improved city prospects as fixing broken windows and filling potholes. After all, survey data consistently indicates that the quality of public education is the *single most important* factor influencing residential choice. This may in fact be one reason why cities are gaining wealthy residents but losing middle-class ones: The wealthy can afford educational options that those of modest means cannot. The average private-school tuition in the United States exceeds six thousand dollars per year. Tuition rates, however, are kept low by the fact that most private schools in the United States are affiliated with, and subsidized by, religious institutions (primarily Roman Catholic churches). The average secular private-school tuition is much higher, more than thirteen thousand dollars per year. The fact that urban private schools, especially nonreligious ones, generally charge much more than that, combined with the fact that urban religious schools, especially Catholic ones, are closing at an alarming rate does not paint a favorable picture for middle-class individuals who would like to raise their families in cities but are unhappy with the quality of urban public-schooling options. Education reforms that make quality schools accessible to the middle class may be, ultimately, what convinces them to choose urban over suburban life.

Finally, from the Progressive era through today, city officials have believed that land-use planning can address, or rather bypass, the root causes of urban decay. As chapter 7 highlights, although planners have sometimes made bad choices about which land-use patterns correlate with urban health, they continue to engage in efforts to perfect them. By exploring the connections, often overlooked, between land-use and policing policies, this book has sought to understand land-use policy, along with order-maintenance policies, as Wilson and Kelling urged. That is, it has explored the feedback effects of different land-use patterns, and the land-use policies that dictate them, in an effort to understand what kinds of land-use policies contribute to the renewal of urban neighborhood life. The book has given particular attention to how the perceived need to impose order and suppress disorder play out in land-use and policing policies; it asks policymakers to consider whether, and under what circumstances, a single-minded quest for "order" may undermine, rather than complement, efforts to improve the health of urban neighborhoods. An awareness of the role that long-standing conceptions of order play in land-use policies is especially critical today, when urban leaders are focused both on curbing disorder and reshaping urban neighborhoods in ways that run contrary to nearly a century of thinking about the proper order of our cities. Just as some order-maintenance-policing policies may have helped our urban centers turn the corner, so, I believe, can innovative land-use policies that recognize that, at least in some circumstances, the order constructed by zoning laws is not necessarily synonymous with an absence of harmful disorder.

Notes

INTRODUCTION

Epigraph: Giamatti, *Take Time for Paradise,* 51–52.
1. Wilson and Kelling, "Broken Windows."
2. Kahan, "Social Influence," 351.
3. Berube and Frey, "Decade of Mixed Blessings," 114–30; Jargowsky, "Stunning Progress, Hidden Problems," 142–58.

CHAPTER 1. ORDER IN THE CITY

1. Livingston, "Police Discretion," 595; Bahr, *Skid Row,* 227.
2. Wilson, *Varieties of Police Behavior,* 31; Wilson and Kelling, "Broken Windows," 29, 35; Stuntz, "Crime Talk and Law Talk," 157; Bittner, "Police on Skid-Row," 703.
3. Bittner, "Police on Skid-Row," 709, 713; Ellickson, "Controlling Chronic Misconduct in Public Places," 1209; Stuntz, "Implicit Bargains," 560; Dubin and Robinson, "Vagrancy Concept Reconsidered," 133–35; Livingston, "Police Discretion," 596.
4. Foote, "Vagrancy-Type Law," 604.
5. Dan-Cohen, "Decisional Rules and Conduct Rules," 626; Steiker, "Counter-Revolution in Criminal Procedure?" 2469, 2488; *Brown v. Texas,* 443 U.S. 47

(1979); *Papachristou v. City of Jacksonville,* 405 U.S. 156, 162 (1972). See also *Shut-tlesworth v. Birmingham,* 382 U.S. 87 (1965); *Wright v. Georgia,* 373 U.S. 284 (1963); *Coates v. Cincinnati,* 402 U.S. 611 (1971).

6. Foote, "Vagrancy-Type Law," 648. For a short history of the "reform" movement, see Kelling and Coles, *Fixing Broken Windows,* 80–90; Livingston, "Police Discretion," 565–73.

7. National Advisory Commission on Civil Disorders ("Kerner Commission"), *Final Report,* 57–60. For a description of the gradual disillusionment with "reform-style" policing, see Kelling and Coles, *Fixing Broken Windows,* 85–89.

8. Grogan and Proscio, *Comeback Cities,* 152; Kelling and Moore, "From Political to Reform to Community," 15; Kelling and Coles, *Fixing Broken Windows,* 40–60; Ellickson, "Controlling Chronic Misconduct in City Spaces," 1209–14.

9. Kelling, *Newark Foot Patrol Experiment,* 124–28; Wilson and Kelling, "Broken Windows," 30; Pate et al., *Reducing Fear of Crime in Houston and Newark,* 30–35.

10. Wilson and Kelling, "Broken Windows."

11. On the dissatisfaction with reform-style policing, see, e.g., Kelling and Coles, *Fixing Broken Windows,* 102–7; Kelling, *Police and Communities,"* 1; Goldstein, *Problem-Oriented Policing,* 13.

12. For a catalog of various order-maintenance-policing and community-policing strategies, see Livingston, "Police Discretion," 573–78.

13. For the definition of "social influence," see Aronson, *Social Animal,* 6. For comprehensive treatments of the "social influence" justification for order-maintenance policing, see, e.g., Kahan, "Social Influence, Social Meaning, and Deterrence," 367–73; Kahan, "Reciprocity, Collective Action, and Community Policing," 1527–38.

14. Kelling and Coles, *Fixing Broken Windows,* 169–75; Kahan and Meares, "Coming Crisis of Criminal Procedure," 1159–71; Meares and Kahan, "When Rights Are Wrong," 3–30; Kennedy, "State, Criminal Law, and Racial Discrimination," 1256; Livingston, "Police Discretion," 561.

15. Harcourt, *Illusion of Order,* 128–29, 299; Dershowitz, "Rights and Interests," 33–39; Steiker, "More Wrong than Rights," 49–57; Burnham, "Twice Victimized," 63–69.

16. Sampson and Raudenbush, "Seeing Disorder," 332–37.

17. *City of Chicago v. Morales,* 527 U.S. 31 (1999); Chicago Gang Loitering Ordinance; Ferkhenhoff, "Anti-Gang Ordinance Passes Test." For a description of legislative efforts to narrow police discretion with "for the purpose of" or "with intent to" statutes, see, e.g., Kelling and Coles, *Fixing Broken Windows,* 60–64, 176–77; Livingston, "Police Discretion," 624–25. See also *People v. Lee,* 2004 WL 98584 (Ill. Ct. App., 2004); *E. L. v. State,* 619 So.2d 252, 253 (Fla. 1993); *City of Akron v. Rowland,* 618 N.E.2d 128, 145–46 (Ohio 1993); *Christian v. City of Kansas City,* 710 S.W.2d 11 (Mo. Ct. App. 1986); *Profit v. City of Tulsa,* 617 P.2d 250 (Okla. Crim. App. 1980); *Coleman v. City of Richmond,* 364 S.E.2d 239, 243–44 (Va. Ct. App. 1988).

18. Cases considering the constitutionality of juvenile curfew laws include *Hodgkins v. Peterson,* 355 F.3d 1048 (7th Cir. 2004); *Ramos v. Town of Vernon,* 331 F.3d 315 (2d Cir. 2003); *Nunez v. City of San Diego,* 114 F.3d 935 (9th Cir. 1997); *Hutchins v. District of Columbia,* 188 F.3d 531 (D.C. Cir. 1999); *Qutb v. Strauss,* 11 F.3d 488 (5th Cir. 1993). Cases

considering challenges to ordinances targeting the homeless include *Berkeley Community Health Project v. City of Berkeley,* 1995 WL 293899, at 4–7 (N.D. Calif. 1995); *Blair v. Shanahan,* 775 F. Supp. 1315 (N.D. Calif. 1991), rev'd and remanded, 38 F.3d 1514 (9th Cir. 1994); *Loper v. New York City Police Department,* 999 F.2d 699 (2d Cir. 1993). See also Hershkoff and Cohen, "Begging to Differ," 896–916; Milnich, "Compassion Fatigue and the Homeless," 255–356.

19. Reiss, "Consequences of Compliance and Deterrence Models of Law Enforcement," 83–122; Sampson and Cohen, "Deterrent Effects of the Police on Crime," 169, 176; Kelling, *Newark Foot Patrol Experiment,* 122–24; Trojanowicz, *Evaluation of the Neighborhood Foot Patrol Program in Flint, Michigan,* 85–87. Harcourt, *Illusion of Order,* 300–309; Greene and Taylor, "Community-Based Policing and Foot Patrols," 195, 201–3; Sherman, "Attacking Crime," 198–99.

20. Skogan, *Disorder and Decline,* 65–84; Harcourt, *Illusion of Order,* 67–75.

21. Sampson and Raudenbush, "Systematic Social Observation."

22. Harcourt and Ludwig, "Broken Windows: New Evidence," 271–77.

23. See, e.g., Kahan, "Social Influence," 367–68.

24. Kelling and Sousa Jr., "Do Police Matter?" 10–16.

25. Corman and Mocan, "Carrots, Sticks, and Broken Windows," 251–63.

26. Harcourt and Ludwig, "Broken Windows: New Evidence," 276; Harcourt and Ludwig, "Reefer Madness," 1–2.

27. Levitt, "Understanding Why Crime Fell in the 1990s," 163; Sampson and Raudenbush, "Systematic Social Observation," 608; Harcourt, *Illusion of Order,* 68.

CHAPTER 2. ORDERING THE CITY

1. *City of Chicago v. Morales,* 527 U.S. 31, 28–49 (1999); Schragger, "The Limits of Localism."

2. Jacobs, *Death and Life of Great American Cities,* 45; Constance Perin, *Everything in Its Place.*

3. Chused, "*Euclid*'s Historical Imagery," 601.

4. Jackson, *Crabgrass Frontier,* 47; Cott, *Bonds of Womanhood,* 19.

5. Cott, *Bonds of Womanhood;* Jackson, *Crabgrass Frontier,* 48–49; Hayden, *Redesigning the American Dream,* 68–74; Hayden, *Grand Domestic Revolution,* 13; Wright, *Building the Dream,* 75–79; Houghton, *Victorian Frame of Mind,* 341–47; Olsen, "Family and the Market," 1497; Siegel, "Home as Work,"1092–94; Proverbs 31:10, 13, 16, 18, 24–25, 28–29 (Revised Standard Version).

6. See generally, e.g., Cott, *Bonds of Womanhood,* 4; see also, e.g., Siegel, "Home as Work," 1093; Kerber, "Separate Spheres, Female Worlds, Woman's Place," 9; Houghton, *Victorian Frame of Mind,* 341–47; Wright, *Building the Dream,* 108. The quotation from the nineteenth-century sermon is found in Jackson, *Crabgrass Frontier,* 48.

7. Mishnah, Baba Batra 2:8–9; Bruegmann, *Sprawl,* 15–16.

8. Olmsted, *Civilizing American Cities,* 39–40.

9. Jackson, *Crabgrass Frontier,* 45–60, 72; Fishman, *Bourgeois Utopias,* 4, 117–33; Wright, *Building the Dream,* 97; Jeffrey, "Family as Utopian Retreat from the City," 22–39.

10. Fishman, *Bourgeois Utopias,* 129 (quoting Olmsted); Jackson, *Crabgrass Frontier,* 117 (noting that "it had . . . been the dream of Andrew Jackson Downing in the 1840s to re-settle 'honest workingmen' in the distant open spaces"), 136 (noting that "for the first time in the history of the world, middle-class families in the late nineteenth century could reasonably expect to buy a detached home on an accessible lot in a safe . . . environment"); Wright, *Building the Dream,* 103–6 (discussing the availability of affordable suburban homes in the early twentieth century).

11. Chused, "Euclid's Historical Imagery," 601; Marsh, *Introduction to City Planning,* 19; Toll, *Zoned American,* 51.

12. The most complete history of the New York City experience is Toll, *Zoned American,* 130–90.

13. Ibid., 20; Jackson, *Crabgrass Frontier,* 242; Ellickson, "Alternatives to Zoning," 692.

14. Fischel, "Economic History of Zoning," 317. For further discussion, see also Fischel, *Homevoter Hypothesis,* ch. 10; *Village of Euclid v. Ambler Realty Co.,* 297 F. 307, 316 (N.D. Ohio 1924); Whitten, "Zoning of Residential Sections," 34; Wright, *Building the Dream,* 194; Lees, "Preserving Property Values? Preserving Proper Homes? Preserving Privilege?" 413–18.

15. *Village of Euclid v. Ambler Realty Co.,* 272 U.S. 365, 394–95 (1926); *State ex rel. Civello v. City of New Orleans,* 154 La. 271, 282 (La. 1923).

16. *Miller v. Board of Public Works,* 234 P. 381, 386 (Cal. 1925); *Wulfson v. Burden,* 150 N.E. 120, 123 (N.Y. 1925); *Brief for the National Conference on City Planning et al. as Amici Curiae Supporting Appellants, Village of Euclid v. Ambler Realty Co.* 272 U.S. 365 (1926) (no. 31), 15.

17. Veiller, "Protecting Residential Districts," 92; *Pritz v. Messer,* 149 N.E. 30, 35 (Ohio 1925).

18. Wright, *Building the Dream,* 125 (quoting Riis), 269 (quoting Olmsted); Boyer, *Urban Masses and Moral Order in America,* 275 (quoting Burnham).

19. *State ex rel. Civello,* 154 La. at 282; *State ex rel. Max Morris v. East Cleveland,* 22 Ohio N. 549 (1920); *Pritz,* 149 N.E. at 35.

20. Marsh, *Introduction to City Planning,* 26; Veiller, "Districting by Municipal Regulation," 163.

21. Wright, *Building the Dream,* 196; Brief for the National Conference on City Planning et al., *Village of Euclid v. Ambler Realty Co.,* 272 U.S. 365 (1926).

22. Jackson, *Crabgrass Frontier,* 241–43; Weiss, *Rise of the Community Builders,* 143–54; Wright, *Building the Dream,* 195–97 (quoting Hoover).

23. Jackson, *Crabgrass Frontier,* 190–218.

24. Ibid.; U.S. Census Bureau, "Housing Vacancies and Homeownership: Annual Statistics 2005," at http://www.census.gov/hhes/www/housing/hvs/annual05/ann05t20.html; Urban Institute, "The Subprime Mortgage Crisis," at http://www.urban.org/decisionpoints08/archive/04subprimemortgage.cfm.

25. Gamm, *Urban Exodus,* 40–41; Wright, *Building the Dream,* 248; Weiss, *Rise of the Community Builders,* 68–72.

26. Wright, *Building the Dream,* 217, 248; Weiss, *Rise of the Community Builders,* 4, 140–51.

27. Jackson, *Crabgrass Frontier,* 207–14 (quoting the FHA *Underwriting Manual*); Wright, *Building the Dream,* 247; Weiss, *Rise of the Community Builders,* 154.

28. See generally, e.g., Wilson, ed., *Urban Renewal, the Record and the Controversy;* Teaford, *Rough Road to Renaissance,* 82–122; Frieden and Sagalyn, *Downtown, Inc.,* 15–38; Glaab, *History of Urban America;* Miller, *Urbanization of Modern America;* Weiss, *Rise of the Community Builders,* 154; Teaford, *Rough Road to Renaissance,* 105; Frieden and Sagalyn, *Downtown, Inc.,* 23–29; Mumford, *From the Ground Up,* 226–29 (quoting Bauer).

29. Justement, *New Cities for Old,* 3; Short, *Alabaster Cities,* 25; Hilberseimer, *New City,* 158.

30. Jacobs, *Death and Life of Great American Cities,* 5; Frieden and Sagalyn, *Downtown, Inc.,* 33; Fried, "Grieving for a Lost Home," 359–79; Gans; *Urban Villagers,* 320–21; Thursz, *Where Are They Now?* 100–101.

31. Frieden and Sagalyn, *Downtown, Inc.,* 15–60; Hartman, "Relocation: Illusory Promises and No Relief," 745–817; Anderson, *Federal Bulldozer,* 73–91, 194–213; Stull, "From Urban Renewal to CDBG," 185.

32. Brownfield, "Disposition Problem in Urban Renewal," 740. See also "Unrealized Profits in Urban Renewal," 101; U.S. National Commission on Urban Problems, *Building the American City;* "Urban Renewal Wastelands," 86–87; Montgomery, "Improving the Design Process in Urban Renewal," 456–66; Accordino and Johnson, "Addressing the Vacant and Abandoned Property Problem," 303; Schill, "Deconcentrating the Inner City Poor," 808.

33. See generally Newman, *Defensible Space;* Schill, "Distressed Public Housing," 500–504; Wright, *Building the Dream,* 235; National Commission on Urban Problems, *More Than Shelter,* 58.

CHAPTER 3. A FOUR-CATEGORY TAXONOMY OF DISORDER

1. See generally Jacobs, *Death and Life of Great American Cities.*

2. Skogan, *Disorder and Decline,* 7.

3. Jacobs, *Death and Life of Great American Cities,* 15.

4. *Jacobellis v. Ohio,* 378 U.S. 184, 197 (1964) (Stewart, J., concurring); Skogan, *Disorder and Decline,* 2–4; Livingston, "Police Discretion," 551; Kelling and Coles, *Fixing Broken Windows,* 14–15.

5. Sampson and Raudenbush, "Systematic Social Observation," 617–18; Perkins and Taylor, "Ecological Assessment of Community Disorder," 63.

6. *State ex rel. Gallo v. Acuna,* 929 P.2d 596 (Cal. 1997); Sampson and Raudenbush, "Systematic Social Observation," 608.

7. Taylor, "Toward an Environmental Psychology of Disorder," 953. *City of Chicago v. Morales,* 527 U.S. 41 (1999).

8. Venkatesh, *Off the Books,* 8–9.

9. Holloway, "Street Vendors Roll Their Way Back to Some Corners"; Editorial, "Street Peddlers in New York"; McNatt, "Council Peddles Plans to Limit Vendors"; Editorial, "New York Changes Command"; Hinkley, "Quality of Life: The Mayor Who Understood"; Polner, "Fighter at Heart."

10. On the regulation of street vending, both in the United States and internationally, see Kettles, "Regulating Vending," 6–8.

11. Bluestone, " 'Pushcart Evil' " is an excellent history of New York City's efforts to regulate street vendors prior to the 1940s. The quote from La Guardia is found on page 88.

12. Kettles, "Regulating Vending," 15–18; Levine, "On the Sidewalks, Business Is Booming"; Brooks and Perkins, "Retailing Spills into Streets of New York"; "Peddlers Irk Stores in Harlem"; Hicks, "Giuliani Broadens Crackdown to Banish All Illegal Vendors"; Hicks, "Many 125th Street Vendors Say They Will Resist Move"; McNatt, "Council Peddles Plans to Limit Vendors"; Bluestone," 'Pushcart Evil,' " 78.

13. Editorial, "Street Peddlers in New York"; Dunier, *Sidewalk,* 42; Williams, "Crackdown on Ave. C Peddlers."

14. Hicks, "Many 125th Street Vendors Say They Will Resist Move"; Hicks, "Vendors' Ouster and Boycott Divide Harlem."

15. Hicks, "Amid Calm, Anger Lingers on 125th Street"; Bloom, "Year Later, 'Model' Market Called a Failure"; Oser, "At Lenox and 116th, Co-Ops and Stores Are Rising"; McNatt, "Harlem on My Mind," 109.

16. Martin, "City Begins Enforcement of Food Cart Restrictions"; Hernandez, "City's Right to Bar Vendors from Streets Is Upheld"; Allen, "Giuliani to Bar Food Vendors on 144 Blocks"; Allen, "Sidewalk Food Vendors Face a New Set of Critics."

17. Editorial, "And Now, the Hot-Dog War"; Allen, "Sidewalk Vendors Rally to Protest Street Restrictions"; Allen, "Giuliani to Bar Food Vendors on 144 Blocks"; Allen, "City Pursuing Negotiations with Street Food Vendors"; "Giuliani Says a New Plan Will Not Please Vendors"; Barnes, "Compromise Plan on Vendors Approved."

18. Jacobs, *Death and Life of Great American Cities,* 187–233; Putnam, *Bowling Alone,* 22–24.

19. See, e.g., Bruegmann, *Sprawl,* 151–53 (describing new urbanism's influence on suburban design); "Hope VI Funds New Urban Neighborhoods" (asserting that the Congress for the New Urbanism shaped many HOPE VI projects and trains participating developers); Garnett, "Ordering (and Order in) the City," 58.

20. Taylor et al., "Street Blocks," 120; Greenberg, Rohe, and Williams, "Safety in Urban Neighborhoods," 141; Wilcox et al., "Busy Places and Broken Windows," 185; Sampson and Raudenbush, "Systematic Social Observation," 610; Greenberg, Rohe, and Williams, "Safety in Urban Neighborhoods," 162.

21. See generally Newman, *Defensible Space;* Katyal, "Architecture as Crime Control"; Taylor et al., "Street Blocks," 122; Taylor, "Toward an Environmental Psychology of Disorder," 954, Kurtz, Koons, and Taylor, "Land Use," 135.

22. Venkatesh, *Off the Books,* 200–202.

23. Taylor et al., "Street Blocks," 122.

24. On the other hand, the cities that grew the fastest during the 1990s were newer, western, "car friendly" cities. Most older, eastern, pedestrian- and public-transportation-oriented cities did not gain population during the last decade. Glaeser and Shapiro, "City Growth," 1; Simmons and Lang, "Urban Turnaround," 51; Sohmer and Lang, "Downtown Rebound," 63.

25. Harcourt, *Illusion of Order,* 130; Roberts, "Foreword," 805; Sampson and Raudenbush, "Seeing Disorder," 335–36; Kelling and Coles, *Fixing Broken Windows*, 16.

26. Kettles, "Regulating Vending," 25.

27. Wilcox et al., "Busy Places and Broken Windows," 200; Venkatesh, *Off the Books,* 178, 198–204.

28. On the effects of economic stagnation in inner-city communities, see generally Wilson, *When Work Disappears.* On the negative effects of vacant storefronts, see Kurtz, Koons, and Taylor, "Land Use," 137.

29. Editorial, "Fair Food Vending in Midtown"; Seifman, "Rudy Bending on Vending Ban"; Fosmoe, "Council Approves Eddy Street Commons."

30. Sennett, *Uses of Disorder;* Frug, *City Making,* 143–54; Glaeser and Gottlieb, "Urban Resurgence and the Consumer City."

31. Lafferty and Frech, "Community Environment and the Market Value of Single-Family Homes," 387–89.

CHAPTER 4. ORDER CONSTRUCTION AS DISORDER SUPPRESSION

1. Perl, "Building Inspector with a Bulletproof Vest."

2. Skogan, *Disorder and Decline,* 37; Spellman, "Abandoned Buildings," 481; Accordino and Johnson, "Addressing the Vacant and Abandoned Property Problem," 301.

3. See, for example, Kotlowitz, "All Boarded Up."

4. Alexander, *Land Bank Authorities,* 4–10; Wilgoren, "Detroit Urban Renewal without the Renewal"; Editorial, "Broken Windows Are a Clue to Livability"; Nelson, "City Trains Sights on Neighborhood Blight"; McWhirter, "Archer Tries to Balance Budget and Re-Election."

5. Ross, "Housing Code Enforcement as Law in Action," 141.

6. State of Connecticut, Division of Criminal Justice, Nuisance Abatement Unit, at http://www.ct.gov/csao/cwp/view.asp?a=1798&q=285774; City of Fort Collins, Public Nuisance Ordinance, at http://fcgov.com/cityattorney/public-nuisance.php; City of Fremont, Report a Hazard/Nuisance, at http://www.ci.fremont.ca.us/PublicSafety/ReportAHazard/default.htm; City of St. Louis, Mayor's Office Press Releases, "Mayor Slay's Neighborhood Life Initiatives," at http://stlcin.missouri.org/release/getpressdetails.cfm?Auto=387; Enkoji, "Californians Get Say in Cases Involving Those Convicted of Nuisance Laws." For a thorough discussion of the "special injury" requirement, see Restatement (Second) of Torts (1979) § 821B; *Armory Park Neighborhood Association v. Episcopal Cemetery Services,* 712 P.2d 914 (Ariz. 1985); Maag, "Cleveland Sues 21 Lenders."

7. Chused, "Euclid's Historical Imagery," 601.

8. Hall et al., "*Non-Plan: An Experiment in Freedom,*" 435–43; Hall, "British Enterprise Zones."

9. Hall, "British Enterprise Zones," 180; Callies, "An American Perspective on UK Planning," 268–69.

10. Butler, *Enterprise Zones,* 32; 54–56 (quoting Siegan); Booth, "Discretion in Planning versus Zoning," 31; *Omnibus Budget Reconciliation Act of 1993,* 26 U.S.C. §§ 1391–1397D (1993), amended by *Taxpayer Relief Act of 1997,* Pub. L. No. 105–34, 951–52, 111 *Stat.* 788, 885 (1997).

11. Wolf, "Enterprise Zones," 3–4; Briffault, "Rise of Sublocal Structures in Urban Governance," 509; James, "Evaluation of Enterprise Zone Programs," 180; Wolf, "Enterprise Zones," 5–6; Erickson and Friedman, "Comparative Dimensions of State Enterprise Zone Policies," 155, 164.

12. Garnett, "Ordering (and Order in) the City," 26–31; 42 U.S.C. § 1397f(a)(2)(B) (2000); U.S. Department of Housing and Urban Development, "Tax Incentive Guide for Businesses in the Renewal Communities, Empowerment Zones, and Enterprise Communities," at http://www.hud.gov/offices/cpd/economicdevelopment/library/taxguide2003 .pdf; U.S. Department of Housing and Urban Development, "Empowerment Zone / Enterprise Community Initiative: Round II: Building Communities Together," at http://www.hud.gov/nofa/ez/urbanforms.pdf.

13. Langdon, *Better Place to Live,* 15–16.

14. See, e.g., Bruegmann, *Sprawl,* 152–53.

15. Wilson, *When Work Disappears,* 4–5.

16. Katyal, "Architecture as Crime Control," 1109.

17. New York City Department of City Planning, "East Harlem Rezoning Proposal— Approved!: Proposed Zoning Changes Affecting Use," at http://home.nyc.gov/html/ dcp/html/eastharlem/eastharlem3b.shtml; East Harlem Online, "New Directions: An Introduction: A 197-A Plan," at http://www.east-harlem.com/cb11_197A_intro.htm; Salins, "Reviving New York City's Housing Market," 54–55; Souccar, "El Barrio: Left Behind and Angry."

18. New York City Department of City Planning, "East Harlem Zoning Proposal— Approved!"; Salins, "Reviving New York City's Housing Market," 62, 68.

19. Skogan, *Disorder and Decline,* 7; Dubin, "From Junkyards to Gentrification," 742. On Houston, see Berry, "Land Use Regulation," 260–63.

20. See generally Tiebout, "A Pure Theory of Local Expenditures"; Garnett, "Ordering (and Order in) the City," 43–44 (reviewing literature on economic development incentives).

21. Briffault, "Our Localism: Part I," 3.

22. Garnett, "Suburbs as Exit," 290–92, 302; Kotkin, "Suburbia"; Kasarda, "Industrial Restructuring and the Changing Location of Jobs," 235.

23. Bruegmann, *Sprawl,* 58–59, 65–67; Kotkin, "Suburbia."

24. Simmons and Lang, "Urban Turnaround," 51; Sohmer and Lang, "Downtown Rebound," 65; Kruse and Sugrue, "Introduction," 6–10.

25. See, e.g., Sanger, "Fighting Poverty, President and Speaker Find a Moment of Unity."

26. University of Chicago, "West and South Campus Plan," at http://southcampusplan .uchicago.edu/index.html; Howes, "Englewood Leaders Urge City to Create Jobs"; Roeder, "Englewood Project Has Backing of Big Names"; Byrne, "Two Cheers for Gentrification," 405; Hogan, "Cincinnati: Race in the Closed City," 59; Cottle, "Boomerang," 26. But see MacDonald, "What Really Happened in Cincinnati," 28.

27. Erez and Earley, *Culture, Self-Identity, and Work,* 99; Tienda and Stier, "Joblessness and Shiftlessness," 135–54; Bandura, "Self-Efficacy Mechanism in Human Agency," 122; Schill, "Distressed Public Housing," 502–22.

28. Wilson, *When Work Disappears,* 50–75; Jahoda, Lazarsfeld, and Zeisel, *Marienthal,* 52–65; Cohen and Dawson, "Neighborhood Poverty and African American Politics," 292.

29. Wilson, *When Work Disappears,* 70; Corcoran et al., "Association between Men's Economic Status and Their Family and Community Origins," 592; Hill and Dun-

can, "Parental Family Income and the Socioeconomic Attainment of Children," 48–49.

30. On the spatial mismatch hypothesis, see generally Jargowsky, *Poverty and Place*; Arnott, "Economic Theory and the Spatial Mismatch Hypothesis," 1171–72; Holzer, "Spatial Mismatch Hypothesis," 107; Ihlanfeldt and Sjoquist, "Effect of Job Access on Black and White Youth Employment," 256; Kasarda, "Urban Industrial Transition and the Underclass," 26–47; Kain, "Spatial Mismatch Hypothesis," 371; Schill, "Deconcentrating the Inner City Poor," 798–808.

31. Kahan, "Social Influence, Social Meaning, and Deterrence," 387.

32. Meares and Kahan, "When Rights Are Wrong," 3–31; Kennedy, *Race, Crime, and the Law,* 25–28; Kelling and Coles, *Fixing Broken Windows,* 96–97; Scott, "Benefits and Consequences of Police Crackdowns," 16–17; Livingston, "Police Discretion," 575–84.

33. Livingston, "Police Discretion," 584.

CHAPTER 5. RELOCATING DISORDER

1. Department of Human Services, "HSD Homepage," at http://www.hsd.maricopa.gov; Maricopa County, *Human Services Campus: Capital Business Plan,* 8–10; "Second Phase of Downtown's Human Services Campus to Begin"; Robertson, "Downtown Human Services Campus Comes to Fruition."

2. Kelling and Coles, *Fixing Broken Windows,* 49–64; Ellickson, "Controlling Chronic Misconduct in City Spaces," 1243; Kahan, "Social Influence, Social Meaning, and Deterrence," 389.

3. Kelling and Coles, *Fixing Broken Windows,* 4; Kahan and Meares, "Coming Crisis of Criminal Procedure," 1159–71.

4. On Orlando, see Coalition for the Homeless of Central Florida, at http://www.centralfloridahomeless.org; Hess, "Helping People Off the Streets." For a closer look at particular homeless campuses see, e.g., Banks, "Shelter's Leader Called 'a Model of Tenacity' "; DeParle, " 'Safety Net' for Anchorage Homeless"; Jewett, "Homeless Programs May Face Cuts"; Moller, "LV Chips in to Keep Crisis Center Open"; Editorial, "Hard Bargain"; Emery, "Ideas to Aid Homeless Unveiled"; Gonser, "Homeless Center Appears Doomed"; McCormick, "Homeless Campus Site Best of Few Options."

5. Ellickson, "Controlling Chronic Misconduct," 1167–68; Hess, "Helping People Off the Streets." On Kansas City's effort, see Hendricks, "Homeless Zone of Their Own"; Diuguid, "Compassion Often Evades the Less Fortunate among Us."

6. *Moden v. United States,* 60 Fed. Cl. 275, 280 (2004); Bell and Parchomovsky, "Givings," 559.

7. *Armory Park Neighborhood Association v. Episcopal Cemetery Services,* 712 P.2d 914 (Ariz. 1985); "Liability for Creation or Maintenance of a Nuisance"; Ellickson and Been, *Land Use Controls,* 618.

8. Accordino and Johnson, "Addressing the Vacant and Abandoned Property Problem," 301; *City of Chicago v. Morales,* 527 U.S. 31 (1999).

9. Perl, "Building Inspector with a Bulletproof Vest"; *Armendariz v. Penman*, 31 F.3d 860, 872 (9th. Cir. 1994).

10. Ellickson, "Controlling Chronic Misconduct," 1220–23.

11. New York City Housing Authority, "NYCHA Residents' Corner: Trespass Policy," at http://www.nyc.gov/html/residents/trespass_new.shtml; Logan, "Shadow Criminal Law of Municipal Governance," 1430; Strosnider, "Anti-Gang Ordinances after City of Chicago v. Morales," 129; Flanagan, "Trespass-Zoning," 327; Smith, "Civil Banishment of Gang Members," 1465–68.

12. On the importance of the right to exclude, see *Kaiser Aetna v. United States,* 444 U.S. 164, 176 (1979); see also *Dolan v. City of Tigard,* 512 U.S. 374, 384 (1994); *Nollan v. California Coastal Communication,* 483 U.S. 825, 831 (1987); *Loretto v. Teleprompter Manhattan CATV Corporation,* 458 U.S. 419, 433 (1982). On drug exclusion laws, see *Johnson v. City of Cincinnati,* 310 F.3d 484, 487 (6th Cir. 2002), *cert. denied,* 539 U.S. 915; *State v. Johnson,* 988 P.2d 913 (Or. Ct. App. 1999).

13. *Virginia v. Hicks,* 539 U.S. 113 (2003); *U.S. Department of Housing and Urban Development v. Rucker,* 535 U.S. 125 (2002).

14. *Brief for Petitioner, Virginia v. Hicks,* 539 U.S. 113 (2003) (No. 02–371), 32–43; *Dallas v. Stanglin,* 490 U.S. 19, 25 (1989).

15. *Johnson,* 310 F.3d at 484; *Thompson v. Ashe,* 250 F.3d 399, 406 (6th Cir. 2001) (upholding public housing no-trespass policy); *Hutchins v. District of Columbia,* 188 F.3d 531, 536–39 (D.C. Cir. 1999); *Nunez v. City of San Diego,* 114 F.3d 935, 944 (9th Cir. 1997).

16. *Johnson,* 310 F.3d at 488; see also *Roberts v. United States Jaycees,* 468 U.S. 609, 617 (1984); *State v. Burnett,* 755 N.E.2d 857, 862–63 (Ohio 2001).

17. *Johnson v. City of Cincinnati,* 119 F. Supp. 2d 735, 748 (S.D. Ohio 2000); *State v. James,* 978 P.2d 415, 419 (Or. Ct. App. 1999).

18. Bahr, *Skid Row,* 31; Anderson, *Hobo,* 250–60; Hoch and Slayton, *New Homeless and Old,* 10–35; Bahr, *Skid Row,* 27; Ellickson, "Controlling Chronic Misconduct," 1208; Levinson, "Skid Row in Transition," 81; Schneider, "Skid Row as an Urban Neighborhood," 11–13.

19. Anderson, *Hobo,* 87, 163; Hoch and Slayton, *New Homeless and Old,* 39–45; Schneider, "Skid Row as an Urban Neighborhood," 11–13. Rossi, *Down and Out in America,* 21 n.6, notes that Anderson later regretted his glamorization of the hobo lifestyle.

20. Anderson, *Hobo,* 3–13; Hoch and Slayton, *New Homeless and Old,* 88; Rossi, *Down and Out in America,* 25–35. For the histories of particular skid rows, see generally Bahr and Caplow, *Old Men, Drunk and Sober;* Blumberg, Shipley, and Shandler, *Skid Row and Its Alternatives;* Bogue, *Skid Row in American Cities.*

21. Bittner, "Police on Skid-Row," 704; Hoch and Slayton, *New Homeless and Old,* 104–5; Schneider, "Skid Row as an Urban Neighborhood," 17; Rossi, *Down and Out in America,* 28–29 (discussing objectives of the studies).

22. Jencks, *Homeless,* 61–74 (linking decline in number of SRO units and homelessness); Rossi, *Down and Out in America,* 33–34 (noting that bizarre behavior of the homeless was previously "acted out on Skid Row"); Levinson, "Skid Row in Transition," 88 (linking destruction of skid row with dispersal of homeless population).

23. Ellickson, "Controlling Chronic Misconduct," 1167–68, 1215.

24. Neuman, "Anomalous Zones," 1209; Mackey, *Red Lights Out,* 211.

25. Best, *Controlling Vice,* 17; Connelly, *Response to Prostitution in the Progressive Era,* 136–50; Rosen, *Lost Sisterhood,* 14–37. Cases addressing the legality of official vice districts include *L'Hote v. City of New Orleans,* 177 U.S. 587, 594–600 (1900); *Baker v. Coman,* 198 S.W. 141 (Tex. 1917); *Spence v. Fenchler,* 180 S.W. 597, 602–3 (Tex. 1915); *Brown Cracker & Candy Co. v. City of Dallas,* 137 S.W. 342, 343 (Tex. 1911).

26. Decker, *Prostitution: Regulation and Control,* 61–67; Best, *Controlling Vice,* 19.

27. Best, *Controlling Vice,* 113; Rosen, *Lost Sisterhood,* 33.

28. On Times Square, see Decker, *Prostitution: Regulation and Control,* 49–60. On Boston, see Marcus, "Zoning Obscenity," 3–4; Kennedy, *Planning the City upon a Hill,* 208; Leung, "Chinatown Enjoys a Renaissance."

29. Wilson, *Varieties of Police Behavior,* 240; Kennedy, *Planning the City upon a Hill,* 208–09; Reichl, *Reconstructing Times Square,* 58–61; Sagalyn, *Times Square Roulette,* 7; Bailey, "Build 'Em High."

30. *City of Renton v. Playtime Theatres, Inc.,* 475 U.S. 41, 51 (1985); *Young v. American Mini Theatres, Inc.,* 427 U.S. 50, 52 (1976); Perlman, "Pornosprawl," 48.

31. Kahan, "Social Influence, Social Meaning, and Deterrence," 370.

32. Emery, "Homeless Center Draws Praise, Ire"; Been, "What's Fairness Got to Do with It?" 1001; Been and Gupta, "Coming to the Nuisance or Going to the Barrios," 33–34; Been, "Locally Undesirable Land Uses in Minority Neighborhoods," 1398–1406; Collin, "Review of the Legal Literature on Environmental Racism," 121.

33. Anchors, "Agency Stirs Safety Concerns for School."

34. Jencks, *Homeless,* 21–74; Maier, "Homeless in the Post-Industrial City," 357–63; Burt et al., *Evaluation of Continuums of Care for Homeless People,* 3–4; Hoch and Slayton, *New Homeless and Old,* 225.

35. Bonilla, "Judge Calls Halt to Skid Row Searches"; Central City Association of Los Angeles, *Downtown's Human Tragedy"*; Bring Los Angeles Home! *Draft Framework for the 10-Year Strategic Plan to End Homelessness,* at http://www.bringlahome.org/docs/BLAH_Draft_Framework.pdf"; Mac Donald, "Skid Row in Rehab"; Los Angeles Homeless Services Authority, "2007 Greater Los Angeles Homeless Count," at http://www.lahsa.org/homelesscount.asp; Harcourt, "Policing L.A.'s Skid Row."

36. Lazare, "Cincinnati and the X-Factor," 43.

37. On "singling out" in takings law, see Levmore, "Takings, Torts, and Special Interests," 1344–45; Lunney, "Critical Reexamination," 1954. On Cincinnati, see Lazare, "Cincinnati and the X-Factor," 43–44; Hogan, "Cincinnati," 49–50; Cottle, "Boomerang," 26; Mac Donald, "What Really Happened in Cincinnati," 28. On Chicago, see Constitutional Rights Foundation Chicago, "CRFC Focus Issue: Gangs," at http://crfc.org/gangs.html; Einzmann, "Chicago Police to Broaden Area for Loitering Arrests."

38. On expressive theories of law, see McAdams, "An Attitudinal Theory of Expressive Law," 340; Kornhauser, "No Best Answer?" 1624–25; Anderson and Pildes, "Expressive Theories of Law," 1531; Cooter, "Expressive Law and Economics," 586; Sunstein, "On the Expressive Function of Law," 2024–25. On the relative merits of targeted sweeps, see Kelling and Coles, *Fixing Broken Windows,* 166; Thatcher, "Conflicting Values in Community Policing," 769.

39. *Armendariz v. Penman,* 31 F.3d 860, 872 (9th Cir. 1994) (Trott, J., dissenting).

CHAPTER 6. THE ORDER-MAINTENANCE AGENDA AS LAND-USE POLICY

Epigraph: *City of Chicago v. Morales,* 527 U.S. 41, 100–102 (Thomas, J., dissenting).

1. Kotkin, *City,* xix–xxii, 11, 32–33, 66, 154–55. See generally Glaeser and Gottlieb, "Urban Resurgence."

2. Wilson and Kelling, "Broken Windows," 29, 35. On the perception of security versus its reality, see Chicago Community Policing Evaluation Consortium, *Community Policing in Chicago,* 66. On safety as a factor influencing housing choice, see National Association of Home Builders, "NAHB: 2005 Multifamily Renter and Condo Buyer Preference Survey," at http://www.nahb.org/generic.aspx?genericContentID=46103, 20–21; Baldassare, *Special Survey on Land Use,* 7; Sigelman and Henig, "Crossing the Great Divide," 7–8.

3. Wilson and Kelling, "Broken Windows," 29.

4. Chicago Community Policing Evaluation Consortium, *Community Policing in Chicago,* iv–v, 6, 54–55, 66–71.

5. Moore and Trojanowicz, "Policing and Fear of Crime," 3; Glassner, *Culture of Fear,* 44–45; Miethe, "Fear and Withdrawal from Urban Life," 14–17; Lee, "Urban Unease Revisited," 4.

6. Skogan, "Measuring What Matters," 47–48; Carroll, "Gallup Reviews Americans' Attitudes About Crime," at http://www.gallup.com/poll/23365/Gallup-Reviews-Americans-Attitudes-About-Crime.aspx"; Miethe, "Fear and Withdrawal from Urban Life," 17–18; Warr and Stafford, "Fear of Victimization," 1033.

7. Skogan and Maxfield, *Coping with Crime,* 203–29; Covington and Taylor, "Fear of Crime in Urban Residential Neighborhoods," 231–32; Gates and Rohe, "Fear and Reactions to Crime," 439; Gibson et al., "Social Integration," 540; Liska, Sanchirico, and Reed, "Fear of Crime and Constrained Behavior," 827; Skogan, "Impact of Victimization on Fear," 135; Miethe, "Fear and Withdrawal from Urban Life," 19; McGarrell, Giacomazzi, and Thurman, "Neighborhood Disorder," 480.

8. Wilson, "Urban Unease," 25. On private precautions, see Mikos, " 'Eggshell' Victims," 307; Ben-Sharhar and Harel, "Economics of the Law of Criminal Attempts," 299; Shavell, "Individual Precautions to Prevent Theft," 123.

9. See, e.g., Black and Baumgartner, "On Self-Help in Modern Society," 195–99.

10. Putnam, *Bowling Alone,* 18–24.

11. Wilson, "Urban Unease," 34. On collective efficacy, see generally Sampson, Raudenbush, and Earls, "Neighborhoods and Violent Crime," 918; Meares, "Praying for Community Policing," 1604. On the connection between collective efficacy and safety, see Gibson et al., "Social Integration," 542; Hunter and Baumer, "Street Traffic, Social Integration, and Fear of Crime," 123–31; Rountree and Land, "Burglary Victimization," 147–80.

12. Calabresi, *Cost of Accidents,* 26.

13. Chicago Community Policing Evaluation Consortium, "Community Policing in Chicago," 92; Wilson, "Urban Unease," 34; Sampson and Raudenbush, "Systematic Social Observation," 612–13; McGarrell, Giacomazzi, and Thurman, "Neighborhood Disorder,"494.

14. Tiebout, "Pure Theory of Local Expenditures," 416–24. See generally Fischel, ed., *Tiebout Model at Fifty.*

15. Cullen and Levitt, "Crime, Urban Flight, and the Consequences for Cities," 159–69; Sampson and Wooldredge, "Evidence that High Crime Rates Encourage Migration Away from Central Cities," 4; Katzman, "Contribution of Crime to Urban Decline," 277; DeFrances and Smith, "Perceptions of Neighborhood Crime, 1995," 5.

16. Sampson, Raudenbush, and Earls, "Neighborhoods and Violent Crime," 918, 923; McGarrell, Giacomazzi, and Thurman, "Neighborhood Disorder,"484; Sampson and Raudenbush, "Systematic Social Observation," 610; Gibson et al., "Social Integration," 552; Cullen and Levitt, "Crime, Urban Flight, and the Consequences for Cities," 159–69.

17. Leland, "On a Hunt for Ways to Put Sex in the City"; see generally Florida, *Rise of the Creative Class.*

18. Bruegmann, *Sprawl,* 221; Glaeser and Gottlieb, "Urban Resurgence," 3.

19. Wells is quoted in Kotkin, *City,* 151. On the economic profile of city residents, see Jargowsky, "Stunning Progress, Hidden Problems," 137; Berube and Frey, "Decade of Mixed Blessings," 111; Booza, Cutsinger, and Galster, *Where Did They Go?* 1.

20. LaGrange, Ferraro, and Supancic, "Perceived Risk and Fear of Crime," 311–34; McGarrell, Giacomazzi, and Thurman, "Neighborhood Disorder,"493; Gibson et al., "Social Integration," 541; Covington and Taylor, "Fear of Crime in Urban Residential Neighborhoods," 241–43.

21. Sampson and Raudenbush, "Systematic Social Observation," 624–26; Gibson et al., "Social Integration," 552.

22. Meares and Corkran, "When 2 or 3 Come Together," 1334, 1350.

23. Kelling et al., *Kansas City Preventive Patrol Experiment,* vii; Trojanowicz, *Evaluation of the Neighborhood Foot Patrol Program in Flint, Michigan,* 19–20. On Newark, see generally Kelling, *Newark Foot Patrol Experiment.*

24. Weisburd and Eck, "What Can Police Do to Reduce Crime, Disorder, and Fear?" 42–65; Pate et al., *Reducing Fear of Crime in Houston and Newark,* 11–13; Cordner, "Fear of Crime and the Police," 223; Zhao, "Effect of Police Presence," 273; Renauer, "Reducing Fear of Crime?" 41–47.

25. Harcourt and Ludwig, "Broken Windows: New Evidence," 314–15.

26. Moore, "Problem Solving and Community Policing," 145; Mastrofski and Uchida, "Transforming the Police," 348; Meares and Corkran, "When 2 or 3 Come Together," 1315; Livingston, "Review: Brutality in Blue," 1556; Mastrofski and Greene, "Community Policing and the Rule of Law," 80–81.

27. Skolnick and Fyfe, *Above the Law,* 114; Moore, "Problem Solving and Community Policing," 145, see n. 59.

28. *Use of Force by Police: Overview of National and Local Data,* vii; Adams, Rohe, and Arcury, "Implementing Community-Oriented Policing," 413–24.

29. Renauer, "Reducing Fear of Crime," 46.

30. Zhao, "Effect of Police Presence" 280–95; Scheider, Rowell, and Bezdikian, "Impact of Citizen Perceptions of Community Policing on Fear of Crime," 363–77; Chicago Community Policing Evaluation Consortium, "Community Policing in Chicago," 43; Sampson and Raudenbush, "Systematic Social Observation," 611.

31. Sherman, "Fair and Effective Policing." 389.

CHAPTER 7. REORDERING THE CITY

1. According to the 2000 Census, the Chicago metropolitan area is the fifth most segregated in the United States (following Detroit, Gary, Milwaukee, and New York). The racial isolation of African Americans in Chicago is more severe than in all but three other metro areas (Detroit, New York, and Gary). U.S. Census Bureau, "Housing Patterns," at http://www.census.gov/hhes/www/housing/housing_patterns/housing_patterns.html. On Gautreaux and Moving to Opportunity, see Polikoff, *Waiting for Gautreaux; Hills v. Gautreaux,* 425 U.S. 284 (1976); *Gautreaux v. City of Chicago,* 480 F.2d 210 (7th Cir. 1973); *Gautreaux v. Chicago Housing Authority,* 342 F. Supp. 827 (N.D. Ill. 1972); Cohen and Taylor, *American Pharaoh,* 549–50; Harcourt and Ludwig, "Broken Windows: New Evidence," 271. Information about the Chicago Housing Authority's "Plan for Transformation," including descriptions of all of the proposed HOPE VI projects, is available at http://www.thecha.org.

2. Hirsch, *Making the Second Ghetto,* 215–58; Bauman, *Public Housing, Race, and Renewal,* 169; Bratt, *Rebuilding a Low-Income Housing Policy,* 70–71; Freidman, *Government and Slum Housing.*

3. Schill, "Distressed Public Housing," 504. See generally Newman, *Defensible Space.*

4. National Commission on Severely Distressed Public Housing, *Final Report,* 47–48.

5. Schill, "Distressed Public Housing," 500–525; National Commission on Severely Distressed Public Housing, *Final Report,* 2–3; *U.S. Department of Housing and Urban Development v. Rucker,* 535 U.S. 125 (2002).

6. For a summary of the program, see Clancy and Quigley, "HOPE VI: A Vital Tool," 527.

7. On vertical and horizontal equity, see Schill, "Distressed Public Housing," 539–40. For a summary of HOPE VI criticisms, see FitzPatrick, "Disaster in Every Generation" 443–46. See generally National Housing Law Project, *False Hope*; Scheehle, Kane, and Hockett, *Report on the Loss of Subsidized Housing in the U.S.*

8. Massey and Kanaiaupuni, "Public Housing and the Concentration of Poverty," 114–15.

9. Buron et al., *Hope VI Resident Tracking Study,* 78–93; Popkin, *Hope VI Program—What about the Residents?*; Buron, "An Improved Living Environment?" 1–2.

10. Hirsch, *Making the Second Ghetto,* 18–35; Cohen and Taylor, *American Pharaoh,* 67–68, 76; Polikoff, *Waiting for Gautreaux,* 27–29.

11. Hirsch, *Making the Second Ghetto,* 179, 218–21; Patillo, *Black on the Block,* 32–44; Cohen and Taylor, *American Pharaoh,* 79.

12. Hirsch, *Making the Second Ghetto,* 122–27, 220–23; Patillo, *Black on the Block,* 187–88; Cohen and Taylor, *American Pharaoh,* 79–85.

13. Hirsch, *Making the Second Ghetto,* 225–30; Cohen and Taylor, *American Pharaoh,* 84–86, 101, 108–11.

14. Hirsch, *Making the Second Ghetto,* 243, 257; Cohen and Taylor, *American Pharaoh,* 112–13, 183–90, 487–89; Patillo, *Black on the Block,* 188, 191–93; see also generally Polikoff, *Waiting for Gautreaux,* 31–32.

15. Patillo, *Black on the Block,* 193–257; Lake Park Crescent, "Lake Park Crescent: Come Home to the Lakefront," at http://www.lakeparkcrescent.com. For information on Jazz

on the Boulevard, see Thrush Real Estate, "Jazz on the Boulevard," at http://www
.thrushhomes.com/html/jazzhome.htm.

16. *Pratt v. Chicago Housing Authority,* 848 F. Supp. 792 (N.D. Ill. 1994); see also Lane,
"Public Housing Sweep Stakes," 68.

17. Cohen and Taylor, *American Pharaoh,* 184–89.

18. *Berman v. Parker,* 348 U.S. 26 (1954).

19. Garnett, "Neglected Political Economy of Eminent Domain," 101; Peñalver, "Property
Metaphors and Kelo v. New London," 2971; Albrook, "High Court Go-Ahead Sparks
RLA Action on SW Project"; Roberts, "Progress or Decay? I—"Downtown Blight'";
Roberts, "Progress or Decay? I—"Two Redevelopment Ideas for Southwest D.C."; Ed-
itorial, "Instead of Slums"; Roberts, "Blueprint for Progress in Southwest Washington";
Editorial, "Bold Approach in Southwest."

20. See generally Lewis, *District of Columbia,* 121–39; District of Columbia Redevelopment
Land Agency, *Community Services and Family Relocation.*

21. Lewis, *District of Columbia,* 132–35; Gutheim, *Worthy of the Nation,* 235–38 (discussing
abandoned efforts to redevelop the Barry Farms and Marshall Heights sections of Anacostia).

22. Gutheim, *Worthy of the Nation,* 314–20; Gillette, *Between Justice and Beauty,* 161–63.

23. See generally Thursz, *Where Are They Now?;* see also Gillette, *Between Justice and Beauty,*
163–65; Lewis, *District of Columbia,* 136.

24. Waterfront, "Waterfront: The Project," at http://www.waterfrontdc.com/project/.

25. Information on the Arthur Capper and Carrollsburg projects is available at District of -
Columbia Housing Authority, at http://www.dchousing.org/hope6/arthur_capper_
hope6.html; on the Capitol Quarter, at http://www.eya.com/index.cfm?neighborhoodid=
390B1CD5–96B6–175C-95D06031216C458B&fuseaction=microsites.view&sectionid=
329DB7D9–1125-AADA-EAE0376CC103A6E5; and on the Capper/Carrollsburg Housing
Redevelopment, at http://www.jdland.com/dc/capper.cfm.

26. Lewis, "Now Comes the Real Test"; Stewart, "Council Votes to Close 2 Waterfront
Agencies."

27. *Cobb v. Milwaukee County,* 207 N.W.2d 848 (Wis. 1973); Preservation Institute, "Removing Freeways," at http://www.preservenet.com/freeways/FreewaysParkEast.html.

28. Preservation Institute, "Removing Freeways," at http://www.preservenet.com/freeways/
FreewaysParkEast.html; Gurwitt, "Mayor as Missionary," 32; Caro, *Power Broker,* 523–25.

29. Schreibman, "Looking for Land?" 10.

30. Preservation Institute, "Removing Freeways," at http://www.preservenet.com/freeways/
FreewaysParkEast.html; Schreibman, "Looking for Land?" 10; "Freeway Razing Sets Stage
for $250 Million in Development."

31. Daykin, "Study Discourages City Funds"; Daykin, "Park East Project Trimmed";
Daykin, "Cost of Park East Upgrades Soaring"; Daykin, "Pace Picking Up After Coun-
cil's Vote"; Daykin, "Park East Land Is Cleared and Projects Are in the Works"; Resler,
"Park East Corridor."

32. On Norquist's ideology, see generally Gurwitt, "Mayor as Missionary."

33. Emerson, "Making Main Street Legal Again," 637; Duany and Talen, "Transect Planning," 247–49; Davis, Duany, and Plater-Zyberk, *Lexicon of New Urbanism;* Duany

and Talen, "Transect Planning," 247–49; Duany, Wright, and Sorlein, *SmartCode and Manual*, C2.

34. Department of City Development, "Park East Redevelopment Plan," at http://www .mkedcd.org/parkeast/PEplan.html, Document Two: Master Plan.

35. Ibid., "Document Three: Development Code," 7–8.

36. Daykin, "Tenant Leaves Park East Plan," D1.

37. Cohen and Taylor, *American Pharaoh*, 184–85.

38. See generally Rosin, "American Murder Mystery"; Venkatesh, *Off The Books*, 302–5; Galster, "Consequences from the Redistribution of Urban Poverty," 121–23; Kingsley and Pettit, "Comment on George C. Galster," 129–31; Grotto, Cohen, and Olkon. "Public Housing Limbo."

39. On the costs and benefits of "managed" diversity of various types, see generally Fainstein, "Cities and Diversity," and Smolla, "In Pursuit of Racial Utopias"; Joseph, "Is Mixed-Income Development an Antidote to Urban Poverty?"; Berube, "Comment on Mark Joseph."

40. Putnam, "E Pluribus Unum." For a historical example of an effort to achieve racial integration by limiting it in Chicago's Hyde Park neighborhood, see Hirsch, *Making the Second Ghetto*, 135–70. On the costs of inclusionary zoning, see generally, Ellickson, "Irony of Inclusionary Zoning."

41. Fischel, "Political Economy of Public Use," 943–49; Garnett, "Neglected Political Economy," 140–42.

CHAPTER 8. LETTING GO?

1. Hedgpeth, "Southwest Waterfront Will Finally Get Over the '60s."

2. See generally "Tiebout, Pure Theory of Local Expenditures"; Garnett, "Save the Cities, Stop the Suburbs?"; Garnett, "Suburbs as Exit, Suburbs as Entrance"; Garnett, "Trouble Preserving Paradise."

3. *Village of Euclid v. Ambler Realty Co.*, 272 U.S. 365 (1926); *Hawaii Housing Authority v. Midkiff*, 467 U.S. 229, 244 (1984); Robert C. Ellickson, "Controlling Chronic Misconduct in City Spaces," 1243–46.

4. Briffault, "Localism and Regionalism" 8–10; Briffault, "Our Localism: Part II," 352; Buzbee, "Urban Sprawl," 374; Garnett, "Trouble Preserving Paradise," 181; Fischel, *Do Growth Controls Matter?* 2–3.

5. See generally Komesar, *Law's Limits;* Ellickson, "Suburban Growth Controls," Fischel, *Homevoter Hypothesis.*

6. Bruegmann, *Sprawl,* 57, 69–70; Pollard, "Greening the American Dream?"; Twomey, "Here Comes (There Goes) a Neighborhood"; Steinhauer, "Ending a Long Battle, New York Lets Housing and Gardens Grow"; Schill, "Comment of Richard P. Voith and David Crawford"; Confessore, "Cities Grow Up, and Some See Sprawl."

7. DeParle, "The 'W' Word Re-Engaged"; Rector, "Secretly Ending Welfare Reform."

8. Shaver, "For the Muffin Lady."

9. Pratt, *Homebased Business,* 38, 86–88; Presser and Bamberger, "American Women Who Work at Home for Pay," 832–33; *Chicago, Illinois, Zoning Code* §§ 17-9-0202 (2006).

10. Ientilucci, "Pigs in the Parlor or Diamonds in the Rough?"

11. See, e.g., Seidel, *Housing Costs and Government Regulations,* 73–77, 90; Salins, "Reviving New York City's Housing Market," 53. On rehabilitation codes, see Galvan, "Rehabilitating Rehab through State Building Codes" 1757–70; Ellickson and Been, *Land Use Controls,* 449.

12. See, e.g., City of Colorado Springs, "Mixed-Use Zoning," at http://www.springsgov .com/Page.asp?NavID=4107; City of Fort Worth, "Mixed-Use Zoning Standards," at http://www.fortworthgov.org/uploadedFiles/Planning/Zoning_Review/MU_Zoning Guide2006.pdf; Georgia Quality Growth Partnership, "Toolkit of Best Practices," at http://www.dca.state.ga.us/toolkit/toolkit.asp; Lewis, "Zoning Trends"; American Planning Association, "Model Mixed-Use Zoning District Ordinance," at http://www .planning.org/research/smartgrowth/pdf/section41.pdf; Pickels, "Mixed-Use Zoning, Greater Density Would Raise Pittsburgh Region's Quality of Life."

13. *Oxford English Dictionary,* 2nd ed., s.v. "subsidiarity"; Briffault, "Rise of Sublocal Structures in Urban Governance," 509.

14. See generally, Ellickson, "New Institutions for Old Neighborhoods"; Liebmann, "Devolutions of Power"; Nelson, "Privatizing the Neighborhood."

15. Liebmann, *Little Platoons,* 143; Ellickson, "New Institutions for Old Neighborhoods," 75, 77–80; Liebmann, "Devolution of Power to Community and Block Associations," 343–46; Nelson, "Privatizing the Neighborhood," 866–67; Reich, "Secession of the Successful." On business-improvement districts, see generally Briffault, "Government for Our Time?" 370. On the influence of neighborhoods in land-use policy, see, e.g., Rose, "Planning and Dealing," 893–909.

16. Kelling and Coles, *Fixing Broken Windows,* 158; Livingston, "Police Discretion," 575–77.

17. Kelling and Coles, *Fixing Broken Windows,* 197–98, see n. 14; Garnett, "Ordering (and Order in) the City," 53–58.

18. Ellickson, "Alternatives to Zoning," 762.

19. Clowney, "Invisible Businessmen"; Garnett, "Neglected Political Economy of Eminent Domain," 125–26; U.S. Department of Transportation, *Relocation Retrospective Study,* 17–18; U.S. Department of Transportation, *Business Relocation Study,* §§ 1-1.

20. See generally Briffault, "Government for Our Time"; Mac Donald, "BIDs Really Work."

21. See generally Viteritti, *Choosing Equality;* Lake, *Hopes, Fears, and Reality;* Yudof, *Educational Policy and the Law;* Howell et al., *Education Gap;* Garnett and Garnett, "School Choice, the First Amendment, and Social Justice"; Ryan and Heise, "Political Economy of School Choice."

Bibliography

BOOKS AND ARTICLES

Accordino, John and Gary T. Johnson. "Addressing the Vacant and Abandoned Property Problem." *Journal of Urban Affairs* 22, (2000): 301.

Adams, Charles F., Howard B. Fleeter, Yul Kim, Mark Freeman, and Imgon Cho. "Flight from Blight and Metropolitan Suburbanization Revisited." *Urban Affairs Review* 31, no. 4 (1996): 529.

Adams, Richard E., William M. Rohe, and Thomas A. Arcury. "Implementing Community-Oriented Policing: Organizational Change and Street Officer Attitudes." *Crime and Delinquency* 48, (2002): 399.

Alba, Richard, and Victor Nee. *Remaking the American Mainstream: Assimilation and Contemporary Immigration.* Cambridge, MA: Harvard University Press, 2003.

Albrook, Robert C. "High Court Go-Ahead Sparks RLA Action on SW Project." *Washington Post,* November 24, 1954, 21.

Alexander, Frank S. *Land Bank Authorities: A Guide for the Creation and Operation of Local Land Banks.* New York: Local Initiatives Support Corporation, 2005.

Allen, Mike. "City Pursuing Negotiations with Street Food Vendors." *New York Times,* June 15, 1998, sec. B.

———. "Giuliani to Bar Food Vendors on 144 Blocks." *New York Times,* May 24, 1998, sec. 1.

———. "Sidewalk Food Vendors Face a New Set of Critics." *New York Times,* May 31, 1998, sec. 1.

———. "Sidewalk Vendors Rally to Protest Street Restrictions." *New York Times,* June 4, 1998, sec. B.

Alstott, Anne L. "Tax Policy and Feminism: Competing Goals and Institutional Choices." *Columbia Law Review* 96, no. 8 (1996): 2001.

Anchors, Sarah. "Agency Stirs Safety Concerns for School." *Arizona Republic,* February 26, 2003.

Anderson, Elizabeth S., and Richard H. Pildes. "Expressive Theories of Law: A General Restatement." *University of Pennsylvania Law Review* 148, no. 5 (2000): 1503.

Anderson, Martin. *The Federal Bulldozer: A Critical Analysis of Urban Renewal, 1949–1962.* Cambridge, MA: MIT Press, 1964.

Anderson, Nels. *The Hobo: The Sociology of the Homeless Man.* Chicago: University of Chicago Press, 1923.

Applebome, Peter. "For Youths, Fear of Crime Is Pervasive and Powerful." *New York Times,* January 12, 1996, sec. A.

Arnott, Richard. "Economic Theory and the Spatial Mismatch Hypothesis." *Urban Studies* 35, no. 7 (1998): 1171.

Aronson, Elliot. *The Social Animal.* 7th ed. New York: Freeman, 1995.

Austin, Regina. "'An Honest Living': Street Vendors, Municipal Regulation, and the Black Public Square." *Yale Law Journal* 103, no. 8 (1994): 2119.

Babcock, Richard F. "The Chaos of Zoning Administration." *Zoning Digest* 12 (1960): 1.

———. *The Zoning Game: Municipal Practices and Policies.* Madison, WI: University of Wisconsin Press, 1966.

Babcock, Richard F., and Charles L. Siemon. *The Zoning Game Revisited.* Boston, MA: Oelgeschlager, Gunn & Hain, 1985.

Bahr, Howard M. *Skid Row: An Introduction to Disaffiliation.* New York: Oxford University Press, 1973.

Bahr, Howard M., and Theodore Caplow. *Old Men, Drunk and Sober.* New York: NYU Press, 1974.

Bailey, Steve. "Build 'Em High." *Boston Globe,* December 17, 2003, sec. C1.

Baker, Newman F. "Zoning Legislation." *Cornell Law Quarterly* 11, no. 2 (1926): 164.

Baldassare, Mark. *Special Survey on Land Use.* San Francisco: Public Policy Institute of California, 2002.

Baldassare, Mark, and Georjeanna Wilson. "Changing Sources of Suburban Support for Local Growth Controls." *Urban Studies* 33, no. 3 (1996): 459.

Bandura, Albert. "Self-Efficacy Mechanism in Human Agency." *American Psychologist* 37, no. 2 (1983): 122.

Banks, Bill. "Shelter's Leader Called 'a Model of Tenacity.'" *Atlanta Journal and Constitution,* September 23, 1999, sec. J1–7.

Barnes, Julian E. "Compromise Plan on Vendors Approved." *New York Times,* January 23, 1999, sec. B.

Barron, David J. "Reclaiming Home Rule." *Harvard Law Review* 116, no. 8 (2003): 2257.

Bauman, John F. *Public Housing, Race, and Renewal: Urban Planning in Philadelphia, 1920–1974.* Philadelphia: Temple University Press, 1987.

Bayley, David H. "Community Policing: A Report from the Devil's Advocate." In *Community Policing: Rhetoric or Reality,* edited by Jack Greene and Stephen Mastrofski. New York: Praeger, 1988.

Been, Vicki. "Comment on Professor Jerry Frug, 'The Geography of Community.' " *Stanford Law Review* 48, no. 5 (1996): 1109.

———. "Exit as Constraint on Land Use Exactions: Rethinking the Unconstitutional Conditions Doctrine." *Columbia Law Review* 91, no. 3 (1991): 473.

———. "Impact Fees and Housing Affordability." *Cityscape* 8, no. 1 (2005): 139.

———. "Locally Undesirable Land Uses in Minority Neighborhoods: Disproportionate Siting or Market Dynamics?" *Yale Law Journal* 103, no. 6 (1994): 1383.

———. "What's Fairness Got to Do with It? Environmental Justice and the Siting of Locally Undesirable Land Uses." *Cornell Law Review* 78, no. 6 (1993): 1001.

Been, Vicki, and Francis Gupta. "Coming to the Nuisance or Going to the Barrios? A Longitudinal Analysis of Environmental Justice Claims." *Ecology Law Quarterly* 24, no. 1 (1997): 1.

Bell, Abraham, and Gideon Parchomovsky. "Givings." *Yale Law Journal* 111, no. 3 (2001): 547.

Bennett, Julie. "Home Bodies; Home-Based Businesses and Zoning Laws." *Planning* 65, no. 5 (1999): 10.

Ben-Shahar, Omri, and Alon Harel. "Blaming the Victim: Optimal Incentives for Private Precautions Against Crime." *Journal of Law, Economics, and Organization* 11, no. 2 (1995): 434.

———. "The Economics of the Law of Criminal Attempts: A Victim-Centered Perspective." *University of Pennsylvania Law Review* 145, no. 2 (1996): 299.

Berry, Brian J. L. "Ghetto Expansion and Single-Family Housing Prices: Chicago, 1968–1972." *Journal of Urban Economics* 3, no. 4 (1976): 397.

Berry, Christopher R. "Land Use Regulation and Residential Segregation: Does Zoning Matter?" *American Law and Economics Review* 3, no. 2 (2001): 251–74.

Berube, Alan. "Comment on Mark Joseph's 'Is Mixed-Income Development an Antidote to Urban Poverty?' " *Housing Policy Debate* 17, no. 2 (2006): 235.

———. "Gaining but Losing Ground: Population Change in Large Cities and Their Suburbs." In *Redefining Urban and Suburban America,* edited by Bruce Katz and Robert E. Lang. Vol. 1, 33.Washington, DC: Brookings Institution Press, 2003.

Berube, Alan, and William H. Frey. "A Decade of Mixed Blessings: Urban and Suburban Poverty in the 1990s." In *Redefining Urban and Suburban America,* edited by Alan Berube, Bruce Katz, and Robert E. Lang. Vol. 2, 111. Washington, DC: Brookings Institution Press, 2003.

Best, Joel. *Controlling Vice: Regulating Brothel Prostitution in St. Paul.* Columbus, OH: Ohio State University Press, 1998.

Bittner, Egon. "The Police on Skid-Row: A Study of Peace Keeping." *American Sociological Review* 32, no. 5 (1967): 699.

Black, Donald, and M. P. Baumgartner. "On Self-Help in Modern Society." In *The Manners and Customs of the Police*, 193, 195–99. New York: Academic Press, 1980.

Bloom, Jennifer Kingson. "A Year Later, 'Model' Market Called a Failure." *New York Times*, December 11, 1994, sec. 13.

Bluestone, Daniel M. "'The Pushcart Evil': Peddlers, Merchants, and New York City's Streets, 1890–1940." *Journal of Urban History* 18, (1991): 68.

Blumberg, Leonard, Thomas E. Shipley Jr., and Irving W. Shandler. *Skid Row and Its Alternatives: Research and Recommendations from Philadelphia*. Philadelphia: Temple University Press, 1973.

Boeck, David. "The Enterprise Zone Debate." *Urban Lawyer* 16, no. 1 (1984): 71.

Bogue, Donald J. *Components of Population Change, 1940–1950: Estimates of Net Migration and Natural Increase for Each Standard Metropolitan Area and State Economic Area*. Oxford, OH: Scripps Foundation for Research in Population Problems, 1957.

———. *Skid Row in American Cities*. Chicago: University of Chicago, 1963.

Bonilla, Denise M. "Judge Calls Halt to Skid Row Searches." *Los Angeles Times*, April 15, 2003, sec. B4.

Booth, Philip. "Discretion in Planning versus Zoning." In *British Planning: 50 Years of Urban and Regional Policy*, edited by Barry Cullingworth, 31. London: Athlone Press, 1999.

Booza, Jason C., Jackie Cutsinger, and George Galster. *Where Did They Go?: The Decline of Middle-Income Neighborhoods in Metropolitan America*. Washington, DC: Brookings Institution, July 28, 2006.

Boyer, Paul. *Urban Masses and Moral Order in America, 1820–1920*. Cambridge, MA: Harvard University Press, 1978.

Bratt, Rachel G. *Rebuilding a Low-Income Housing Policy*. Philadelphia: Temple University Press, 1989.

Brauner, Sarah, and Pamela Loprest. *Where Are They Now? What States' Studies of People Who Left Welfare Tell Us*. Washington, DC: Urban Institute, 1999.

Briffault, Richard. "A Government for Our Time? Business Improvement Districts and Urban Governance." *Columbia Law Review* 99, no. 2 (1999): 365.

———. "The Local Government Boundary Problem in Metropolitan Areas." *Stanford Law Review* 48, no. 5 (1996): 1115.

———. "Localism and Regionalism." *Buffalo Law Review* 48, no. 1 (2000): 1.

———. "Our Localism: Part I—The Structure of Local Government Law." *Columbia Law Review* 90, no. 1 (1990): 1.

———. "Our Localism: Part II—Localism and Legal Theory." *Columbia Law Review* 90, no. 2 (1990): 346.

———. "The Rise of Sublocal Structures in Urban Governance." *Minnesota Law Review* 82, no. 2 (1997): 503.

Brooks, Carole A., and Stafford Perkins. "Retailing Spills into Streets of New York." *Newsday*, December 17, 1990, 45.

Brownfield, Lyman. "The Disposition Problem in Urban Renewal." *Law and Contemporary Problems* 25, no. 4 (1960): 732–40.

Bruegmann, Robert. *Sprawl: A Compact History*. Chicago: University of Chicago Press, 2005.

Bullard, Robert D. *Invisible Houston: The Black Experience in Boom and Bust.* College Station, TX: Texas A&M University Press, 1987.

Burchell, Robert W., and David Listokin. *The Adaptive Reuse Handbook: Procedures to Inventory, Control, Manage, and Reemploy Surplus Municipal Properties.* New Brunswick, NJ: Rutgers University, Center for Urban Policy Research, 1981.

Burnham, Margaret A. "Twice Victimized." In *Urgent Times: Policing and Rights in Inner-City Communities,* edited by Tracey L. Meares and Dan M. Kahan. Boston: Beacon Press, 1999.

Burns, Nancy. *The Formation of American Local Governments: Private Values in Public Institutions.* New York: Oxford University Press, 1994.

Buron, Larry. "An Improved Living Environment? Neighborhood Outcomes for Hope VI Relocatees." *Metropolitan Housing and Community Center,* Brief no. 3 (September 2004).

Buron, Larry, Susan J. Popkin, Diane Levy, Laura E. Harris, and Jill Khadurri. *Hope VI Resident Tracking Study.* Washington, DC: Urban Institute (2002).

Burt, Martha R. et al., U.S. Department of Housing and Urban Development, *Evaluation of Continuums of Care for Homeless People.* Washington, D.C.: Government Printing Office, 2002.

Butler, Stuart. *Enterprise Zones: Greenlining the Inner Cities.* New York: Universe Books, 1981.

Buzbee, William W. "Sprawl's Dynamics: A Comparative Institutional Analysis." *Wake Forest Law Review* 35, no. 3 (2000): 509.

———. "Urban Sprawl, Federalism, and the Problem of Institutional Complexity." *Fordham Law Review* 68, no. 1 (1999): 57.

Byrne, Peter. "Two Cheers for Gentrification." *Howard Law Journal* 46, no. 3 (2003): 405.

Calabresi, Guido. *The Cost of Accidents.* New Haven, CT: Yale University Press, 1970.

Callies, David L. "An American Perspective on UK Planning." In *British Planning: 50 Years of Urban and Regional Policy,* edited by Barry Cullingworth. New York: Praeger, 1988.

Calthorpe, Peter. *The Next American Metropolis: Ecology, Community, and the American Dream.* New York: Princeton Architectural Press, 1993.

Caro, Robert A. *The Power Broker: Robert Moses and the Fall of New York.* New York: Knopf, 1974.

Carsky, Mary L., Elizabeth M. Dolan, and Rhona K. Free. "An Integrated Model of Home-based Work Effects on Family Quality of Life." *Journal of Business Research* 23, no. 1 (1991): 37.

Cashin, Sheryll D. "Localism, Self-Interest, and the Tyranny of the Favored Quarter: Addressing the Barriers to New Regionalism." *Georgetown Law Journal* 88, no. 7 (2000): 1985.

Central City Association of Los Angeles. *Downtown's Human Tragedy: It's Not Acceptable Anymore: A Public Health and Safety Plan.* Los Angeles: 2002.

Cheney, Charles H. "Removing Social Barriers by Zoning." In *The Survey 44, no. 11* (1920): 275.

Chicago Community Policing Evaluation Consortium. *Community Policing in Chicago, Year Ten: An Evaluation of Chicago's Alternative Policing Strategy.* Chicago: Illinois Criminal Justice Information Authority, 2004.

Chused, Richard H. "Euclid's Historical Imagery." *Case Western Reserve Law Review* 51, no. 4 (2001): 597.

Clancy, Patrick E., and Leo Quigley. "HOPE VI: A Vital Tool for Comprehensive Neighborhood Revitalization." *Georgetown Journal on Poverty Law and Policy* 8, no. 2 (2001): 527.

Clotfelter, Charles T. *After Brown: The Rise and Retreat of School Desegregation.* Princeton, NJ: Princeton University Press, 2004.

Clowney, Stephen. "Invisible Businessman: Undermining Black Enterprise with Land Use Rules." *University of Illinois Law Review* (forthcoming).

Cohen, Adam, and Elizabeth Taylor. *American Pharaoh: Mayor Richard J. Daley, His Battle for Chicago and the Nation.* Chicago: Back Bay Books, 2000.

Cohen , Cathy J., and Michael C. Dawson. "Neighborhood Poverty and African American Politics." *American Political Science Review* 87, no. 2 (1993): 286.

Cole, David. "Forward: Discretion and Discrimination Reconsidered: A Response to the New Criminal Justice Scholarship." *Georgetown Law Journal* 87, no. 5 (1999): 1059.

Collin, Robert W. "Review of the Legal Literature on Environmental Racism, Environmental Equity, and Environmental Justice." *Journal of Environmental Law and Litigation* 9, no. 1 (1994): 121.

Confessore, Nicholas. "Cities Grow Up, and Some See Sprawl." *New York Times,* August 6, 2006.

Connelly, Mark Thomas. *The Response to Prostitution in the Progressive Era.* Chapel Hill, NC: University of North Carolina Press, 1980.

Cooter, Robert. "Expressive Law and Economics." *Journal of Legal Studies* 27, no. 2 (1998): 585.

Cooter, Robert, and Thomas Ulen. *Law and Economics.* 4th ed. Boston: Pearson Publishing, 2004.

Corcoran, Mary, Roger Gordon, Deborah Laren, and Gary Solon. "The Association between Men's Economic Status and Their Family and Community Origins." *Journal of Human Resources* 27, no. 4 (1992): 575.

Cordner, G. W. "Fear of Crime and the Police: An Evaluation of a Fear-Reduction Strategy." *Journal of Police Science and Administration* 14, no. 3 (1986): 223.

Corman, Hope, and Naci Mocan. "Carrots, Sticks, and Broken Windows." *Journal of Law and Economics* 48, no. 1 (April 2005): 235.

Cott, Nancy F. *The Bonds of Womanhood: "Woman's Sphere" in New England, 1780–1830.* 2nd ed. New Haven, CT: Yale University Press, 1997.

Cottle, Michelle. "Boomerang: Did Integration Cause the Cincinnati Riots?" *New Republic,* May 7, 2001, 26.

Council on Environmental Quality. *The Costs of Sprawl: Case Studies and Further Research.* Chicago: Real Estate Research Corporation, 1975.

Covington, Jeannette, and Ralph Taylor. "Fear of Crime in Urban Residential Neighborhoods: Implications of between- and within-Neighborhoods for Current Models." *Sociological Quarterly* 32, no. 2 (1991): 231.

Crecine, John P., Otto A. Davis, and John E. Jackson. "Urban Property Markets: Some Empirical Results and Their Implications for Zoning." *Journal of Law and Economics* 10, no. 1 (1967): 79.

Cronon, William. *Nature's Metropolis: Chicago and the Great West.* New York: Norton, 1991.

Cullen, Julie Berry, and Steven D. Levitt. "Crime, Urban Flight, and the Consequences for Cities." *Review of Economics and Statistics* 81, no. 2 (1999).

Dana, David A. "Land Use Regulations in an Age of Heightened Scrutiny." *North Carolina Law Review* 75, no. 4 (1997): 1243.

Dan-Cohen, Meir. "Decisional Rules and Conduct Rules: On Acoustic Separation in Criminal Law." *Harvard Law Review* 97, no. 3 (1984): 626.

Davis, Robert, Andrés Duany, and Elizabeth Plater-Zyberk. *Lexicon of the New Urbanism.* Ed. 3.1. Miami: Duany Plater-Zyberk, 2002.

Daykin, Tom. "Cost of Park East Upgrades Soaring; Increase Likely to Fuel Debate Over Wages, Affordable Housing." *Milwaukee Journal Sentinel,* May 10, 2004, sec. D1.

———. "Pace Picking Up after Council's Vote; Unity Urged in Pushing Park East Development." *Milwaukee Journal Sentinel,* June 21, 2004, sec. D1.

———. "The Park East Land Is Cleared and Projects Are in the Works, but Developers Say They Need to Know What the City Will Give; Building Impatience." *Milwaukee Journal Sentinel,* May 1, 2007, sec A..

———. "Park East Project Trimmed; Developer also Drops Pursuit of Aid from City." *Milwaukee Journal Sentinel,* July 21, 2007, sec. D1.

———. "Study Discourages City Funds; Park East Development Could Hurt Other Projects, It Says." *Milwaukee Journal Sentinel,* June 7, 2007, sec. D1.

———. "Tenant Leaves Park East Plan: Development Too Slow, Firm Says." *Milwaukee Journal Sentinel,* July 6, 2007, sec. D1.

Decker, John F. *Prostitution: Regulation and Control.* Littleton, CO: Fred B. Rothman, 1979.

DeFrances, Carol J., and Steven K. Smith. "Perceptions of Neighborhood Crime, 1995." *Bureau of Justice Statistics: Special Report,* April 1998.

DeParle, Jason. " 'Safety Net' for Anchorage Homeless Is Seen as Both a Lifesaver and a Trap." *New York Times,* September 24, 1992, sec. B12.

———. "The 'W' Word Re-Engaged." *New York Times,* February 8, 2009, 1.

Dershowitz, Alan M. "Rights and Interests." In *Urgent Times: Policing and Rights in Inner-City Communities,* edited by Tracey L. Meares and Dan M. Kahan. Boston: Beacon Press, 1999.

Dilworth, Richardson. *The Urban Origins of Suburban Autonomy.* Cambridge, MA: Harvard University Press, 2005.

District of Columbia Redevelopment Land Agency. *Community Services and Family Relocation.* Washington, DC: 1964.

Diuguid, Lewis W. "Compassion Often Evades the Less Fortunate Among Us." *Kansas City Star,* March 10, 2005, Commentary.

Donohue, John D. "Tiebout? Or Not Tiebout? The Market Metaphor and America's Devolution Debate." *Journal of Economic Perspectives* 11, no. 3 (1997): 73.

Downs, Anthony. *New Visions for a Metropolitan America.* Washington, DC: Brookings Institution Press, 1994.

———. *Stuck in Traffic.* Washington, DC: Brookings Institution Press, 1992.

Duany, Andrés, Elizabeth Plater-Zyberk, and Jeff Speck. *Suburban Nation: The Rise of Sprawl and the Decline of the American Dream.* New York: North Point Press, 2000.

Duany, Andrés, and Emily Talen. "Transect Planning." *Journal of the American Planning Association* 68, no. 3 (2002): 247

Duany, Andrés, William Wright, and Sandy Sorlein. *SmartCode and Manual.* Ed. 8.0. Ithaca, NY: New Urban Publications, 2006, C2.

Dubin, Gary V., and Richard H. Robinson. "The Vagrancy Concept Reconsidered: Problems and Abuses of Status Criminality." *New York University Law Review* 37, no. 2, 102 (1962).

Dubin, Jon C. "From Junkyards to Gentrification: Explicating a Right to Protective Zoning in Low-Income Communities of Color." *Minnesota Law Review* 77, no. 4 (1993): 739.

Dunier, Mitchell. *Sidewalk.* New York: Farrar, Straus, and Giroux, 1999.

Dunn, James L., Jr. "Bureaucracy and the Bulldozer: Every City Has Plenty of Houses That Would Be Better Off Torn Down but a Maze of Legal Complications Often Keeps Them Standing." *Governing Magazine,* July 1994, 22.

Editorial. "And Now, the Hot-Dog War." *New York Times,* June 4, 1998, sec. A.

———. "Bold Approach in Southwest." *Washington Post,* October 19, 1952, sec. B4.

———. "Broken Windows Are a Clue to Livability." *Indianapolis Star,* January 18, 2002, sec. 14A.

———. "Fair Food Vending in Midtown." *New York Times,* April 22, 1994, sec. A.

———. "A Hard Bargain." *Salt Lake Tribune,* September 12, 2004, sec. AA2.

———. "Instead of Slums." *Washington Post,* September 10, 1952, 12.

———. "New York Changes Command; Mayor Giuliani Bows Out." *New York Times,* December 30, 2001, sec. 4.

———. "Street Peddlers in New York." *New York Times,* May 28, 1994, sec. 1.

Einzmann, David. "Chicago Police to Broaden Area for Loitering Arrests." *Chicago Tribune,* May 2, 2004, Metro sec.

Ellickson, Robert C. "Alternatives to Zoning: Covenants, Nuisance Rules, and Fines as Land Use Controls." *University of Chicago Law Review* 40, no. 4, 683 (1973).

———. "Controlling Chronic Misconduct in City Spaces: Of Panhandlers, Skid Rows, and Public-Space Zoning." *Yale Law Journal* 105, no. 5 (1996): 1165.

———. "Monitoring the Mayor: Will the New Information Technologies Make Local Officials More Responsible?" *Urban Lawyer* 32, no. 3 (2000): 391.

———. "New Institutions for Old Neighborhoods." *Duke Law Journal* 48, no. 1 (1998): 75.

———. *Order without Law: How Neighbors Settle Disputes.* Cambridge: Harvard University Press, 1991.

———. "Suburban Growth Controls: An Economic and Legal Analysis." *Yale Law Journal* 86, no. 3 (1977): 385.

Ellickson, Robert C., and Vicki L. Been. *Land Use Controls.* 3rd ed. New York: Aspen Publishers, 2005.

Elling, Richard C., and Ann Workman Sheldon. "Determinants of Enterprise Zone Success: A Four State Perspective." In *Enterprise Zones: New Directions in Economic Development,* edited by Roy Green, 136. Newbury Park, CA: Sage Publications, 1991.

Elwood, John P. "Rethinking Government Participation in Urban Renewal: Neighborhood Revitalization in New Haven." *Yale Law and Policy Review* 12, no. 1 (1994): 138.

Emerson, Chad. "Making Main Street Legal Again: The SmartCode Solution to Sprawl."
    Missouri Law Review 71, no. 3 (2006): 637

Emery, Erin. "Homeless Center Draws Praise, Ire." *Denver Post,* June 25, 2000, sec. B4.

———. "Ideas to Aid Homeless Unveiled: Colorado Springs Panel Calls for 3 Shelters."
    Denver Post, April 3, 2002, sec. B4.

Enkoji, M. S. "Californians Get Say in Cases Involving Those Convicted of Nuisance
    Laws." *Sacramento Bee,* October 29, 2002.

Enrich, Peter D. "Saving the States from Themselves: Commerce Clause Constraints on
    State Tax Incentives for Business." *Harvard Law Review* 110, no. 2 (1996): 377.

Epstein, Richard A. *Bargaining with the State.* Princeton, NJ: Princeton University Press,
    1993.

———. "The Moral and Practical Dilemmas of an Underground Economy." *Yale Law
    Journal* 103, no. 8 (1994): 2157.

———. *Takings: Private Property and the Power of Eminent Domain.* Cambridge, MA:
    Harvard University Press, 1985.

Erez, Miriam, and P. Christopher Earley. *Culture, Self-Identity, and Work.* New York: Ox-
    ford University Press, 1993.

Erickson, Rodney A., and Susan W. Friedman. "Comparative Dimensions of State Enter-
    prise Zone Policies." In *Enterprise Zones: New Directions in Economic Development,* ed-
    ited by Roy E. Green, 180. Newbury Park, CA: Sage Publications, 1991.

Fainstein, Susan S. "Cities and Diversity: Should We Want It? Can We Plan for It?" *Urban
    Affairs Review* 41, no. 1 (2005): 3.

Fannie Mae. *The 1997 Fannie Mae National Housing Survey: City Life, Homeownership, and
    the American Dream.* Washington, DC, 1997.

Farber, Daniel A., and Philip P. Frickey. *Law and Public Choice.* Chicago: University of
    Chicago Press, 1991.

Fennell, Lee Anne. "Exclusion's Attraction: Land Use Controls in Tieboutian Perspective."
    In *The Tiebout Model at Fifty: Essays in Public Economics in Honor of Wallace Oates,* ed-
    ited by William A. Fischel, 163. Cambridge, MA: Lincoln Institute of Land Policy, 2006.

———. "Homes Rule." *Yale Law Journal* 112, no. 3 (2002): 617.

Ferkhenhoff, Eric. "Anti-Gang Ordinance Passes Test," *Chicago Tribune,* March 20, 2002.

Fischel, William A. *Do Growth Controls Matter?: A Review of Empirical Evidence on the Ef-
    fectiveness and Efficiency of Local Government Land Use Regulation.* Cambridge, MA: Lin-
    coln Institute of Land Policy, 1989.

———. "An Economic History of Zoning and a Cure for Its Exclusionary Effects." *Urban
    Studies* 41, no. 2 (2004): 317.

———. *The Economics of Zoning Laws: A Property Rights Approach to American Land Use
    Controls.* Baltimore: Johns Hopkins University Press, 1985.

———. *The Homevoter Hypothesis: How Home Values Influence Local Government Taxation,
    School Finance, and Land-Use Policies.* Cambridge, MA: Harvard University Press, 2001.

———. "The Political Economy of Public Use in Poletown: How Federal Grants Encourage
    Excessive Use of Eminent Domain." *Michigan State Law Review 2004,* no. 4 (2004): 929.

———, ed. *The Tiebout Model at Fifty: Essays in Public Economics in Honor of Wallace
    Oates.* Cambridge, MA: Lincoln Institute of Land Policy, 2006.

Fishman, Robert. *Bourgeois Utopias: The Rise and Fall of Suburbia.* New York: Basic Books, 1987.

FitzPatrick, Michael S. "A Disaster in Every Generation: An Analysis of HOPE VI: HUD's Newest Big Budget Development Plan." *Georgetown Journal on Poverty Law and Policy* 7, no. 2 (2000): 421.

Flanagan, Peter M. "Trespass-Zoning: Ensuring Neighborhoods a Safer Future by Excluding Those with a Criminal Past." *Notre Dame Law Review* 79, no. 1 (2003): 327.

Florida, Richard. *The Rise of the Creative Class.* New York: Basic Books, 2002.

Foote, Caleb, "Vagrancy-Type Law and Its Administration." *University of Pennsylvania Law Review* 104, no. 5 (1956): 604.

Ford, Richard Thompson. "The Boundaries of Race: Political Geography in Legal Analysis." *Harvard Law Review* 107, no. 8 (1994): 1841.

Fosmoe, Margaret. "Council Approves Eddy Street Commons." *South Bend Tribune,* July 17, 2007, sec. A.

"Freeway Razing Sets Stage for $250 Million in Development." *New Urban News,* July/August 2004.

Freidman, Lawrence W. *Government and Slum Housing: A Century of Frustration.* Chicago: Rand McNally, 1968.

French, Susan. "There Goes the Neighborhood: To Spark Urban Renewal, Some Towns Dynamite History." *Preservation Magazine,* January 4, 2002.

Frey, William H. *Diversity Spreads Out: Metropolitan Shifts in Hispanic, Asian, and Black Populations since 2000.* Washington, DC: Metropolitan Policy Program, Brookings Institution, 2006.

Fried, Marc. "Grieving for a Lost Home: Psychological Costs of Relocation" In *Urban Renewal: The Record and the Controversy,* 359, edited by James Q. Wilson. Cambridge, MA: MIT Press, 1966.

———. "Urban Renewal: The Record and the Controversy." In *Urban Renewal: The Record and the Controversy,* edited by James Q. Wilson, 359–79. Cambridge, MA: MIT Press, 1966.

Frieden, Bernard J., and Lynne B. Sagalyn. *Downtown, Inc.: How America Rebuilds Cities.* Cambridge, MA: MIT Press, 1989.

Frug, Gerald E. "The City as Legal Concept." *Harvard Law Review* 93, no. 6 (1980): 1057.

———. *City Making: Building Communities without Building Walls.* Princeton, NJ: Princeton University Press, 1999.

———. "City Services." *New York University Law Review* 73, no. 1 (1998): 23.

———. "Decentering Decentralization." *University of Chicago Law Review* 60, no. 2 (1993): 253.

———. "Surveying Law and Borders: The Geography of Community." *Stanford Law Review* 48, no. 5 (1996): 1047.

Galster, George C. "Consequences from the Redistribution of Urban Poverty during the 1990s: A Cautionary Tale." *Economic Development Quarterly* 19, no. 2 (2005): 119.

Galvan, Sara C. "Rehabilitating Rehab through State Building Codes." *Yale Law Journal* 115, no. 7 (2006): 1744.

Gamm, Gerald. *Urban Exodus: Why the Jews Left Boston and the Catholics Stayed.* Cambridge, MA: Harvard University Press, 1999.

Gans, Herbert J. *The Urban Villagers: Group and Class in the Life of Italian-Americans.* New York: Free Press of Glencoe, 1962.

Gardiner, John A., and Theodore R. Lyman. *Decisions for Sale: Corruption and Reform in Land-Use and Building Regulation.* New York: Praeger, 1978.

Garnett, Nicole Stelle. "The Neglected Political Economy of Eminent Domain." *Michigan Law Review* 105, no. 1 (2006): 101.

———. "On Castles and Commerce: Zoning Law and the Home-Business Dilemma." *William and Mary Law Review* 42, no. 4 (2001): 1191.

———. "Ordering (and Order in) the City." *Stanford Law Review* 57, no. 1 (2004): 1.

———. "The Public-Use Question as a Takings Problem." *George Washington Law Review* 71, no. 6 (2003): 934.

———. "Relocating Disorder." *Virginia Law Review* 91, no. 5 (2005): 1075.

———. "The Road from Welfare to Work: Informal Transportation and the Urban Poor." *Harvard Journal on Legislation* 38, no. 1 (2001): 173.

———. "Save the Cities, Stop the Suburbs?" *Yale Law Journal* 116, (2006): 599.

———. "Suburbs as Exit, Suburbs as Entrance." *Michigan Law Review* 106, no. 2 (2007): 277.

———. "Trouble Preserving Paradise." *Cornell Law Review* 87, no. 1 (2001): 158.

———. "Unsubsidizing Suburbia." *Minnesota Law Review* 90, no. 2 (2005): 459.

Garnett, Richard W., and Nicole Stelle Garnett. "School Choice, the First Amendment, and Social Justice." *Texas Review of Law and Politics* 4, no. 2 (2000): 301.

Garofalo, J., and J. Laub. "The Fear of Crime: Broadening Our Perspective." *Victimology* 3, no. 3/4 (1978): 242.

Gates, Lauren B., and William M. Rohe. "Fear and Reactions to Crime: A Revised Model." *Urban Affairs Quarterly* 22, no. 3 (1987): 425.

Giamatti, A. Bartlett. *Take Time for Paradise: Americans and Their Games.* New York: Summit, 1989.

Gibson, Chris L., Jihong Zhao, Nicholas P. Lovrich, and Michael J. Gaffney. "Social Integration, Individual Perceptions of Collective Efficacy, and Fear of Crime in Three Cities." *Justice Quarterly* 19, no. 3 (2002): 537.

Gillette, Clayton P. "Courts, Covenants, and Communities." *University of Chicago Law Review* 61, no. 4 (1994): 1375.

———. "The Law and Economics of Federalism: Business Incentives, Interstate Competition, and the Commerce Clause." *Minnesota Law Review* 82, no. 2 (1997): 447.

———. "Plebiscites, Participation, and Collective Action in Local Government Law." *Michigan Law Review* 86, no. 5 (1988): 930.

———. "Regionalization and Interlocal Bargains." *New York University Law Review* 76, no. 1 (2001): 190.

Gillette, Howard, Jr. *Between Justice and Beauty: Race, Planning and the Failure of Urban Policy in Washington, D.C.* Baltimore: Johns Hopkins University Press, 1995.

"Giuliani Says a New Plan Will Not Please Vendors." *New York Times,* June 19, 1998, sec. B.

Glaab. Charles N. *A History of Urban America.* 3rd ed. New York: Macmillan, 1983.

Glaeser, Edward L., and Joshua D. Gottlieb. "Urban Resurgence and the Consumer City." Urban Studies 43, no. 8, 1275.

Glaeser, Edward L., and Jessie Shapiro. "City Growth: Which Places Grew and Why." In *Redefining Urban and Suburban America: Evidence from Census 2000,* edited by Bruce Katz and Robert E. Lang. Washington, DC: Brookings Institution Press, 2003.

Glaeser, Edward L., and Jacob L. Vigdor. "Racial Segregation: Promising News." In *Redefining Urban and Suburban America,* edited by Bruce Katz and Robert Lang. Vol. 1, 211. Washington, DC: Brookings Institution Press, 2003.

Glassner, Barry. *The Culture of Fear: Why Americans Are Afraid of the Wrong Things.* New York: Basic Books, 1999.

Goetz, Edward G. "Land Use and Homeless Policy in Los Angeles." *International Journal of Urban and Regional Research* 16, (1992): 540.

Goldstein, Herman. *Problem-Oriented Policing.* New York: McGraw-Hill, 1990.

———. "Toward Community-Oriented Policing: Potential, Basic Requirements, and Threshold Questions." *Crime and Delinquency* 33, no. 1 (1987): 6.

Goldstein, Joseph. "Police Discretion Not to Invoke the Criminal Process." *Yale Law Journal* 69, no. 4 (1960): 543.

Gonser, James. "Homeless Center Appears Doomed." *Honolulu Advertiser,* June 1, 2004, sec. A1.

Good Jobs First. *Minding the Candy Store: State Audits of Economic Development.* Washington, DC: Institute on Taxation and Economic Policy, 2000.

Grasmick, Harold G., and Donald E. Green. "Legal Punishment, Social Disapproval, and Internalization as Inhibitors of Illegal Behavior." *Journal of Criminal Law and Criminology* 71, no. 3 (1980): 325.

Gratz, Roberta Brandes, and Norman Mintz. *Cities Back from the Edge: New Life for Downtown.* Washington, DC: Preservation Press, 1998.

Greenbaum, Susan D. "Housing Abandonment in Inner-City Black Neighborhoods: A Case Study of the Effects of the Dual Housing Market." In *The Cultural Meaning of Urban Space,* edited by Robert Rotenberg and Gary McDonogh. Westport, CT: Bergin & Garvey, 1993.

Greenberg, Stephanie W., William M. Rohe, and Jay R. Williams. "Safety in Urban Neighborhoods: A Comparison of Physical Characteristics and Informal Territorial Control in High and Low Crime Neighborhoods." *Population and Environment* 5, no. 3 (1982): 141.

Greene, Jack R., and Ralph B. Taylor, "Community-Based Policing and Foot Patrol: Issues of Theory and Evaluation." In *Community Policing: Rhetoric or Reality,* edited by Jack Greene and Stephen Mastrofski. New York: Praeger, 1988.

Grogan, Paul, and Tony Proscio. *Comeback Cities: A Blueprint for Urban Neighborhood Revival.* Boulder, CO: Westview Press, 2000, 152.

Grotto, Jason, Laurie Cohen, and Sara Olkon. "Public Housing Limbo." *Chicago Tribune* July 6, 2008, 1.

Gunther, Gerald. "The Supreme Court, 1971 Term—Foreword: In Search of Evolving Doctrine on a Changing Court: A Model for a Newer Equal Protection." *Harvard Law Review* 86, no. 1 (1972): 1.

Gurwitt, Rob. "The Mayor as Missionary." *Governing Magazine,* July 1999, 32.

Gutheim, Frederick Albert. *Worthy of the Nation: The History of Planning for the National Capital.* Washington, DC: Smithsonian Institution Press, 1977.

Haar, Charles M., and Jerold S. Kayden, eds. *Zoning and the American Dream: Promises Still to Keep.* Chicago: Planners Press, 1989.

Haar, Charles M., and Michael Allen Wolf. "Euclid Lives: The Survival of Progressive Jurisprudence." *Harvard Law Review* 115, no. 8 (2002): 2158.

Hall, Peter. "The British Enterprise Zones." In *Enterprise Zones: New Directions in Economic Development,* edited by Roy E. Green, 180. Newbury Park, CA: Sage Publications, 1991.

Hall, Peter, Paul Barker, Reyner Banham, and Cedric Price. "Non-Plan: An Experiment in Freedom." *New Society* 26, (1968): 435–43.

Handlin, Oscar, and Mary Flug Handlin. *Commonwealth: A Study of the Role of Government in the American Economy: Massachusetts, 1774–1861.* Cambridge, MA: Harvard University Press, 1969.

Harcourt, Bernard E. *Illusion of Order: The False Promise of Broken Windows Policing.* Cambridge, MA: Harvard University Press, 2001.

———. "Policing L.A.'s Skid Row: Crime and Real Estate Development in Downtown Los Angeles." *University of Chicago Legal Forum* 2005, 2325 (2005).

———. "Reflecting on the Subject: A Critique of the Social Influence Conception of Deterrence, the Broken Windows Theory, and Order-Maintenance Policing New York Style." *Michigan Law Review* 97, no. 2 (1998): 291.

Harcourt, Bernard E., and Jens Ludwig. "Broken Windows: New Evidence from New York City and a Five-City Social Experiment." *University of Chicago Law Review* 73, no. 1 (2006): 271.

———. "Reefer Madness: Broken Windows Policing and Misdemeanor Marijuana Arrests in New York City, 1989–2000." *Criminology and Public Policy* 6, no. 1 (February 2007): 165.

Hartman, Chester. "Relocation: Illusory Promises and No Relief." *Virginia Law Review* 57, no. 5 (1971): 745.

Hayden, Dolores. *The Grand Domestic Revolution: A History of Feminist Designs for American Homes, Neighborhoods, and Cities.* Cambridge, MA: MIT Press, 1981.

———. *Redesigning the American Dream: The Future of Housing, Work, and Family Life.* New York: Norton, 1984.

Hedgpeth, Dana. "Southwest Waterfront Will Finally Get Over the '60s: Development Plan Would Shun Tall Towers, Dead-End Streets." *Washington Post,* October 9, 2006, sec. D1.

Heen, Mary L. "Welfare Reform, Child Care Costs, and Taxes: Delivering Increased Work-Related Child Care Benefits to Low-Income Families." *Yale Law and Policy Review* 13, no. 2 (1995): 173.

Held, Margaret Beebe. "Developing Microbusinesses in Public Housing: Notes from the Field." *Harvard Civil Rights–Civil Liberties Law Review* 31, no. 2 (1996): 473.

Heller, Michael A., and James E. Krier. "Deterrence and Distribution in the Law of Takings." *Harvard Law Review* 112, no. 5 (1999): 997.

Hendricks, Mike. "A Homeless Zone of Their Own." *Kansas City Star,* December 31, 2003, sec. B1.

Hernandez, Raymond. "City's Right to Bar Vendors from Streets Is Upheld." *New York Times,* June 18, 1997, sec. B.

Hershkoff, Helen, and Adam S. Cohen. "Begging to Differ: The First Amendment Right to Beg." *Harvard Law Review* 104, no. 4 (1991): 896.

Hess, Robert V. "Helping People Off the Streets: Real Solutions to Urban Homelessness." *USA Today Magazine,* January 2000, 18.

Hicks, Jonathan P. "Amid Calm, Anger Lingers on 125th St." *New York Times,* October 31, 1994, sec. B.

———. "Giuliani Broadens Crackdown to Banish All Illegal Vendors." *New York Times,* May 9, 1994, sec. B.

———. "Many 125th Street Vendors Say They Will Resist Move." *New York Times,* October 17, 1994, sec. B.

———. "Vendors' Ouster and Boycott Divide Harlem." *New York Times,* October 23, 1994, sec. 1.

Hilberseimer, Ludwig. *The New City: Principles of Planning.* Chicago: P. Theobald, 1944.

Hill, Martha S., and Greg J. Duncan. "Parental Family Income and the Socioeconomic Attainment of Children." *Social Science Research* 16, no. 1 (1987): 39.

Hinkley, David. "Quality of Life: The Mayor Who Understood." *Daily News,* December 20, 2001.

Hirsch, Arnold R. *Making the Second Ghetto: Race and Housing in Chicago, 1940–1960.* New York: Cambridge University Press, 1983.

Hoch, Charles, and Robert A. Slayton. *New Homeless and Old: Community and the Skid Row Hotel.* Philadelphia: Temple University Press, 1989.

Hogan, Wesley. "Cincinnati: Race in the Closed City." *Social Policy* 32, no. 2 (2001): 49.

Holloway, Lynette. "Street Vendors Roll Their Way Back to Some Corners." *New York Times,* June 19, 1997, sec. B8.

Holzer, Harry J. "The Spatial Mismatch Hypothesis: What Has the Evidence Shown?" *Urban Studies* 28, no. 1 (1991): 105.

"Hope VI Funds New Urban Neighborhoods." *New Urban News,* Jan./Feb. 2002.

Houghton, Walter E. *The Victorian Frame of Mind, 1830–1870.* New Haven, CT: Yale University Press, 1957.

Howell, William G., Paul E. Peterson, Patrick J. Wolf, and David E. Campbell. *The Education Gap: Vouchers and Urban Schools.* Washington, DC: Brookings Institution Press, 2002.

Howes, Joshua. "Englewood Leaders Urge City to Create Jobs." *Chicago Tribune,* July 29, 2003, sec. C2.

Hunter, Albert, and Terry L. Baumer. "Street Traffic, Social Integration, and Fear of Crime." *Sociological Inquiry* 52, no. 2 (1982): 123.

Hylton, Keith N. "Optimal Law Enforcement and Victim Precaution." *RAND Journal of Economics* 27, no. 1 (1996): 197.

Ientilucci, Arthur. "Pigs in the Parlor or Diamonds in the Rough? A New Vision for Nonconformity Regulation." *Zoning News,* April 2003, 1.

Ihlanfeldt, Keith R., and David L. Sjoquist. "The Effect of Job Access on Black and White Youth Employment: A Cross-Sectional Analysis." *Urban Studies* 28, no. 2 (1991): 255.

Inman, Robert, and Daniel Rubinfeld. "The Judicial Pursuit of Local Fiscal Equity." *Harvard Law Review* 92, no. 8 (1979): 1662.

Jackson, Kenneth T. *Crabgrass Frontier: The Suburbanization of the United States.* New York: Oxford University Press, 1985.

Jacobs, Eugene B. "Land Drafting Problems in Redevelopment and Urban Renewal Projects." *Real Property, Probate and Trust Journal* 5, no. 3 (1970): 373.

Jacobs, Jane. *The Death and Life of Great American Cities.* New York: Vintage Books, 1961.

Jahoda, Marie, Paul F. Lazarsfeld, and Hans Zeisel. *Marienthal: The Sociography of an Unemployed Community.* Edison, New York: Transaction Publishers, 1971.

James, Franklin J. "Economic Development: A Zero-Sum Game?" In *Urban Economic Development,* edited by Richard D. Bingham and John P. Blair, 157. Beverly Hills, CA: Sage Publications, 1984.

———. "The Evaluation of Enterprise Zone Programs." In *Enterprise Zones: New Directions in Economic Development,* edited by Roy E. Green, 180. Newbury Park, CA: Sage Publications, 1991.

Jargowsky, Paul A. *Poverty and Place.* New York: Russell Sage Foundation, 1997.

———. "Stunning Progress, Hidden Problems: The Dramatic Decline of Concentrated Poverty in the 1990s." In *Redefining Urban and Suburban America,* edited by Alan Berube, Bruce Katz, and Robert E. Lang. Vol. 2, 137. Washington, DC: Brookings Institution Press, 2003.

Jeffrey, Kirk. "The Family as Utopian Retreat from the City: The Nineteenth-Century Contribution." *Soundings,* Spring 1972, 22.

Jencks, Christopher. *The Homeless.* Cambridge, MA: Harvard University Press, 1994.

———. *Rethinking Social Policy: Race, Poverty, and the Underclass.* Cambridge, MA: Harvard University Press, 1992.

Jewett, Christina. "Homeless Programs May Face Cuts." *Sacramento Bee,* March 15, 2004, sec. B1.

Joseph, Mark L. "Is Mixed-Income Development an Antidote to Urban Poverty?" *Housing Policy Debate* 17, no. 2 (2006): 209.

Justement, Louis. *New Cities for Old: City Building in Terms of Space, Time, and Money.* New York: McGraw-Hill, 1946.

Kahan, Dan M. "Between Economics and Sociology: The New Path of Deterrence." *Michigan Law Review* 95, no. 8 (1997): 2477.

———. "Reciprocity, Collective Action, and Community Policing." *California Law Review* 90, no. 5 (2002): 1527.

———. "Social Influence, Social Meaning, and Deterrence." *Virginia Law Review* 83, no. 2 (1997): 349.

———. "Social Norms, Social Meaning, and the Economic Analysis of Crime." *Journal of Legal Studies* 27, no. 2 (1998): 609.

Kahan, Dan M., and Tracey L. Meares. "The Coming Crisis of Criminal Procedure." *Georgetown Law Journal* 86, no. 5 (1998): 1159.

Kain, John F. "The Spatial Mismatch Hypothesis: Three Decades Later." *Housing Policy Debate* 3, no. 2 (1994): 371.

Kasarda, John D. "Industrial Restructuring and the Changing Location of Jobs." In *State of the Union: America in the 1990s,* edited by Reynolds Farley. Vol. 1, 215. New York: Russell Sage Foundation, 1995.

————. "Urban Industrial Transition and the Underclass." *Annals of the American Academy of Political and Social Science* 501, no. 1 (1989): 26.

Katyal, Neal Kumar. "Architecture as Crime Control." *Yale Law Journal* 111, no. 5 (2002): 1039.

Katz, Peter, Vincent Joseph Scully, and Todd W. Bressi. *The New Urbanism: Toward an Architecture of Community.* New York: McGraw-Hill, 1994.

Katzman, Martin D. "The Contribution of Crime to Urban Decline." *Urban Studies* 17, no. 3 (1980): 277.

Kelling, George L. *Newark Foot Patrol Experiment.* Washington, DC: Police Foundation, 1981.

————. "Police and Communities: The Quiet Revolution." *Perspectives on Policing 1.* Washington, DC: National Institute of Justice, U.S. Department of Justice, June 1988.

Kelling, George L., and Catherine M. Coles. *Fixing Broken Windows: Restoring Order and Reducing Crime in Our Communities.* New York: Martin Kessler Books, 1996.

Kelling, George L., and Mark Moore. "From Political to Reform to Community: The Evolving Strategy of Police." In *Police and Society,* edited by David H. Bayley, 15. Beverly Hills, CA: Sage Publications, 1977.

Kelling, George L., Antony Pate, Duane Dieckman, and Charles E. Brown. *The Kansas City Preventive Patrol Experiment: A Summary Report.* Washington, DC: Police Foundation, 1974.

Kelling, George L., and William H. Sousa Jr. "Do Police Matter? An Analysis of the Impact of New York City's Police Reforms." Civic Report 22. New York: Manhattan Institute, Center for Civic Innovation, December 2001.

Kelly, Eric D. *Managing Community Growth: Policies, Techniques, and Impacts.* Westport, CT: Praeger, 1993.

Kendig, Lane. *Performance Zoning.* Chicago: Planners Press, 1980.

Kennedy, Lawrence W. *Planning the City upon a Hill: Boston Since 1630.* Amherst, MA: University of Massachusetts, 1992.

Kennedy, Randall. *Race, Crime, and the Law.* New York: Pantheon Books, 1997.

————. "The State, Criminal Law, and Racial Discrimination: A Comment." *Harvard Law Review* 107, no. 6 (1994): 1255.

Kerber, Linda K. "Separate Spheres, Female Worlds, Woman's Place: The Rhetoric of Women's History." *Journal of American History* 75, no. 1 (1982): 9.

Kettles, Gregg W. "Regulating Vending in the Sidewalk Commons." *Temple Law Review* 77, no. 1 (2004): 1–45.

Kingsley, Thomas, and Kathryn L. S. Pettit. "Comment on George C. Galster's 'Consequences from the Redistribution of Urban Poverty during the 1990s: A Cautionary Tale.'" *Economic Development Quarterly* 19, no. 2 (2005): 126.

Klein, Michael R. "Eminent Domain: Judicial Response to the Human Disruption." *Journal of Urban Law* 46, no. 1 (1968): 1.

Kmiec, Douglas W. "Deregulating Land Use: An Alternative Free Enterprise Development System." *University of Pennsylvania Law Review* 130, no. 1 (1981): 28.

Knaap, Gerrit, and Arthur C. Nelson. *The Regulated Landscape: Lessons on State Land Use Planning from Oregon.* Cambridge, MA: Lincoln Institute of Land Policy, 1992.

Komesar, Neil K. *Law's Limits: The Rule of Law and the Supply and Demand of Rights.* New York: Cambridge University Press, 2001.

Kornhauser, Lewis A. "No Best Answer?" *University of Pennsylvania Law Review* 146, no. 5 (1998): 1599.

Kosman, Joel. "Toward an Inclusionary Jurisprudence: A Reconceptualization of Zoning." *Catholic University Law Review* 43, no. 1 (1993): 59.

Kotkin, Joel. *The City: A Global History.* New York: Modern Library, 2005.

———. "Suburbia: Homeland of the American Future." *Next American City,* August 2006.

Kotlowitz, Alex. "All Boarded Up," *New York Times Magazine,* March 4, 2009.

Krasnowiecki, Jan Z. "Abolish Zoning." *Syracuse Law Review* 31, no. 3 (1980): 719.

Kriemer, Seth F. "Allocational Sanctions: The Problem of Negative Rights in a Positive State." *University of Pennsylvania Law Review* 132, no. 6 (1984): 1293.

Krist, John. "State Air Guidelines Conflict with 'Smart Growth.' " *California Planning and Development Report* 20, no. 6 (2005): 6.

Kruse, Kevin M. *White Flight: Atlanta and the Making of Modern Conservatism.* Princeton, NJ: Princeton University Press, 2005.

Kruse, Kevin M., and Thomas J. Sugrue. "Introduction." In *The New Suburban History,* edited by Kevin M. Kruse and Thomas J. Sugrue, 1. Chicago: University of Chicago Press, 2006.

Kunstler, James Howard. *Home from Nowhere: Remaking Our Everyday World for the Twenty-First Century.* New York: Simon & Schuster, 1996.

Kurtz, Ellen M., Barbara A. Koons, and Ralph B. Taylor. "Land Use, Physical Deterioration, Resident-Based Control, and Calls for Service on Urban Streetblocks." *Justice Quarterly* 15, no. 1 (1998): 121–35.

LaFave, Wayne. "The Police and Nonenforcement of the Law—Part I." *Wisconsin Law Review* 1962, no. 1 (1962): 104.

LaFave, Wayne R., and Jerold H. Israel. *Criminal Procedure.* 2nd ed. St. Paul, MN: West Publishing, 1992.

Lafferty, Ronald N., and H. E. Frech III. "Community Environment and the Market Value of Single-Family Homes: The Effect of the Dispersion of Land Uses." *Journal of Law and Economics* 21, no. 2 (1978): 381.

LaGrange, Randy L., Kenneth F. Ferraro, and Michael Supancic. "Perceived Risk and Fear of Crime: Role of Social and Physical Incivilities." *Journal of Research in Crime and Delinquency* 29, no. 3 (1992): 311–34.

Lake, Robin. *Hopes, Fears, and Reality: A Balanced Look at American Charter Schools in 2007.* Washington, DC: National Charter Schools Research Project, 2007.

Lane, Vincent. "Public Housing Sweep Stakes: My Battle with the ACLU." *Policy Review* 69, (1994): 68.

Langdon, Philip. *A Better Place to Live: Reshaping the American Suburb.* Amherst, MA: University of Massachusetts Press, 1994.

Lasker, Bruno. "Unwalled Towns." *The Survey* 43, no. 19 (1920): 675–77.

Lazare, Daniel. "Cincinnati and the X-Factor." *Columbia Journalism Review* 40 (2001): 43.

Le Corbusier. *The City of To-morrow and Its Planning.* London: John Rodker Publishing, 1929.

Lee, Barrett A. "The Urban Unease Revisited: Perceptions of Local Safety and Neighborhood Satisfaction among Metropolitan Residents." *Social Science Quarterly* 62, no. 4 (1981): 4.

Lee, Matthew R., and Terri L. Earnest. "Perceived Community Cohesion and Perceived Risk of Victimization." *Justice Quarterly* 20, no. 1 (2003): 131–38.

Lees, Martha A. "Preserving Property Values? Preserving Proper Homes? Preserving Privilege?: The Pre-Euclid Debate Over Zoning for Exclusively Private Residential Areas, 1916–1926." *University of Pittsburgh Law Review* 56, no. 2 (1994): 367.

Leland, John. "On a Hunt for Ways to Put Sex in the City." *New York Times,* December 11, 2003, sec. F1.

Leoussis, Fay. "The New Constitutional Right to Beg—Is Begging Really Protected Speech?" *St. Louis Public University Law Review* 14, no. 2 (1995): 529.

Lessig, Lawrence. "The Regulation of Social Meaning." *University of Chicago Law Review* 62, no. 3 (1995): 943.

Leung, Shirley. "Chinatown Enjoys a Renaissance." *Boston Globe,* April 9, 1997, sec. A1.

Levine, Richard. "On the Sidewalks, Business Is Booming." *New York Times,* September 24, 1990, sec. B1.

Levinson, David. "Skid Row in Transition." *Urban Anthropology* 3, no. 1 (1974): 79.

Levitt, Steven D. "Understanding Why Crime Fell in the 1990s: Four Factors That Explain the Decline and Six That Do Not." *Journal of Economic Perspectives* 18, no. 1 (2004): 163.

Levmore, Saul. "Changes, Anticipations, and Reparations." *Columbia Law Review* 99, no. 7 (1999): 1657.

———. "Just Compensation and Just Politics." *Connecticut Law Review* 22, no. 2 (1990): 285.

———. "Takings, Torts, and Special Interests." *Virginia Law Review* 77, no. 7 (1991): 1333.

Lewis, Dan A., and Greta Salem. *Fear of Crime: Incivility and the Production of a Social Problem.* New Brunswick: Transaction Books, 1986.

Lewis, David L. *District of Columbia: A Bicentennial History.* New York: Norton, 1976.

Lewis, Roger K. "Now Comes the Real Test: Putting the Southwest Development Plan into Action." *Washington Post,* November 11, 2006, sec. F5.

Lewis, Steve. "Zoning Trends: The Mixed-Use Puzzle." *Real Traffic Magazine,* May 1, 2002.

"Liability for Creation or Maintenance of a Nuisance." *American Jurisprudence 2d,* State and Federal, 57, § 120 et seq. Minnesota: Thompson-West, 2001.

Liebmann, George W. "Devolution of Power to Community and Block Associations." *Urban Lawyer* 25, no. 2 (1993): 335.

———. *The Little Platoons: Sub-Local Governments in Modern History.* Westport, CT: Praeger, 1995.

Lind, H. C. "What Constitutes a 'Home Occupation' or the Like within Accessory Use Provisions of Zoning Regulation." *American Law Reports, Federal 2d.* 73, (1960): 439.

Liska, Allen E., Andrew Sanchirico, and Mark D. Reed. "Fear of Crime and Constrained Behavior: Specifying and Estimating the Reciprocal Effects Model." *Social Forces* 66, no. 3 (1988): 827.

Livingston, Debra Ann. "Police, Community Caretaking, and the Fourth Amendment." *University of Chicago Legal Forum* 1998, no. 1 (1998): 261.

———. "Police Discretion and the Quality of Life in Public Places: Courts, Communities, and the New Policing." *Columbia Law Review* 97, no. 3 (1997): 551.

————. "Review: Brutality in Blue: Community, Authority, and the Elusive Promise of Police Reform." *Michigan Law Review* 92, no. 6 (1994): 1556.

Logan, Wayne A. "The Shadow Criminal Law of Municipal Governance." *Ohio State Law Journal* 62, no. 4 (2001): 1409.

Lunney, Glynn S., Jr. "A Critical Reexamination of the Takings Jurisprudence." *Michigan Law Review* 90, no. 7 (1992): 1892.

Maag, Christopher. "Cleveland Sues 21 Lenders Over Subprime Mortgages." *New York Times,* January 12, 2008.

Mabry, Cynthia R. "Brother Can You Spare Some Change—and Your Privacy Too?: Avoiding a Fatal Collision Between Public Interests and the Beggar's First Amendment Rights." *University of San Francisco Law Review* 28, no. 2 (1994): 309.

Mac Donald, Heather. "BIDs Really Work." *City Journal,* Spring 1996.

————. "Skid Row in Rehab." *Los Angeles Times,* November 18, 2007.

————. "What Really Happened in Cincinnati." *City Journal,* Summer 2001, 28.

Mackey, Thomas C. *Red Lights Out: A Legal History of Prostitution, Disorderly Houses, and Vice Districts, 1870–1917.* New York: Garland, 1987.

Maier, Andrew. "The Homeless in the Post-Industrial City." *Political Geography* 5, no. 5 (1986): 357–63.

Makielski, S. J. *The Politics of Zoning: The New York Experience.* New York: Columbia University Press, 1966.

Mallamud, Jonathan. "Begging and the First Amendment." *South Carolina Law Review* 46, no. 2 (1995): 215.

Mandelker, Daniel R. *Land Use Law.* 4th ed. Charlottesville, VA: LEXIS Law Publishers, 1997.

————. *The Zoning Dilemma: A Legal Strategy for Urban Change.* Indianapolis: Bobbs-Merrill, 1971.

Marcus, Norman. "Zoning Obscenity: Or, the Moral Politics of Porn." *Buffalo Law Review* 27, no. 1 (1979): 1.

Maricopa County. *Human Services Campus: Capital Business Plan.* Phoenix, 2002.

Marsh, Benjamin C. *An Introduction to City Planning.* 1904. Reprint, New York: Arno Press, 1974.

Martin, Douglas. "City Begins Enforcement of Food Cart Restrictions." *New York Times,* April 21, 1994, sec. B.

Maser, Steven M., William H. Riker, and Richard N. Rosett. "The Effects of Zoning and Externalities on the Price of Land: An Empirical Analysis of Monroe County, New York." *Journal of Law and Economics* 20, no. 1 (1977): 111.

Massey, Douglas S., and Shawn M. Kanaiaupuni. "Public Housing and the Concentration of Poverty." *Social Science Quarterly* 74, no. 1 (1993): 109.

Mastrofski, Stephen D., and Jack Greene. "Community Policing and the Rule of Law." In *Police Innovation and Control of the Police,* edited by David Weisburd and Craig Uchida. New York: Springer-Verlag, 1993.

Mastrofski, Stephen D., and Craig D. Uchida. "Transforming the Police." *Journal of Research in Crime and Delinquency* 30, no. 3 (1993): 330.

McAdams, Richard H. "An Attitudinal Theory of Expressive Law." *Oregon Law Review* 79, no. 2 (2000): 339.

McBain, Howard Lee. *American City Progress and the Law.* New York: Columbia University Press, 1918.

McCaffery, Edward. "Slouching Toward Equality: Gender Discrimination, Market Efficiency, and Social Change." *Yale Law Journal* 103, no. 3 (1993): 595.

McCormick, Cynthia. "Homeless Campus Site Best of Few Options." *Cape Cod Times,* September 21, 2003.

McGarrell, Edmund F., Andrew L. Giacomazzi, and Quint C. Thurman. "Neighborhood Disorder, Integration, and the Fear of Crime." *Justice Quarterly* 14, no. 3 (1997): 479.

McGreevy, John T. *Parish Boundaries: The Catholic Encounter with Race in the Twentieth-Century Urban North.* Chicago: University of Chicago Press, 1996.

McNatt, Robert. "Council Peddles Plans to Limit Vendors." *Crain's New York Business,* February 1, 1993.

———. "Harlem on My Mind: Black America's Cultural Capital Is Thriving Again." *Business Week,* September 20, 2004, 109.

McNichol, Dan, and Andy Ryan. *The Big Dig.* New York: Silver Lining Books, 2000.

McUsic, Molly. "The Ghost of Lochner: Modern Takings Doctrine and Its Impact on Economic Legislation." *Boston University Law Review* 76, no. 4 (1996): 605.

———. "Looking Inside Out: Institutional Analysis and the Problem of Takings." *Northwestern University Law Review* 92, no. 2 (1998): 591.

McWhirter, Cameron. "Archer Tries to Balance Budget and Re-Election." *Detroit News,* March 4, 2001, sec. 1A.

Meares, Tracey L. "Praying for Community Policing." *California Law Review* 90, no. 5 (2002): 1593–1604.

Meares, Tracey L., and Kelsi Brown Corkran. "When 2 or 3 Come Together." *William and Mary Law Review* 48, no. 4 (2007): 1315.

Meares, Tracey L., and Dan M. Kahan. "Law and (Norms of) Order in the Inner City." *Law and Society Review* 32, no. 4 (1998): 805.

———, eds. *Urgent Times: Policing and Rights in Inner-City Communities.* Boston: Beacon Press, 1999.

———. "When Rights Are Wrong: The Paradox of Unwanted Rights." In *Urgent Times: Policing and Rights in Inner-City Communities,* edited by Tracey L. Meares and Dan M. Kahan. Boston: Beacon Press, 1999.

Merrill, Thomas. "The Economics of Public use." *Cornell Law Review* 72, no. 1 (1986): 61.

———. "Rent Seeking and the Compensation Principle." *Northwestern University Law Review* 80, no. 6 (1986): 1561.

Metzenbaum, James. *The Law of Zoning.* 2nd ed. New York: Baker, Voorhis, 1930.

Michelman, Frank. "The Jurisprudence of Takings." *Columbia Law Review* 88, no. 8 (1988): 1600.

———. "Property, Utility, and Fairness: Comments on the Ethical Foundations of 'Just Compensation' Law." *Harvard Law Review* 80, no. 6 (1967): 1165.

Miethe, Terance D. "Fear and Withdrawal from Urban Life." *Annals of the American Academy of Political and Social Science* 539, no. 1 (1995): 14.

Mikos, Robert A. "'Eggshell' Victims, Private Precautions, and the Societal Benefits of Shifting Crime." *Michigan Law Review* 105, no. 2 (2006): 307.

Miller, Gary J. *Cities by Contract: The Politics of Municipal Incorporation.* Cambridge, MA: MIT Press, 1981.

Miller, Zane L. *The Urbanization of Modern America: A Brief History.* New York: Harcourt Brace Jovanovich, 1973.

Milnich, Nancy A. "Compassion Fatigue and the Homeless: Are the Homeless Constitutional Castaways?" *UC Davis Law Review* 27, no. 2 (1994): 255.

Moller, Jan. "LV Chips in to Keep Crisis Center Open." *Las Vegas Review Journal,* February 20, 2003, sec. 5B.

Montgomery, Roger. "Improving the Design Process in Urban Renewal." In *Urban Renewal: The Record and the Controversy,* edited by James Q. Wilson, 454. Cambridge, MA: MIT Press, 1966.

Moore, Mark H. "Problem Solving and Community Policing." *Crime and Justice: A Review of Research* 15, no. 1 (1992): 99.

Moore, Mark H., and George L. Kelling. " 'To Serve and Protect': Learning from Police History." *Public Interest* 70 (Winter 1983): 49.

Moore, Mark H., and Robert C. Trojanowicz. "Policing and Fear of Crime." *Perspectives on Policing* 3 (June 1988): 3.

Muller, Peter O. *Contemporary Suburban America.* Englewood Cliffs, NJ: Prentice-Hall, 1981.

Mumford, Lewis. *From the Ground Up: Observations on Contemporary Architecture, Housing, Highway Building, and Civic Design.* New York: Harcourt Brace, 1956.

Munch, Patricia. "An Economic Analysis of Eminent Domain." *Journal of Political Economy* 84, no. 3 (1976): 473.

Murphy, Jane C. "Legal Images of Motherhood: Conflicting Definitions from Welfare 'Reform,' Family, and Criminal Law." *Cornell Law Review* 83, no. 3 (1998): 688.

Murray, Charles A. *Losing Ground: American Social Policy, 1950–1980.* New York: Basic Books, 1984.

National Advisory Commission on Civil Disorders. *Final Report.* Washington, DC: U.S. Government Printing Office, 1968.

National Commission on Severely Distressed Public Housing. *The Final Report.* Washington, DC: Government Printing Office, 1992.

National Commission on Urban Problems. *Building the American City.* H.R. Doc. 91–34 (1969).

National Commission on Urban Problems. *More Than Shelter: Social Needs in Low and Moderate-Income Housing.* Washington, DC: Government Printing Office, 1968.

National Housing Law Project. *False Hope: A Critical Assessment of the Hope VI Public Housing Redevelopment Program.* Oakland, CA: 2002.

National Institute of Justice. *Use of Force by Police: Overview of National and Local Data.* Washington, DC, 1999.

Nelson, Arthur C., and James B. Duncan. *Growth Management Principles and Practices.* Chicago: Planners Press, 1988.

Nelson, Arthur C., Rolf Pendall, Casey J. Dawkins, and Gerritt J. Knapp. "The Link between Growth Management and Housing Affordability: The Academic Evidence." In *Growth Management and Affordable Housing,* edited by Anthony Downs, 117. Washington, DC: Brookings Institution Press, 2004.

Nelson, Colleen McCain. "City Trains Sights on Neighborhood Blight." *Dallas Morning News,* May 6, 2002, sec. 1A.

Nelson, Robert. "Privatizing the Neighborhood: A Proposal to Replace Zoning with Private Collective Property Rights to Existing Neighborhoods." *George Mason Law Review* 7, no. 4 (1999): 827.

———. *Zoning and Property Rights: An Analysis of the American System of Land-Use Regulation.* Cambridge, MA: MIT Press, 1977.

Neuman, Gerald L. "Anomalous Zones." *Stanford Law Review* 48, no. 5 (1996): 1197.

Newman, Oscar. *Defensible Space: Crime Prevention through Urban Design.* New York: Macmillan, 1972.

Noam, Eli M. "The Interaction of Building Codes and Housing Prices." *Real Estate Economics* 10, no. 4 (1982): 394.

Norquist, John O. *The Wealth of Cities: Revitalizing the Centers of American Life.* Reading, MA: Addison-Wesley, 1998.

Office of the Mayor, City of Los Angeles Press Release. "City Launches Initiative to Reduce Crime on Skid Row: 50 More Police Officers Deployed to Area." September 24, 2006.

Olmsted, Frederick Law. *Civilizing American Cities: A Selection of Frederick Law Olmsted's Writings on City Landscapes,* edited by S. B. Sutton. Cambridge, MA: MIT Press, 1971.

Olsen, Francis E. "The Family and the Market: A Study of Ideology and Legal Reform." *Harvard Law Review* 96, no. 7 (1983): 1497.

Orfield, Myron. *Metropolitics: A Regional Agenda for Community and Stability.* Washington, DC: Brookings Institution Press, 1997.

Oser, Alan S. "At Lenox and 116th, Co-Ops and Stores Are Rising." *New York Times,* August 8, 1999, sec. 11.

Paglin, Morton. "The Underground Economy: New Estimates from Household Income and Expenditure Surveys." *Yale Law Journal* 103, no. 8 (1994): 2239.

Pate, Antony M., Mary Ann Wycoff, Wesley G. Skogan, and Lawrence W. Sherman. *Reducing Fear of Crime in Houston and Newark: A Summary Report.* Washington, DC: Police Foundation, 1986.

Patillo, Mary. *Black on the Block: The Politics of Race and Class in the City.* Chicago: University of Chicago Press, 2007.

"Peddlers Irk Stores in Harlem." *New York Times,* September 24, 1990, sec. B.

Peirce, Neal R., Curtis W. Johnson, and John Stuart Hall. *Citistates: How Urban America Can Prosper in a Competitive World.* Washington, DC: Seven Locks Press, 1993.

Peñalver, Eduardo Moises. "Property Metaphors and Kelo v. New London: Two Views of the Castle." *Fordham Law Review* 74, no. 6 (2003): 2971.

Perin, Constance. *Everything in Its Place: Social Order and Land Use in America.* Princeton, NJ: Princeton University Press, 1977.

Perkins, Douglas D., and Ralph B. Taylor. "Ecological Assessment of Community Disorder: Their Relationship to Fear of Crime and Theoretical Implications." *American Journal of Community Psychology* 24, no. 1 (1996): 63.

Perl, Peter. "Building Inspector with a Bulletproof Vest." *Washington Post,* June 27, 1999, sec. W8.

Perlman, Ellen. "Pornosprawl: X-Rated Businesses Are Leaving the City for the Suburbs: The Suburbs Aren't Ready." *Governing Magazine,* October 1997, 48.

Phelan, Thomas J., and Mark Schneider. "Race, Ethnicity, and Class in American Suburbs." *Urban Affairs Review* 31, no. 5 (1996): 659.

Pickels, Dwayne. "Mixed-Use Zoning, Greater Density Would Raise Pittsburgh Region's Quality of Life." *Pittsburgh Tribune-Review,* April 1, 2005.

Platt, Rutherford H. *Land Use and Society: Geography, Law, and Public Policy.* Washington, DC: Island Press, 1996.

Polikoff, Alexander. *Waiting for Gautreaux: A Story of Segregation, Housing, and the Black Ghetto.* Evanston, IL: Northwestern University Press, 2006.

Pollard, Trip. "Greening the American Dream?" *Planning* 67, no. 10 (2001): 10.

Polner, Robert. "A Fighter at Heart: Rudy Never Mild in Pursuit of Goals." *Newsday,* December 23, 2001, sec. A7.

Popkin, Susan J. *The Hope VI Program: What about the Residents?* Washington, DC: Urban Institute, December 2002.

Posner, Richard. *Economic Analysis of the Law.* 4th ed. Boston: Little, Brown, 1992.

———. "Social Norms, Social Meaning, and the Economic Analysis of Law: A Comment." *Journal of Legal Studies* 27, s.2 (1998): 553.

Poyner, Barry. *Design Against Crime: Beyond Defensible Space.* Boston: Butterworths, 1983.

Pratt, Joanne H. *Homebased Business: The Hidden Economy.* Washington, DC: Office of Advocacy, U.S. Small Business Administration, 1999.

Presser, Harriet B., and Elizabeth A. Bamberger. "American Women Who Work at Home for Pay: Distinctions and Determinants." *Social Science Quarterly* 74, no. 4 (1993): 815.

"The Public Use Limitation on Eminent Domain: An Advance Requiem." *Yale Law Journal* 58, no. 4 (1949): 599.

Putnam, Robert D. *Bowling Alone: The Collapse and Revival of American Community.* New York: Touchstone, 2000.

———. "E Pluribus Unum: Diversity and Community in the Twenty-first Century: The 2006 Johan Skytte Prize Lecture." *Scandinavian Political Studies* 30, no. 2 (2007): 137.

Rabin, Yale. "Expulsive Zoning: The Inequitable Legacy of Euclid." In *Zoning and the American Dream: Promises Still to Keep,* edited by Charles M. Haar and Jerold S. Kayden. Chicago: Planners Press, 1989.

Radin, Margaret Jane. "Property and Personhood." *Stanford Law Review* 34, no. 5 (1982): 957.

Ramsey, Sarah H., and Fredrick Zolna. "A Piece in the Puzzle of Providing Adequate Housing: Court Effectiveness in Code Enforcement." *Fordham Urban Law Journal* 18, no. 4 (1991): 605.

Rector, Robert. "Secretly Ending Welfare Reform." *Washington Times,* February 26, 2009.

Reich, Robert B. "Secession of the Successful." *New York Times,* January 20, 1991.

Reichl, Alexander J. *Reconstructing Times Square: Politics and Culture in Urban Development.* Lawrence, KS: University Press of Kansas, 1999.

Reiss, Albert J., Jr. "Consequences of Compliance and Deterrence Models of Law Enforcement for the Exercise of Police Discretion." *Law and Contemporary Problems* 47, no. 4 (Autumn 1984): 83.

Renauer, Brian C. "Reducing Fear of Crime: Citizen, Police, or Government Responsibility?" *Police Quarterly* 10, no. 1 (2007): 41.

Resler, Jerry. "The Park East Corridor: Patience Is a Virtue, Even in Downtown Milwaukee." *Milwaukee Journal Sentinel,* May 13, 2007, sec. J4.

Restatement (Second) of Torts, Philadelphia: American Law Institute (1979) § 821B.

Roberts, Chalmers M. "Blueprint for Progress in Southwest Washington: Bold Planning in Southwest Will Pay Dividends to D.C." *Washington Post,* September 22, 1952, 28.

———. "Progress or Decay? I—'Downtown Blight' in the Nation's Capital." *Washington Post,* January 27, 1952, sec. M1.

———. "Progress or Decay? I—Two Redevelopment Ideas for Southwest D.C." *Washington Post,* February 10, 1952, sec. B1.

Roberts, Dorothy. "Foreword: Race, Vagueness, and the Social Meaning of Order-Maintenance Policing." *Journal of Criminal Law and Criminology* 89, no. 3 (1999): 775.

Robertson, Anne. "Downtown Human Services Campus Comes to Fruition." *Phoenix Business Journal,* August 22, 2003.

Robinson, Paul H., and John M. Darley. *Justice, Liability, and Blame: Community Views and the Criminal Law.* Boulder, CO: Westview Press, 1995.

Roeder, David. "Englewood Project Has Backing of Big Names." *Chicago Sun-Times,* May 30, 2002, Financial sec.

Rose, Carol M. "Planning and Dealing: Piecemeal Land Controls as a Problem of Local Legitimacy." *California Law Review* 71, no. 3 (1983): 837.

Rosen, Ruth. *The Lost Sisterhood: Prostitution in America, 1900–1918.* Baltimore: Johns Hopkins University Press, 1982.

Rosin, Hannah. "American Murder Mystery." *Atlantic,* July/August 2008, 40.

Ross, H. Laurence. "Housing Code Enforcement as Law in Action." *Law and Policy* 17, no. 2 (1995): 133.

Rossi, Peter H. *Down and Out in America: The Origins of Homelessness.* Chicago: University of Chicago Press, 1989.

Rountree, Pamela Wilcox, and Kenneth C. Land. "Burglary Victimization, Perceptions of Crime Risk, and Routine Activities: A Multilevel Analysis across Seattle Neighborhoods and Census Tracts." *Journal of Research in Crime and Delinquency* 33, no. 2 (1996): 147.

Rusk, David. *Cities without Suburbs.* 2nd ed. Washington, DC: Woodrow Wilson Center Press, 1995.

Ryan, James E., and Michael Heise. "The Political Economy of School Choice." *Yale Law Journal* 111, no. 8 (2002): 2043.

Rybczynski, Witold. *City Life: Urban Expectations in a New World.* New York: Scribner, 1995.

Sagalyn, Lynne B. *Times Square Roulette: Remaking the City Icon.* Cambridge, MA: MIT Press, 2001.

Sager, Lawrence Gene. "Tight Little Islands: Exclusionary Zoning, Equal Protection and the Indigent." *Stanford Law Review* 21, no. 4 (1969): 767.

Salins, Peter D. "Reviving New York City's Housing Market." In *Housing and Community Development in New York City,* edited by Michael H. Schill, 53–55. Albany, NY: State University of New York Press, 1999.

Salins, Peter D., and Gerard C. S. Mildner. *Scarcity by Design: The Legacy of New York City's Housing Policies.* Cambridge, MA: Harvard University Press, 1992.

Sampson, Robert J. "Urban Black Violence: The Effect of Male Joblessness and Family Disruption." *American Journal of Sociology* 93, no. 2 (1987): 348.

Sampson, Robert J., and Jacqueline Cohen. "Deterrent Effects of the Police on Crime: A Replication and Theoretical Extension." *Law and Society Review* 22, no. 1 (1988): 169.

Sampson, Robert J., and Stephen W. Raudenbush. "Seeing Disorder: Neighborhood Stigma and the Social Construction of 'Broken Windows.'" *Social Psychology Quarterly* 67, no. 3 (2004): 319.

———. "Systematic Social Observation of Public Spaces: A New Look at Disorder in Public Places." *American Journal of Sociology* 105, no. 3 (1999): 603.

Sampson, Robert J., Stephen W. Raudenbush, and Felton Earls. "Neighborhoods and Violent Crime: A Multilevel Study of Collective Efficacy." *Science* 277, no. 5328 (1997): 918.

Sampson, Robert J., and John D. Wooldredge. "Evidence that High Crime Rates Encourage Migration Away from Central Cities." *Sociology and Social Research* 70, no. 4 (1986): 310.

Sanger, Carol. "Separating from Children." *Columbia Law Review* 96, no. 2 (1996): 375.

Sanger, David E. "Fighting Poverty, President and Speaker Find a Moment of Unity." *New York Times,* November 6, 1999, sec. A10.

Scafidi, Benjamin P., Michael H. Schill, Susan M. Wachter, and Dennis P. Culhane. "An Economic Analysis of Housing Abandonment." *Journal of Housing Economics* 7, no. 4 (1998): 287.

Schaefer, Matthew. "State Investment Attraction Subsidy Wars Resulting from a Prisoner's Dilemma." *New Mexico Law Review* 28, no. 2 (1998): 303.

Scheehle, Peter, Michael Kane, and Dushaw Hockett. *Report on the Loss of Subsidized Housing in the U.S.* Washington, DC: National Alliance of HUD Tenants, October 4, 2002.

Scheider, Matthew C., Tawandra Rowell, and Veh Bezdikian. "The Impact of Citizen Perceptions of Community Policing on Fear of Crime: Findings from Twelve Cities." *Police Quarterly* 6, no. 4 (2003): 363.

Schill, Michael H. "Comment of Richard P. Voith and David Crawford's Smart Growth and Affordable Housing." In *Growth Management and Affordable Housing: Do They Conflict?* edited by Anthony Downs. Washington, DC: Brookings Institution Press, 2004.

———. "Deconcentrating the Inner City Poor." *Chicago-Kent Law Review* 67, no. 3 (1991): 795–808.

———. "Distressed Public Housing: Where Do We Go from Here?" *University of Chicago Law Review* 60, no. 2 (1993): 497.

Schill, Michael H., and Benjamin P. Scafidi. "Housing Conditions and Problems in New York City." In *Housing and Community Development in New York City,* edited by Michael H. Schill, 11. Albany, NY: State University of New York Press, 1999.

Schneider, David J. *Introduction to Social Psychology.* San Diego, CA: Harcourt, Brace, Jovanovich, 1988.

Schneider, John C. "Skid Row as an Urban Neighborhood, 1880–1960." *Urbanism Past and Present* 9, no. 1 (1984): 11.

Schneider, Mark. *The Competitive City: The Political Economy of Suburbia.* Pittsburgh, PA: University of Pittsburgh Press, 1989.

Schragger, Richard C. "The Limits of Localism." *Michigan Law Review* 100, no. 2 (2001): 371.

Schreibman, Lisa. "Looking for Land? Try Tearing Down a Highway." *Planning* 67, no. 1 (2001): 10.

Schulhofer, Stephen J. "On the Fourth Amendment Rights of the Law-Abiding Public." *Supreme Court Review* 1989, no. 1 (1989): 87.

Scott, Michael S. "The Benefits and Consequences of Police Crackdowns." In *Problem Oriented Guides for Police.* Response Guide Series 1. Washington, DC: U.S. Department of Justice, 2003.

"Second Phase of Downtown's Human Services Campus to Begin." *Phoenix Business Journal,* May 15, 2006.

Seidel, Stephen R. *Housing Costs and Government Regulations: Confronting the Regulatory Maze.* New Brunswick, NJ: Center for Urban Policy Research, 1978.

Seifman, David. "Rudy Bending on Vending Ban." *New York Post,* June 19, 1998, News sec.

Sennett, Richard. *The Uses of Disorder: Personal Identity and City Life.* New York: Knopf, 1970.

Servon, Lisa J. *Bootstrap Capital: Microenterprises and the American Poor.* Washington, DC: Brookings Institution Press, 1999.

Shavell, Steven. "Individual Precautions to Prevent Theft: Private v. Socially Optimal Behavior." *International Review of Law and Economics* 11, no. 2 (1991): 123.

Shaver, Katherine. "For the Muffin Lady, Some Home Baked Troubles." *Washington Post,* February 13, 1997, sec. A1.

Shen, Q. "Spacial Impacts of Locally Enacted Growth Controls: The San Francisco Bay Region in the 1980s." *Environment and Planning B: Planning and Design* 23, no. 1 (1995): 61.

Sherman, Lawrence W. "Attacking Crime: Police and Crime Control." In *Modern Policing,* edited by Michael Tonry and Norval Morris, 198–99. Chicago: University of Chicago Press, 1992.

———. "Fair and Effective Policing." In *Crime: Public Policies for Crime Control,* edited by James Q. Wilson and Joan Petersilia, 383. Oakland, CA: ICS Press, 2002.

Short, John Rennie. *Alabaster Cities: Urban U.S. since 1950.* Syracuse, NY: Syracuse University Press, 2006.

Siegan, Bernard H. *Land Use without Zoning.* Lexington, MA: Lexington Books, 1972.

Siegel, Reva B. "Home as Work: The First Women's Rights Claims Concerning Wives' Household Labor, 1850–1880." *Yale Law Journal* 103, no. 5 (1994): 1073.

Sigelman, Lee, and Jeffrey R. Henig. "Crossing the Great Divide: Race and Preferences for Living in the City versus the Suburbs." *Urban Affairs Review* 37, no. 1 (2001): 3.

Simmons, Patrick A., and Robert E. Lang. "The Urban Turnaround." In *Redefining Urban and Suburban America: Evidence from Census 2000,* edited by Bruce Katz and Robert E. Lang, vol. 1, 51. Washington, DC: Brookings Institution Press, 2003.

Singer, Joseph William. *Introduction to Property.* 2nd ed. New York: Aspen Publishers, 2005.

Skogan, Wesley G. *Disorder and Decline: Crime and the Spiral of Decay in American Neigh-borhoods.* New York: Free Press, 1990.

———. "Fear of Crime and Neighborhood Change." In *Communities and Crime,* edited by Albert J. Reiss Jr. and Michael Tonry. Chicago: University of Chicago Press, 1986.

———. "The Impact of Victimization on Fear." *Crime and Delinquency* 33, no. 1 (1987): 135.

———. "Measuring What Matters: Crime, Disorder, and Fear." In *Measuring What Matters: Proceedings from the Policing Research Institute Meetings,* edited by Robert H. Lang-worthy, 37. Washington, DC: National Institute of Justice, 1999.

Skogan, Wesley G., and Michael G. Maxfield. *Coping with Crime.* Beverly Hills: Sage Pub-lications, 1981.

Skolnick, Jerome H., and David H Bayley. *The New Blue Line: Police Innovation in Six American Cities.* New York: Free Press, 1986.

Skolnick, Jerome H., and James J. Fyfe. *Above the Law: Police and the Excessive Use of Force.* New York: Free Press, 1993.

Smith, Stephanie. "Civil Banishment of Gang Members: Circumventing Criminal Due Process Requirements?" *University of Chicago Law Review* 67, no. 4 (2000): 1461.

Smolla, Rodney A. "In Pursuit of Racial Utopias: Fair Housing, Quotas, and Goals in the 1980s." *Southern California Law Review* 58, no. 4 (1985): 947.

Sohmer, Rebecca R., and Robert E. Lang. "Downtown Rebound." In *Redefining Urban and Suburban America,* edited by Bruce Katz and Robert E. Lang. Vol. 1. Washington, DC: Brookings Institute Press, 2003.

Souccar, Miriam Kreinin. "El Barrio: Left Behind and Angry." *Crain's New York Business,* January 13, 2003, 20.

Sparks, Richard F., Hazel G. Genn, and David J. Dodd. *Surveying Victims.* New York: Wi-ley, 1977.

Spellman, William. "Abandoned Buildings: Magnets for Crime?" *Journal of Criminal Jus-tice* 21, no. 5 (1993): 481.

Staley, Samuel R. "Reforming the Zoning Laws." In *A Guide to Smart Growth: Shattering Myths, Providing Solutions,* edited by Jane S. Shaw and Ronald D. Utt, 61. Washington, DC: Heritage Foundation, 2000.

Steiker, Carol S. "Counter-Revolution in Criminal Procedure? Two Audiences, Two An-swers." *Michigan Law Review* 94, no. 8 (1996): 2469.

———. "More Wrong than Rights." In *Urgent Times: Policing and Rights in Inner-City Com-munities,* edited by Tracey L. Meares and Dan M. Kahan. Boston: Beacon Press, 1999.

Steinhauer, Jennifer. "Ending a Long Battle, New York Lets Housing and Gardens Grow." *New York Times,* September 19, 2002, sec. A1.

Sterk, Stewart E. "Competition among Municipalities as a Constraint on Land Use Exac-tions." *Vanderbilt Law Review* 45, no. 4 (1992): 831.

Stewart, Nikita. "Council Votes to Close 2 Waterfront Agencies." *Washington Post,* June 6, 2007, sec. B2.

Strosnider, Kim. "Anti-Gang Ordinances After City of Chicago v. Morales: The Intersec-tion of Race, Vagueness Doctrine, and Equal Protection in the Criminal Law." *American Criminal Law Review* 39, no. 1 (2002): 101.

Stull, William J. "From Urban Renewal to CDBG: Community Development in Nine Cities." *Research in Real Estate* 2, (1982): 185.

Stuntz, William J. "Crime Talk and Law Talk." *Reviews in American History* 23 (1995): 157.

———. "Implicit Bargains, Government Power, and the Fourth Amendment." *Stanford Law Review* 44, no. 3 (1992): 560.

———. "Privacy's Problem and the Law of Criminal Procedure." *Michigan Law Review* 93, no. 5 (1995): 1016.

Sugarman, Carole. "Muffin Makeover: Recipes and Reflections from Linda Fisher, Rebuilding Her Life One Batch at a Time." *Washington Post,* February 17, 1998, sec. E1.

Sugrue, Thomas J. *The Origins of the Urban Crisis: Race and Inequality in Postwar Detroit.* Princeton, NJ: Princeton University Press, 1996.

Sullivan, Kathleen. "Unconstitutional Conditions." *Harvard Law Review* 102, no. 7 (1989): 1413.

Sunstein, Cass. "Lochner's Legacy." *Columbia Law Review* 87, no. 5 (1987): 873.

———. "On the Expressive Function of Law." *University of Pennsylvania Law Review* 144, no. 5 (1996): 2021.

———. "Social Norms and Social Roles." *Columbia Law Review* 96, no. 4 (1996): 903.

Taylor, Brian D., and Paul M. Ong. "Spatial Mismatch or Automobile Mismatch? An Examination of Race, Residence, and Commuting in U.S. Metropolitan Areas." *Urban Studies* 32, no. 9 (1995): 1453.

Taylor, Ralph B. "Crime, Grime, Fear, and Decline: A Longitudinal Look." *National Institute of Justice: Research in Brief,* July 1999.

———. "Toward an Environmental Psychology of Disorder." In *Handbook of Environmental Psychology,* edited by Daniel Stokols and Irwin Altman. Vol. 2, 954. New York: Wiley, 1987.

Taylor, Ralph, Barbara A. Koons, Ellen M. Kurtz, Jack R. Greene, and Douglas D. Perkins. "Street Blocks with More Nonresidential Land Uses Have More Physical Deterioration." *Urban Affairs Review* 31, no. 2 (1995): 120.

Teaford, Jon C. *The Rough Road to Renaissance: Urban Revitalization in America, 1940–1985.* Baltimore: Johns Hopkins University Press, 1990.

Testa, Mark, and Marilyn Krogh. "The Effect of Employment on Marriage among Black Males in Inner-City Chicago." In *The Decline in Marriage among African Americans: Causes, Consequences, and Policy Implications,* edited by M. Belinda Tucker and Claudia Mitchell-Kerna, 59. New York: Russell Sage Foundation, 1995.

Thatcher, David. "Conflicting Values in Community Policing." *Law and Society Review* 35, no. 4 (2001): 765.

Thernstrom, Stephan, and Abigail Thernstrom. *America in Black and White: One Nation Indivisible.* New York: Simon & Schuster, 1997.

Thomas, Kenneth P. *Competing for Capital: Europe and North America in a Global Era.* Washington, DC: Georgetown University Press, 2000.

Thursz, Daniel. *Where Are They Now?: A Study of the Impact of Relocation on Former Residents of Southwest Washington, Who Were Served in an HWC Demonstration Project.* Washington, DC: Health and Welfare Council of the National Capital Area, 1966.

Tiebout, Charles M. "A Pure Theory of Local Expenditures." *The Journal of Political Economy* 64, no. 5 (1956): 416.

Tienda, Marta, and Haya Stier. "Joblessness and Shiftlessness: Labor Force Activity in Chicago's Inner City, in the Urban Underclass." In *The Urban Underclass,* edited by Christopher Jencks and Paul E. Peterson, 135–54. Washington, DC: Brookings Institution, 1991.

Toll, Seymour I. *Zoned American.* New York: Grossman Publishers, 1969.

Treanor, William Michael. "The Armstrong Principle, the Narratives of Takings, and Compensation Statutes." *William and Mary Law Review* 38, no. 3 (1997): 1151.

Trice, Dawn Turner. "Developer's Vision Thrives in Lakefront Model." *Chicago Tribune,* July 22, 2002.

Trojanowicz, Robert C. *An Evaluation of the Neighborhood Foot Patrol Program in Flint, Michigan.* East Lansing, MI: National Neighborhood Foot Patrol Center, 1982.

Twomey, Steve. "Here Comes (There Goes) a Neighborhood." *Washington Post Magazine,* July 2, 2000, sec. W8.

"The Unrealized Profits in Urban Renewal." *Architectural Forum,* July 1962, 101.

"Urban Renewal Wastelands: Cities' Development Suffering and Bulldozed Acres Lie Idle and Untaxed." *Nation's Business,* April 1965, 86–87.

U.S. Department of Transportation. *Business Relocation Study* (2002).

U.S. Department of Transportation, *Relocation Retrospective Study* (1996).

Veiller, Lawrence. "Districting by Municipal Regulation." In *Proceeds of the Eighth National Conference on City Planning.* Toronto: May 1912, 163.

———. "Protecting Residential Districts." In *Proceeds of the Sixth National Conference on City Planning.* Toronto: 1914, 92.

Venkatesh, Sudhir Alladi. *Off the Books: The Underground Economy of the Urban Poor.* Cambridge, MA: Harvard University Press, 2006.

Viteritti, Joseph P. *Choosing Equality: School Choice, the Constitution, and Civil Society.* Washington, DC: Brookings Institution Press, 1999.

Voith, Richard P., and David L. Crawford. "Smart Growth and Affordable Housing." In *Growth Management and Affordable Housing,* edited by Anthony Downs. Washington, DC: Brookings Institution Press, 2004.

Warr, Mark, and Mark Stafford. "Fear of Victimization: A Look at Proximate Causes." *Social Forces* 61, no. 4 (1983): 1033.

Weicher, John C. "Private Production: Has the Rising Tide Lifted All Boats?" In *Housing America's Poor,* edited by Peter D. Salins, 45. Chapel Hill, NC: University of North Carolina Press, 1987.

Weisburd, David, and John E. Eck. "What Can Police Do to Reduce Crime, Disorder, and Fear?" *Annals of the American Academy of Political and Social Science* 593, no. 1 (2004): 42.

Weiss, Marc A. *The Rise of the Community Builders: The American Real Estate Industry and Urban Land Planning.* New York: Columbia University Press, 1987.

Whitten, Robert H. "The Zoning of Residential Sections." *Proceedings of the National Conference on City Planning* 10 (1918): 34.

Wilcox, Pamela, Neil Quisenberry, Debra T. Cabrera, and Shayne Jones. "Busy Places and Broken Windows: Toward Defining the Role of Physical Structure and Process in Community Crime Models." *Sociological Quarterly* 45, no. 2 (2004): 185.

Wilgoren, Jodi. "Detroit Urban Renewal without the Renewal." *New York Times,* July 7, 2002, sec. 1.

Williams, Monte. "Crackdown on Ave. C Peddlers." *New York Times,* March 12, 1995, sec. 13.

Wilson, James Q., ed. *Urban Renewal, the Record and the Controversy.* Cambridge, MA: MIT Press, 1966.

————. "The Urban Unease: Community v. City." *Public Interest* 12, (Summer 1968): 25.

————. *Varieties of Police Behavior: The Management of Law and Order in Eight Communities.* Cambridge, MA: Harvard University Press, 1968.

Wilson, James Q., and George L. Kelling. "Broken Windows: The Police and Neighborhood Safety." *Atlantic Monthly,* March 1982, 29.

Wilson, William J. *When Work Disappears: The World of the New Urban Poor.* New York: Knopf, 1996.

Wolf, Michael Allen. "Dangerous Crossing: State Brownfields Recycling and Federal Enterprise Zoning." *Fordham Environmental Law Journal* 9, no. 3 (1998): 495.

————. "Enterprise Zones: A Decade of Diversity." *Economic Development Quarterly* 4, no. 1 (1990): 3.

Wright, Gwendolyn. *Building the Dream: A Social History of Housing in America.* New York: Pantheon Books, 1981.

Young, Iris Marion. *Justice and the Politics of Difference.* Princeton, NJ: Princeton University Press, 1990.

Yudof, Mark G. *Educational Policy and the Law.* 4th ed. Belmont, CA: West/Thomson Learning, 2002.

Zhao, J. Solomon. "The Effect of Police Presence on Public Fear Reduction and Satisfaction: A Review of the Literature." *Justice Professional* 15, no. 3 (2002): 273.

LEGAL CASES AND STATUTES

42 U.S.C. § 1397f(a)(2)(B) (2000).

Ambler Realty Co. v. Village of Euclid, 297 F. 307 (N.D. Ohio 1924).

Armendariz v. Penman 31 F.3d 860 (9th. Cir. 1994).

Armendariz v. Penman, 75 F.3d 1311 (9th Cir. 1996) (en banc).

Armory Park Neighborhood Association v. Episcopal Community Services, 712 P.2d 914 (Ariz. 1985).

Baker v. Coman, 198 S.W. 141 (Tex. 1917).

Berkeley Community Health Project v. City of Berkeley, 1995 WL 293899 (N.D. Calif. 1995).

Berman v. Parker, 348 U.S. 26 (1954).

Blair v. Shanahan, 775 F. Supp. 1315 (N.D. Calif. 1991), rev'd and remanded, 38 F.3d 1514 (9th Cir. 1994).

Bray v. Alexandria Women's Health Clinic, 506 U.S. 263 (1993).

Brief for the National Conference on City Planning et al. as Amici Curiae Supporting Appellants, Village of Euclid v. Ambler Realty Co., 272 U.S. 365 (1926) (No. 31).

Brief for Petitioner, Virginia v. Hicks, 539 U.S. 113 (2003) (No. 02–371).

Brown v. Texas, 443 U.S. 47 (1979).

Brown Cracker & Candy Co. v. City of Dallas, 137 S.W. 342 (Tex. 1911).

Burton v. Dupree, 46 S.W. 272 (Tex. Civ. App. 1898).

Chicago, Illinois, Zoning Code §§ 17–9-0202 (2006).

Christian v. City of Kansas City, 710 S.W.2d 11 (Mo. App. 1986).

City of Akron v. Rowland, 618 N.E.2d 128 (Ohio 1993).

City of Chicago v. Morales, 527 U.S. 31 (1999).

City of Milwaukee v. Wilson, 291 N.W.2d 452 (Wis. 1980).

City of Renton v. Playtime Theatres, Inc., 475 U.S. 41 (1985).

City of Tacoma v. Luvene, 827 P.2d 826 (Wash. 1992).

Coates v. Cincinnati, 402 U.S. 611 (1971).

Cobb v. Milwaukee County, 207 N.W.2d 848 (Wis. 1973).

Coleman v. City of Richmond, 364 S.E.2d 239 (Va. Ct. App. 1988).

Dallas v. Stanglin, 490 U.S. 19 (1989).

Dolan v. City of Tigard, 512 U.S. 374 (1994).

E. L. v. State, 619 So.2d 252 (Fla. 1993).

Gallo v. Acuna, 929 P.2d 596 (Cal. 1997).

Gautreaux v. Chicago Housing Authority, 342 F. Supp. 827 (N.D. Ill. 1972).

Gautreaux v. City of Chicago, 480 F.2d 210 (7th Cir. 1973).

Hawaii Housing Authority v. Midkiff, 467 U.S. 229 (1984).

Hills v. Gautreaux, 425 U.S. 284 (1976).

Hodgkins v. Peterson, 2004 WL 99028 (7th Cir. 2004).

The Housing and Community Development Act of 1974, Pub. L. 93–383 § 101(c)(6), *Stat.* 88
    (1974): 633, 634–35.

Hutchins v. District of Columbia, 188 F.3d 531 (D.C. Cir. 1999).

Jacobellis v. Ohio, 378 U.S. 184 (1964).

Johnson v. City of Cincinnati, 119 F. Supp. 2d 735 (S.D. Ohio 2000).

Johnson v. City of Cincinnati, 310 F.3d 484 (6th Cir. 2002), *cert. denied,* 539 U.S. 915.

Kaiser Aetna v. United States, 444 U.S. 164 (1979).

Kolender v. Lawson, 461 U.S. 352 (1983).

L'Hote v. City of New Orleans, 177 U.S. 587 (1900).

Loper v. New York City Police Department, 999 F.2d 699 (2d Cir. 1993).

Loretto v. Teleprompter Manhattan CATV Corporation, 458 U.S. 419 (1982).

Memorial Hospital v. Maricopa County, 415 U.S. 250 (1974).

Miller v. Board of Public Works, 234 P. 381 (Cal. 1925).

Moden v. United States, 60 Fed. Cl. 275 (2004).

Nollan v. California Coastal Communication, 483 U.S. 825 (1987).

Northend Cinema, Inc. v. Seattle, 585 P.2d 1153 (Wash. 1978).

Nunez v. City of San Diego, 114 F.3d 935 (9th Cir. 1997).

Omnibus Budget Reconciliation Act of 1993, 26 U.S.C. §§ 1391–1397D (1993), amended by
    Taxpayer Relief Act of 1997, Pub. L. No. 105–34, 951–52, 111 *Stat.* 788, 995 (1997).

Papachristou v. City of Jacksonville, 405 U.S. 156 (1972).

People v. Lee, 2004 WL 98584 (Ill. App., Jan. 15, 2004).

People v. Smith, 378 N.E.2d 1032 (N.Y. 1978).

Pratt v. Chicago Housing Authority, 848 F. Supp. 792 (N.D. Ill. 1994).

Pritz v. Messer, 149 N.E. 30 (Ohio 1925).

Profit v. City of Tulsa, 617 P.2d 250 (Okla. Crim. App. 1980).

Qutb v. Strauss, 11 F.3d 488 (5th Cir. 1993).

Ramos v. Town of Vernon, 331 F.3d 315 (2d Cir. 2003).

Roberts v. United States Jaycees, 468 U.S. 609 (1984).

Shuttlesworth v. Birmingham, 382 U.S. 87 (1965).

Spence v. Fenchler, 180 S.W. 597 (Tex. 1915).

State v. Burnett, 755 N.E.2d 857 (Ohio 2001).

State v. James, 978 P.2d 415 (Or. Ct. App. 1999).

State v. Johnson, 988 P.2d 913 (Or. Ct. App. 1999).

State ex rel. Civello v. City of New Orleans, 154 La. 271 (1923).

State ex rel. Gallo v. Acuna, 929 P.2d 596 (Cal. 1997).

State ex rel. Max Morris v. East Cleveland, 22 Ohio N. 549 (1920).

Thompson v. Ashe, 250 F.3d 399 (6th Cir. 2001).

U.S. Department of Housing and Urban Development v. Rucker, 535 U.S. 125 (2002).

Village of Euclid v. Ambler Realty Company, 272 U.S. 365 (1926).

Virginia v. Hicks, 539 U.S. 113 (2003).

Wright v. Georgia, 373 U.S. 284 (1963).

Wulfson v. Burden, 150 N.E. 120 (N.Y. 1925).

Young v. American Mini Theatres, Inc., 427 U.S. 50 (1976).

WEB SITES

American Planning Association. "Model Mixed-Use Zoning District Ordinance." http://
    www.planning.org/research/smartgrowth/pdf/section41.pdf.

Bring Los Angeles Home! "Draft Framework for the 10-Year Strategic Plan to End Home-
    lessness." 2004. http://www.bringlahome.org/docs/BLAH_Draft_Framework.pdf.

Carroll, Joseph. "Gallup Reviews Americans' Attitudes about Crime." June 16, 2006. Gallup.
    http://www.gallup.com/poll/23365/Gallup-Reviews-Americans-Attitudes-About-Crime
    .aspx.

Central City Association of Los Angeles. "Downtown's Human Tragedy: It's Not Acceptable
    Anymore: A Public Health and Safety Plan." (2002). http://www.ccala.org/legislative/11
    _02/Public%20Health%20Safety%20White%20Paper%20Final.pdf.

Chicago Housing Authority. "Change: Chicago Housing Authority: Welcome to the
    CHA." http://www.thecha.org.

City of Colorado Springs. "Mixed-Use Zoning." http://www.springsgov.com/Page.asp
    ?NavID=4107.

City of Fort Collins. "Public Nuisance Ordinance." http://fcgov.com/cityattorney/public
    -nuisance.php.

City of Fort Worth. "Mixed Use Zoning." http://www.fortworthgov.org/uploadedFiles/
    Planning/Zoning_Review/MU_ZoningGuide2006.pdf.

City of Fremont. "Report a Hazard/Nuisance." The City Government of Fremont, Cali-
    fornia. http://www.ci.fremont.ca.us/PublicSafety/ReportAHazard/default.htm.

City of St. Louis, Mayor's Office Press Releases (April 23, 2002). "Mayor Slay's Neighborhood Life Initiatives." http://stlcin.missouri.org/release/getpressdetails.cfm?Auto=387.

Coalition for the Homeless of Central Florida. "Welcome to the Coalition for the Homeless of Central Florida." http://www.centralfloridahomeless.org.

Constitutional Rights Foundation Chicago. "CRFC Focus Issue: Gangs." http://crfc.org/gangs.html.

Department of City Development. "Park East Redevelopment Plan." City of Milwaukee. http://www.mkedcd.org/parkeast/PEplan.html.

Department of Human Services. "HSD Homepage." Maricopa County. http://www.hsd.maricopa.gov.

District of Columbia Housing Authority. "District of Columbia Housing Authority: Arthur Capper/Carrollsburg." http://www.dchousing.org/hope6/arthur_capper_hope6.html.

East Harlem Online. "New Directions: An Introduction: A 197-A Plan for Manhattan Community District 11." http://www.east-harlem.com/cb11_197A_intro.htm.

Georgia Quality Growth Partnership. "Toolkit of Best Practices." http://www.dca.state.ga.us/toolkit/toolkit.asp.

JDLand. "Capper/Carrollsburg Housing Redevelopment." http://www.jdland.com/dc/capper.cfm.

Lake Park Crescent. "Lake Park Crescent: Come Home to the Lakefront." Draper and Kramer Incorporated. http://www.lakeparkcrescent.com.

Los Angeles Homeless Services Authority. "2007 Greater Los Angeles Homeless Count." http://www.lahsa.org/homelesscount.asp.

National Association of Home Builders. "NAHB: 2005 Multifamily Renter and Condo Buyer Preference Survey." http://www.nahb.org/generic.aspx?genericContentID=46103.

The Neighborhoods of EYA. "Capitol Quarter: Rowhomes That Combine Classic DC Architecture with Modern Amenities. http://www.eya.com/index.cfm?neighborhoodid=390B1CD5-96B6-175C-95D06031216C458B&fuseaction=microsites.view&sectionid=329DB7D9-1125-AADA-EAE0376CC103A6E5.

New York City Department of City Planning. "East Harlem Rezoning Proposal—Approved!" http://www.nyc.gov/html/dcp/html/eastharlem/eastharlem3a.shtml and http://www.nyc.gov/html/dcp/html/eastharlem/eastharlem3b.shtml.

New York City Housing Authority. "NYCHA: Residents' Corner: Trespass Policy." http://www.nyc.gov/html/residents/trespass_new.shtml.

Preservation Institute. "Removing Freeways, Restoring Cities: Milwaukee, Wisconsin: Park East Freeway." http://www.preservenet.com/freeways/FreewaysParkEast.html.

Saad, Lydia. "Perceptions of Crime Problem Remain Curiously Negative." Gallup, October 22, 2007. http://www.gallup.com/poll/102262/Perceptions-Crime-Problem-Remain-Curiously-Negative.aspx.

State of Connecticut Division of Criminal Justice. "Nuisance Abatement Unit." http://www.ct.gov/csao/cwp/view.asp?a=1798&q=285774.

Thrush Real Estate. "Jazz on the Boulevard: Your Home." The Thrush Companies. http://www.thrushhomes.com/html/jazzhome.htm.

University of Chicago. "West and South Campus Plan." http://southcampusplan.uchicago.edu/index.html.

Urban Institute. "The Subprime Mortgage Crisis." http://www.urban.org/decisionpoints08/ archive/04subprimemortgage.cfm.

U.S. Census Bureau. "Housing Patterns." http://www.census.gov/hhes/www/housing/ housing_patterns/housing_patterns.html.

U.S. Census Bureau. "Housing Vacancies and Homeownership: Annual Statistics 2005." http://www.census.gov/hhes/www/housing/hvs/annual05/ann05t20.html.

U.S. Department of Housing and Urban Development. "Empowerment Zone / Enterprise Community Initiative: Round II: Building Communities Together." www.hud .gov/nofa/ez/urbanforms.pdf.

———. "Tax Incentive Guide for Businesses in the Renewal Communities, Empowerment Zones, and Enterprise Communities." http://www.hud.gov/offices/cpd/economic development/library/taxguide2003.pdf.

———. "Welcome to the Community Renewal Initiative." http://www.hud.gov/offices/ cpd/economicdevelopment/programs/rc/index.cfm.

Waterfront. "Waterfront: The Project." http://www.waterfrontdc.com/project/.

Index

Abandoned and vacant buildings: and community policing, 205; as crime magnets, 78, 79; demolition of, 79; deregulation of as economic development strategy, 207–8; in East Harlem, 88

Accordino, John, 106

ADA (Americans with Disabilities Act of *1990*), 208

Adult-use districts, 115–17

Aesthetic preferences: of elites, 138–39; and new-urbanist regulations, 183–86, 200–201

Affordable housing, 35, 79, 113, 154, 163. *See also* HOPE VI program; Housing affordability; Public housing

African Americans: crime reduction in neighborhoods of, 130; displaced by redevelopment, 171–72; home ownership rates of, 41; and housing segregation in Chicago, 156, 157, 159; and order-

maintenance policing efforts, 19, 25; perceptions of disorder by, 20, 70; perceptions of security by, 130–31; and poverty, 7; in Southwest Washington, 169

"Alternatives to Zoning" (Ellickson), 207

Americans with Disabilities Act of *1990* (ADA), 208

Antigang enforcement efforts, 16, 20–21, 27, 53–54, 123

Anti-panhandling laws, 21, 24

Appraisal practices, postwar, 40–43

Architectural design, 45, 48, 152–53, 184–85. *See also* New urbanism

Arizona: homeless campus in, 101, 104, 107; nuisance remedies in, 106. *See also specific cities*

Atlanta, Georgia, 79, 104

Austin, Texas, abandoned buildings and crime in, 78